M. Gregory Tweedie and Robert C. Johnson
Medical English as a Lingua Franca

Developments in English as a Lingua Franca

Editors
Jennifer Jenkins
Will Baker

Volume 16

M. Gregory Tweedie and Robert C. Johnson

Medical English as a Lingua Franca

DE GRUYTER
MOUTON

ISBN 978-3-11-135553-5
e-ISBN (PDF) 978-3-11-069702-5
e-ISBN (EPUB) 978-3-11-069707-0
ISSN 2192-8177

Library of Congress Control Number: 2021949754

Bibliographic information published by the Deutsche Nationalbibliothek
The Deutsche Nationalbibliothek lists this publication in the Deutsche Nationalbibliografie;
detailed bibliographic data are available on the Internet at http://dnb.dnb.de.

© 2023 Walter de Gruyter GmbH, Berlin/Boston
This volume is text- and page-identical with the hardback published in 2022.
Typesetting: Integra Software Services Pvt. Ltd.
Printing and binding: CPI books GmbH, Leck

www.degruyter.com

Acknowledgements

The contents and writing of this book come heavily indebted to many, many people over the years who have provided thoughts, insights, ideas, mentorship, counsel, challenge, advice, disagreements, friendship, encouragement and practical help.

Our early efforts at researching medical English were inspired and enthusiastically supported by nursing instructors, like Jan Marie Graham, Krista King, Carina Zhu, Pamela Zielinski, Daphne Kennedy, Danaiet Teame, Carolyn Wolsey, Zohra Hasnan-Samnani, and many others. Administrators, like Associate Dean of Teaching and Learning Mahomoud Adam, and all three Deans & CEOs of the University of Calgary in Qatar during our tenure - Carolyn Byrne, Kim Critchley, and Deborah White, were essential in their support. A very special thanks must be made to our ongoing collaborator, Dr. Jessie Johnson, a natural bridge builder, whose passion for supporting students' learning has provided encouragement, challenge and guidance throughout all phases of this research.

Crossing bridges for transdisciplinary research is not easy, but the wonderful nurse-researchers and technicians at the Simulation Lab always seemed to "get" us, and this research would never have taken place without their input, support, encouragement and very practical assistance. We are forever indebted to Julie Hoffart and Arlene Masaba, both directors of the UCQ Clinical Simulation Centre (CSC), and both of whom shocked us with their instant willingness to join our research endeavours. Nursing instructor Hanin Omar was also a valuable member of the research team during her time with the CSC, and staff members Hamza Khene and Nganga Ambi Sinnasamy provided considerable help as well.

The EAP Dream Team continually grounded our research, and indeed us personally, in the everyday realities of language learning for medical purposes. It is impossible to conceive of the concepts in this book ever coming into being without the pragmatic, field-tested insights of Jody Shimoda, Angela Waigand, Marie-Claude Toriida, Simon Heslup, Shannon Blanke, Liet Hellwig, Virginia Christopher, and our first Director of the EAP program, Pamela Kapur. Thank you all for your invaluable advice and ideas, particularly during our very non-golfing Doha Golf Club dinners.

Navigating the intricacies of the research process across jurisdictions presented a challenge, and the authors are grateful for the helpful, constructive and timely feedback from the administrative teams of the Conjoint Faculties Research Ethics Board, and the Research Section of the Primary Health Care Corporation. Colleagues Roswita Dressler, Sylvie Roy, Jennifer Lock, Sarah Eaton, and Barb Brown mixed in sympathetic listening, belief and encouragement with their practical advice for traversing the unfamiliar terrain of academia.

Judi Ringuette worked tirelessly on multiple aspects to support both the research and writing, including transcription, serial form-filling, reporting, editing, managing, coordinating, and chief firefighting duties, and this book would have never been more than an idea without her direct involvement. Natalie Fecher and Kirstin Börgen at De Gruyter have provided engaged, efficient and timely support throughout the publication process.

The authors gratefully acknowledge the support of the Taylor Institute of Teaching and Learning, whose SoTL grant provided initial funding for what would become the foundations of this research.

Contents

Acknowledgements —— V

Introduction: MELF and ELF —— 1
1 Introduction: Distinctives of medical English as a lingua franca —— 1
2 Potential: Being misunderstood —— 7
3 Conceptualizing MELF within ELF —— 13
3.1 ELF and MELF: A backdrop —— 14
3.2 Toward a definition of medical English as a lingua franca —— 17
4 Conclusion —— 18

Chapter 1
Healthcare communication and MELF —— 20
1.1 Healthcare professional migration —— 20
1.2 Medical communication and migration of healthcare professionals —— 22
1.3 Interprofessional communication and medical migration —— 29
1.4 Medical communication and English as a lingua franca —— 31
1.4.1 Social and individual dimensions of MELF —— 32
1.4.2 ELF and norm-development —— 33
1.4.3 ELF and centrist perspectives —— 36
1.5 Summary —— 39

Chapter 2
Tools for analysis: Framing MELF —— 40
2.1 Introduction —— 40
2.2 Community and medical English as a lingua franca —— 41
2.3 Communities of practice and medical English as a lingua franca —— 43
2.3.1 Communities of practice and ELF —— 44
2.3.2 Communities of practice and medicine —— 45
2.3.3 MELF as a community of practice —— 46
2.4 A socio-cognitive approach to MELF —— 58
2.4.1 Medical consultation as an activity type —— 67
2.5 Social network theory and MELF —— 70
2.6 Conclusion —— 72

Chapter 3
The researchers, the research, and the research setting — 73
3.1 Introduction — 73
3.2 Research context — 75
3.2.1 Lingua francas in the State of Qatar — 75
3.2.2 Research context: Institutional setting — 80
3.3 Tracing MELF: An emerging understanding — 80
3.3.1 Intelligibility in MELF — 81
3.3.2 MELF in simulation training — 88
3.4 Practical considerations for data collection: Simulation research — 95
3.4.1 Inside simulation scenarios — 97
3.4.2 Simulation data analysis — 101
3.5 MELF in interprofessional healthcare communication — 105
3.6 Limitations in simulation research for understanding MELF — 108
3.7 Summary — 112

Chapter 4
Strategies for MELF communication — 113
4.1 Introduction — 113
4.2 Pre-emption strategies — 116
4.2.1 Repetition and collaborative repair — 116
4.2.2 Allo-repetition and reformulation — 119
4.2.3 Spelling — 124
4.2.4 Other-initiated repair — 126
4.2.5 Playback and non-verbal communication — 129
4.3 Summary — 132

Chapter 5
Finding common ground in MELF — 134
5.1 Introduction: Health assessment as an activity type — 134
5.2 Lexical simplification, biomedical summaries, and answer-offering — 136
5.3 Playback, queryback and recipient design — 140
5.4 Sociocognitive approach (SCA) — 145
5.4.1 Healthcare providers and linguistic home territory — 147
5.4.2 Biomedical think aloud and common communicative ground — 150
5.5 Summary — 154

Chapter 6
Implications and conclusion: Healthcare education in MELF contexts —— 155
6.1   Introduction —— 155
6.2   Social context and language use —— 157
6.3   Language matters: Implications for patient safety —— 158
6.3.1 Language errors in ELF and MELF —— 160
6.4   Multimodal resources to support effective MELF communication —— 164
6.4.1 Multimodality in simulation training and ESP —— 168
6.5   Implications for healthcare communication training in MELF contexts —— 170
6.5.1 Teaching listening for MELF contexts —— 171
6.6   Closing remarks —— 181

Appendix: Transcription Glossary —— 183

References —— 185

Index —— 217

Introduction: MELF and ELF

Chapter key points:
- MELF differs from ELF in several important ways including the potential for regulatory processes and its exceptionally high stakes nature.
- MELF is broadly defined as any use of English in a healthcare setting, and not limited to the Western biomedical model alone.
- MELF is distinguished by its domain use, and the overall goal of its users (both healthcare professionals and patients): improving human health and medical care.

1 Introduction: Distinctives of medical English as a lingua franca

Though researchers and language teaching professionals, our interest as authors of this book on English as a lingua franca as it is used in the field of medicine is not solely academic or professional in nature. The core of our teaching and research takes place among future and current healthcare professionals being trained for a multicultural and multilingual environment where English (along with Arabic) functions as one of two primary means of interlingual medical communication. However, our interest in medical English as a lingua franca (or MELF) is not just a professional one. We are drawn to this subject because we, our families, and presumably all readers of this volume, are also *patients* – that is, recipients, of healthcare services. And frequently, increasingly, and even typically for many of us, this healthcare provision happens in contexts in which one, many, or all stakeholders are speakers of a first language other than English, but are using English for communication in medical care. MELF, therefore, touches, at a very personal level, a significant segment of the global population, and in a very crucial way. The global prevalence of MELF, and the vital importance of efficient medical communication, are two elements that we believe set this field of study apart. And, as we will claim in this volume, there are others as well.

In fact, at the heart of this book lies a central question: is medical English as a lingua franca (MELF) *different*?

We assert, in the pages that follow, that MELF, while sharing many similarities to the established body of knowledge about English as a lingua franca (ELF), differs in several important ways.

MELF in our view is different because it, among the domains studied where ELF interactions take place, may be the most subject to the process of standardization, regulation, and codification. There is convincing evidence that its stakeholders are demanding that these processes take place, and the nature of medical communication is such that there exists the means to both insist upon standardization, as well as enable and enforce its regulation. This contrasts with the descriptions of variability, fluidity and emergence characterizing ELF interactions in other domains in which it has been studied. Given the unique and historically unprecedented circumstances that have positioned English as a global language, used as a communicative vehicle between speakers of thousands of different languages, its fluidity and variability are multifarious. To illustrate, a business negotiation using ELF between Angolan and Chinese entrepreneurs in Luanda will be shaped by many factors, including the dominant language (L1) of each interlocutor; their relative proficiency in English; the degree to which knowledge of other potential lingua francas are present (e.g., Portuguese; Mandarin); the nature of the speech acts in the particular interaction; and so on. Or, a family of Japanese tourists asking for directions in English to a native of Barcelona will be impacted by a range of similar factors, as well as other differing ones which are introduced by contextual factors that diverge from the first example. The myriad of differing circumstantial factors shaping each of the countless ELF interactions that take place around the world daily ensure fluidity, variability and emergence.

An ELF interaction between a physician (L1 Egyptian Arabic) and a Sri Lankan pharmacist (L1 Sri Lankan Tamil) in a Saudi Arabian hospital also possesses elements of fluidity, variability and emergence, that will set it apart, say, from an ELF patient handover discussion between two nurses (L1s Tagalog and Igbo) at the same hospital. But pressing upon these two medical interactions are influences not present in either of the two non-medical ELF examples above. There is the fact that precise message conveyance is critical, with the consequences of miscommunication potentially dire. There are established communication protocols imposed upon the interlocutors by their respective professions, and their employers. Time pressures are present, as are legal frameworks governing various aspects of the interactions' contents. As opposed to the transient and brief ELF encounters among businesspeople and tourists described above, these medical ELF interactions occur in the unique circumstances of a migrant worker destination, which, as we shall see later, creates a unique environment of extended multilingual language contact where ELF users live, work and interact in close proximity, with daily, face-to-face communication over months and years. All of these factors, along with others which will be discussed in subsequent chapters, push and pull MELF toward processes of language standardization and regulation not present to the same extent in domains in which ELF research has hitherto been investigated.

This is *not* to say that ELF research has ignored interlocutory conditions such as the above. The community of practice framework (Lave & Wenger 1991) has helped frame understandings of ELF (e.g., House 2003; Jenkins 2007; Ehrenreich 2018), where the role of social, non-linguistic contexts is considered central to understanding ELF communication. Indeed, we will argue later that the notion of community of practice, or at least a modified version, has great utility for comprehending MELF. Unlike the transitory encounters said to describe most ELF interactions (Jenkins 2015), the healthcare context provides a relatively fixed community, where (medical) practice is being engaged in, with various levels of formal regulatory bodies – local, national and international – superintending processes and procedures. Our context for the study of MELF – countries of the Gulf Cooperation Council (GCC) – provide special circumstances for frequent, sustained and protracted contact among ELF users, paving the way for further norm stabilization. As Mauranen (2018) asserted, the duration of a community and the relative frequency of its communication will impact upon its propensity to introduce regulatory processes.

Nor are we arguing that MELF is the *only* domain of interaction in which ELF standardization and regulation processes can be examined. Air traffic control is one obvious example, and Mauranen suggests the post-Brexit European Union linguistic community of Brussels as another (2018). What we *are* saying is that MELF provides one such sphere where regulatory processes can be observed, and for reasons discussed in subsequent chapters, provides an exceptionally useful one.

If the global spread of English evidences reclaiming and reinterpretation as it is increasingly appropriated for local use (Pennycook 2007), the domain of MELF may represent a pushback against the forces of localization. We find evidence of MELF users indeed reclaiming the local (Canagarajah 2005), but within the constraints of global regulatory forces which press indelibly upon the forms in which local usage takes shape. The nature of language is understood both as a highly decontextualized and stable global phenomenon, and a considerably contextualized and fluid local one (Kalocsai 2014): for reasons explained in the chapters that follow, we suggest that MELF tilts decidedly toward the former.

One element of these regulatory processes impacting upon MELF, which may be less considered in ELF contexts studied to date, is that of institutional talk. Institutional interaction is characterized, among other things, by the nature of its speech-exchange systems (Hutchby & Wooffitt 2008). Participants in institutional interaction typically situate themselves toward a relatively structured configuration of turn-taking, for example. Pre-allocated turn-taking (Atkinson & Drew 1979), of question-answer sequences, is especially evident in MELF; in the data that will be presented in subsequent chapters, for instance, nurses seemed to instinctively orient themselves, without direct instruction to do so, to the conventional format of a medical interview, and parameterize their language use accordingly. In medical contexts, turn-taking tends to be structured around defined goals (for example, gathering information to make a diagnosis). Normative restrictions are in play: the healthcare professional typically directs the speech exchange, with the patient expected to provide answers in response to queries, and informal sanctions may be utilized if either interlocutor strays too far from the question-answer format (Hutchby & Wooffitt 2008). In a healthcare professional-patient interview, there may be no formal institutional constraints which prevent a patient from initiating new topics or directing the question sequence, but research shows that, overwhelmingly, these tasks are physician-led (Frankel 1984; Frankel 1990). The types of questions healthcare professionals typically ask serve to restrict the kinds of responses patients can offer, and at the same time, patient responses reinforce this asymmetrical sequence of turn-taking (Heath 1992). In fact, an essential feature of medical interactions is their ritual nature, in that they take place to considerable extent in a ritualized, prescribed manner; perhaps a necessity, in that medical encounters ". . . accomplish a social role – the 'provision' of care and the maintenance of public health – and are therefore regulated by legal and social norms" (Bigi and Rossi 2020: 18). In the pages to come, we attempt to understand how conversational restraints such as these impact upon the variable, fluid and emergent nature said to characterize ELF communication.

MELF is also different in that abundant literature detailing interlocutor interactions is available to ELF researchers, having been generated by the medical field itself. Certainly, communication in other domains, such as business, is widely studied, but the sheer volume of research on medical communication is unequalled. Healthcare research has long recognized the importance of effective communication, and the potentially disastrous results when communication is ineffective. The healthcare communication research literature identifies multiple barriers to effective communication, including: unequal power relations between physicians and other medical professionals; organizational culture; poor questioning techniques; time pressures; system failures; inaccessible medical jargon; and fear of litigation, to name only a few. The literature is plentiful and diverse. Of particular interest to ELF are studies on communication impacted upon what the healthcare research literature broadly calls "language barriers". The literature makes wide use of the (decidedly imprecise) term "limited English proficiency" and the challenges this construct poses to the delivery of safe and effective patient care. ELF researchers will also find in healthcare communication literature substantial consideration of the global phenomenon of medical migration, where skilled healthcare professionals cross international borders to practice elsewhere, and indeed through global migration generally, as patients bring different first languages to everyday medical interactions conducted in

English. Communication features prominently among the issues treated in this area of study, and language chief among them.

Another distinguishing feature of MELF is that its interactions are often of a high-stakes, even life-and-death, nature. There may be high-stakes consequences in ELF business negotiations and ELF exchanges among academics (sites of previous ELF research), but they rarely have life-or-death outcomes. In contrast, misunderstood medication names or dosages, or incorrect diagnoses due to language imprecision, do. Medical researchers have said that language barriers increase risks to patient safety (e.g., Divi et al. 2007) and increase the likelihood of serious medical events (e.g., Cohen et al. 2005). Again, we do not claim that MELF is the *only* site of ELF research representing high-stakes, potentially life-or-death outcomes. ELF interactions take place daily in potentially hazardous workplace situations around the world: on construction sites; in air traffic control towers and airline cockpits; on the front lines of war zones in international peacekeeping missions; and in shipping lanes, for example. We do assert that ELF research sites such as these (MELF being only one), where precision communication is paramount, represent latent potential for contributing significantly to our understanding of ELF interaction. Does, for example, the let it pass strategy, observed in ELF business transactions (Firth 1996) apply to the especially time-sensitive and high-stakes situations of hospital emergency rooms or surgical theatres?

The nature of its subject matter means that MELF is also delineated by its wide relevance, a point we alluded to in the opening paragraph. With English as the prominent international language of medicine (Maher 1987), labour migration patterns in general, and of healthcare professionals specifically (Lu & Corbett 2012), the stage is set for healthcare to become a leading site for ELF interactions, and one many readers are likely to encounter at an especially personal level. One indication of wide public interest is perhaps its treatment in the popular media. Though of course not referencing the term MELF as such, (English) language barriers feature regularly in media reports on healthcare, reflecting the growing intersection of medical migration with ELF communication, and how the practicalities of that convergence are perceived to impact daily life. Whether in discussions of language proficiency for medical professionals (e.g., BBC News 2015; BBC News 2016); concerns over medication errors due to language barriers (Bladd 2008); patients' perceptions of language barriers in medical care (Allen 2009); or more sensationalist cases that likely conflate language proficiency with other issues (e.g., BBC News 2010), media discussions can be understood to mirror a wider public recognition.

We also make the point in this volume that several particular elements of MELF hold the potential to contribute significantly to our understanding of ELF. The urgency and immediacy inherent in the communicative context have already been alluded to in this regard, as has the role of regulatory processes. Another area in which MELF may enlarge and expand our conceptualization of ELF is in that of the role of non-verbal forms as elements of ELF communication. Non-verbal forms of communication have received some treatment in previous ELF research, but as Matsumoto (2019: 569) points out, "few researchers have conducted in-depth analyses of nonlinguistic interactional elements in a way that treats them as *integral* to ELF and ELF communicative strategies" (emphasis in original). Matsumoto asserts that non-verbals have been viewed largely as supplemental features, rather than part of the "multimodal ensemble" (Bezemer and Kress 2008: 166) which interlocutors bring to a communicative task, This, Matsumoto argues "is unfortunate because a multimodal orientation has the potential to enrich ELF research and deepen ELF interactional analysis" (2019: 569). MELF communication represents one such avenue for enhancing research enrichment and depth.

Non-verbal forms of communication, such as gestures, are an important part of medical communication in general (Gerwing & Allison 2009; Gerwing & Landmark Dalby 2014), and health assessments in particular, a communicative activity where a healthcare professional seeks to understand a patient's symptoms. Ting and Cogo (in press) make the point that gestures and other non-verbals may contribute significantly to avoiding non-understanding in MELF communication. Doctors often are taking notes on a computer during medical consultations, thus reducing eye contact with patients. In such circumstances, non-linguistic resources play a significant role, and ELF interlocutors may utilize non-verbals such as gestures to ensure engagement in the communication process.

In our data, we find that non-linguistic resources are far from supplemental features of communication. Rather, given the nature of the health assessment activity type (Levinson 1992), non-verbals may be indispensable. Protocols for assessment of medical conditions often require physical tasks to be undertaken by the patient, while the healthcare professional directs and carefully observes performance (e.g., *please move your right arm through its full range of motion*). We find examples in our data of an effective nurse-patient communication loop, where the nurse simultaneously models a desired action and a verbal prompt; the patient attempts the action accompanied by a verbal explanation; the nurse confirms the result verbally; and the patient makes a final acknowledgement, which closes the loop and permits the assessment sequence to proceed. We do not make the claim that this "multimodal ensemble" (Bezemer and Kress 2008: 166) is unique to MELF; the simultaneous use of linguistic and non-linguistic resources are likely part of many healthcare consultations. But we do assert that in a MELF context, this approach proves especially effective at avoiding potential misunderstandings, a finding that has important implications for healthcare education in ELF settings. We also argue that the multimodal resources utilized by MELF interlocutors represent a significant opportunity to extend understanding of ELF communication in general.

2 Potential: Being misunderstood

We do understand that by claiming the uniqueness of MELF among its research site predecessors, we run the risk of being sorely misunderstood. In recounting the medical profession's own description of the risks to patient safety brought on by language barriers, we may be wrongly interpreted as alarmist. We are not. In fact, our own initial research suggests that medical communication among ELF users includes several accommodation strategies, which, by and large, serve to facilitate successful understanding, even in circumstances which present potential risk for serious medical error. As we point out later, if alarm bells are being sounded, it is by healthcare researchers themselves, who identify language barriers as a key source of lowered quality of care, and of an amplified risk of serious medical events.

We also risk being perceived as arguing *for* the pre-eminence of English in international healthcare communication. We are making no such contention. Rather, we affirm the view of the World Health Organization (WHO) in this regard: any trend toward monolingual delivery of healthcare limits access to important public health information for great numbers of the world's population. In the *Bulletin of the World Health Organization*, Adams and Fleck (2015) describe the lack of access to public health information available during the Ebola outbreak in West Africa. Content of critical importance to public health at the time of the outbreak was provided almost exclusively in English, a language spoken by less than 20% of the population. Even though WHO's official documents are published in its six official languages (Arabic, Chinese, English, French, Russian, and Spanish), those who speak these as first languages (L1s) represent less than half of the world's population (Eberhard, Simons & Fennig 2020). In subsequent chapters, we observe that an English-centric perspective does seem prevalent in healthcare communication literature, though we suggest this might be due not to triumphalist bias, but simply a reflection of the high proportion of medical communication studies which, to date, have taken place in countries where English is spoken as a native language (e.g., see Schwei et al. 2016). Contrary to the notion of a single global language for access to healthcare, our ideal is that all patients would have access to care and treatment in the language of their choice (CHIA 2002), a value upheld in the context where out study takes place (HMC).

In asserting the unique nature of MELF, there is in addition the possibility of being wrongly associated with essentialist notions of language and culture. Much of the research we have undertaken on observing interactions in MELF contexts can be broadly subsumed under the heading of intercultural communication, and indeed the relationship between ELF and intercultural communication has been observed elsewhere (e.g., Baker 2015; Baker 2018; Cogo & Dewey 2012; Zhu 2015). In describing MELF, we are recounting instances of communication that are, by very definition, between two or more linguacultures. In our descriptions, we identify broad and imprecise characteristics such as speakers' nationalities, cultures and self-identified first or strongest languages. Such broad-brush descriptions are prone to criticism for being essentialist in nature: assuming clearly defined distinctions between cultures, nations or languages, or that individual characteristics align neatly with presumed national or cultural ones. Many researchers in intercultural communication are quick to eschew such demarcated categories as culture and language, and stress instead their blurred, unbounded and heterogenous nature, with some even arguing for the disuse of such categories altogether (Scollon, Scollon & Jones 2012). With respect to language, and specifically to one of the fields in which we work – the teaching of English to speakers of other languages (TESOL) – authors like Holliday (2005) find a sinister agenda lurking: a reboot of the colonial mission through essentialist stereotyping and cultural chauvinism. Holliday uses scare quotes to frame the terms "native speaker" and "non-native speaker", to draw attention to what he feels are the essentialist nature of such designations. In the phenomenon Holliday calls "native-speakerism", an essentialist view of culture is knowingly or unknowingly disseminated through the work of TESOL professionals: since person *A* (our TESOL colleague or student) is part of nationality *B*, and therefore larger religious/philosophical/language group *C*, we can expect behaviours *D*, *E* and *F*. At the core, Holliday asserts, is the construction of a generalized Other (e.g., *all* language learners from country/language *X*), a stereotype to undergird and reaffirm an unproblematic Self (2005: 19).

We will, admittedly, draw upon broad-gauged categories like language in this volume, but reject the notion that by doing so we are inherently engaging in essentialist stereotyping. First, we are at pains to utilize those categories identified by the participants in our research themselves. We do not assume, for example, that a nurse holding an Egyptian passport therefore considers Modern Standard Arabic to be his L1. Instead, we ask. He may consider himself a native speaker of French, or indicate his strongest language is Mattokki. He may consider two or more languages equally to be his "first". Or he may not be able to identify a mother tongue at all. Our research is framed upon the boundaries – however relatively fixed or unfixed – expressed by *participants*. We affirm the widely-held understanding that the nativeness paradigm primarily describes a social construct, not a linguistic one (e.g., Brutt-Griffler & Samimy 2001; Butcher 2005; Davies 2003), and agree with the assertion of Gupta (2010: 84), that tying the notion of native speaker to "race, ethnicity or citizenship is invidious and unjustifiable". Second, while agreeing that terms like culture and language are too broad, cumbersome and imprecise, and as such are prone to essentialism, alternative appellations are in short supply, and unlikely to be less problematic (Baker 2018).

Similarly, our findings may also be misinterpreted to depict an idealised, homogenous speech community. As will be discussed later, we glimpse in the medical communication research literature an unstated presumption of an imagined community of linguistically homogeneous medical professionals, attempting to communicate with patients whose language barriers preclude equitable access to healthcare. This presumption extends to foreign doctors or nurses struggling to communicate with their local colleagues. However, we caution against immediately identifying in this orientation an *inherently* political interpretation – a tendency to which critical linguistics is prone (Waters 2007a; Waters 2007b). In the main, we find language barriers in the healthcare communication literature described from the standpoint of praxis, with the aim of improving access to care for all, and in the context of the multicultural and multilingual societies in which the care is delivered. We understand Holliday's (2005) depictions of an unproblematic Self alongside a problematized Other to be written in the context of a critique of TESOL, and it would be unwise to view data from healthcare communication research, which our research draws upon extensively, through the same lens.

Finally, we run the risk of being misunderstood in that much of the healthcare literature upon which we draw is based upon a research paradigm which, at times, appears at odds with ELF theorizing. Baker (2016: 71), for example, argues that "ELF studies add to the growing body of *postmodernist thinking and research* in applied linguistics that can inform intercultural communication research" (emphasis ours). In the same article, he goes on to say that the fluidity of identity construction as identified in ELF shares elements "*in common with much postmodern research* in linguistics and outside it" (2106: 75; emphasis ours), and again later, that "ELF research has adopted *postmodernist approaches*" in contrast to binary approaches to language and culture (2016: 75; emphasis ours). We do not wish to decontextualize Baker's comments, because in the article cited here the author is specifically contrasting ELF understandings with the fixed and bounded categories of culture and language evident in previous intercultural research. Nor are we suggesting that Baker is here attempting to characterize *all* research paradigms used in ELF; indeed, a criticism levelled at ELF is that in its earlier development theorists over-relied on positivist-objectivist assumptions (O'Regan 2014). Yet, if Baker is correct in asserting that ELF has much in common with postmodernist approaches, we provide here forewarning.

Readers more at home with a postmodernist orientation should be cautioned that a positivist or post-positivist research paradigm underlies much of medicine and medical research (Brown & Dueñas 2020) and therefore a not insignificant portion of the literature which we draw from in our attempt to understand MELF. In contrast to the scepticism of some of the research paradigms prevalent in qualitative research, medical research historically has assumed universal truth exists. Brown and Dueñas (2020) reference Alderson (1998: 1007) in this regard, "in medicine, the emphasis on . . . body parts, conditions and treatments assumes that these are universally constant replicable facts".

The positivist/post-positivist research paradigm which has dominated medical research, and its specific application in what is known as the biomedical model (Freeman 2016), has led to impressive achievements, particularly in our understanding of control and treatment of infectious diseases. As we write this chapter in early 2020, the world is in the grip of the COVID-19 coronavirus pandemic, and the frantic search for "universally constant replicable facts" is a leading concern of the public, including, presumably, even the most sceptical postmodernists.

While paradigm shifts are well underway which may supplant the biomedical model (Wilson 2000), it still holds considerable influence on healthcare research, and therefore warrants a brief explanation here.

McWhinney's classic textbook on family medicine (Freeman 2016), widely used in medical education and now in its fourth edition, provides the following concise and simplified explanation of the biomedical model.

> Patients suffer from diseases that can be categorized in the same way as other natural phenomena. A disease can be viewed independently from the person who is suffering from it and from his social context. Mental and physical diseases can be considered separately, with provision for a group of psychosomatic diseases in which the mind appears to act on the body. Each disease has a specific causal agent, and it is a major objective of research to discover them. Given a certain level of host resistance, the occurrence of disease can be explained as a result of exposure to a pathogenic agent. The physician's main task is to diagnose the patient's disease and to prescribe a specific remedy aimed at removing the cause or relieving the symptoms.
> (2016: 58)

Needless to say, readers more comfortable with postmodernist research paradigms may not readily identify with the worldview caricaturized above, and may, when encountering some of the literature we draw upon in this volume, mistakenly conclude that as authors our own worldview aligns *exclusively* with this one. It does not. We do, however, conduct our work as language teachers in a professional sphere where variants of the biomedical model figure prominently, and it therefore informs our research and teaching in multiple ways, likely both consciously and subconsciously. Further, we acknowledge being more at home as researchers with quantitative methods, and when it comes to qualitative research, a post-positivist, critical realist position (Maxwell 2012).

In this regard, the reader will note in this volume our methodological pluralism. This non-uniformity in approach was not our original intent but was occasioned as we were confronted by our data. The focus of our research, as conceptualized in its earliest phases, was oriented heavily toward the linguistic code. At the time our research was taking shape, the potential for serious medical errors due to language barriers featured prominently in public debate in our context and was a focus of concern at the institution in which the data collection took place. Perhaps as a result, our earliest exploration of healthcare communication centred around matters of intelligibility and understanding, and with those, attention to the role of linguistic code. Our analyses centred around fine-grained perspectives, such as phoneme- and morpheme-level distinctions, segmental and suprasegmental features and the like which might explain how understanding was achieved among ELF healthcare professionals in our multilingual context, or account for instances when nonunderstanding or misunderstanding occurred.

However, as we reviewed hour-upon-hour of transcribed recordings of ELF nurse interactions, with patients and with each other (47 hours of recordings at the time of writing, with the process ongoing), it became apparent that a wider lens than linguistic code alone would be needed to understand the phenomena we were observing. The social elements of language, its "living social practice" (Eckert & McConnell-Ginet 1992: 462) were in evidence, but apparently sitting astride the structures for conversational interactions characterized by institutional talk (Drew and Heritage 1992a), and in particular the medical interview (Boyd & HeritageI 2006). Yet linguistic code could not be ignored either, as successful medical communication requires exceptional precision. We recognized that a single methodology or theoretical framework would be insufficient, and so opted to accept the perils of drawing upon multiple analytical tools. Readers will find in this book elements of conversation analysis (Sidnell & Stivers 2013) as we sought to understand how meaning-making was achieved across linguacultures within micro-interactional units. On a macro level, we drew inspiration from the thick description of qualitative case study research (Denzin & Lincoln 2018) to interpret the influence of the larger political and economic forces on shaping language contact experiences of our participants. We grappled with the sociological forces underpinning interactions between healthcare professionals and patients (Heritage & Maynard 2006), and to understand the role of language as it functioned in our data in developing a medical community of practice (Thrysoe et al. 2010). Making sense of our interlocutors' linguistic choices required us to dramatically improve our background knowledge of an at times overwhelming amount of discipline-specific medical content, as varied in focus and scope as technical language for health assessment; medication names; nursing practice routines; theory and practice of medical education; interprofessional healthcare delivery; patient safety; medical migration; medical simulation training; biomedical philosophy; and human anatomy. Our reference list reflects this assorted range of disciplines as we sought to understand healthcare communication: readers will find diverse sources consulted in our research, ranging from broad topic coverage (*McWhinney's Textbook of Family Medicine*) to the oddly specific (*Journal of Lower Genital Tract Disease*); the list includes works aimed at decidedly niche audiences ("Perioperative psychoeducational intervention can reduce postoperative delirium in patients after cardiac surgery: a pilot study"), as well as to the likely much broader readership of the *Las Vegas Sun* newspaper ("Foreign nurses can slip into communication gap"). We of course looked as well to sub-disciplines more familiar to us in our training in applied linguistics, and to the conversations and debates within them, including: English for Specific Purposes; English for Academic Purposes; World Englishes; Content-based Language Teaching; Task-Based Language Teaching; language proficiency testing; language policy and planning; Second Language Acquisition; bilingualism and multilingualism; language standardisation; translanguaging practices; pragmatics; native-speakerism; Communicative Language Teaching; and the like. This is of course above all a book in a series on English as a Lingua Franca, so through all and in all we attempted to understand all of our data, irrespective of the diverse methodological and theoretical perspectives found within, in light of the rich scholarship in ELF. Inevitably, attempts to draw from such a broad range of subjects result in incomprehensive treatment of all, and for this we apologize in advance to disciplinary and sub-disciplinary specialists in the fields listed above. Interdisciplinary research for applied linguistics is certainly not without its challenges (Cox 2020), but the nature of this inquiry made it a necessity.

Fortunately, we found precedent for our (overly?) ambitious attempt to integrate such diverse and multiple perspectives within the healthcare field itself. Healthcare researchers who advocate the holistic notion of patient-centred care (PCC) attempt to do so in a profession traditionally dominated by monological epistemology (Kincheloe 2005), focused on one-dimensional ways of knowing. In contrast, the comprehensive view of patient health and wellbeing of PCC requires a multi-dimensional approach to knowledge, engaging with various theoretical frameworks and research methodologies, along with one's own reflexivity as a researcher, and the lived experiences of participants (Warne & McAndrew

2009). Drawing upon a bricolage (Kincheloe 2005) of methods and approaches, we attempt in this volume to weave together multiple paradigms, approaches and methods – at times potentially conflicting in orientation- so as to both interpret our own observational data, and contribute to an emerging theory of the nature of MELF communication. We leave it to the reader to judge, in the pages that follow, the success or failure of what we attempt.

Being misunderstood is one of the risks of engaging with conflicting research orientations, and their at times entirely different cultures of knowing (Snow 1998). Research that crosses the boundaries of disciplinary cultures requires "the capacity to adopt a fundamentally open and experimental approach to disciplines, research questions as well as their potential for addressing societal issues" (Fuchs 2018: s3). We ourselves have attempted to embrace this capacity, and ask readers to adopt a similarly open stance as they consider our work.

3 Conceptualizing MELF within ELF

As an emerging site of study within the larger field of ELF, our conceptualisation of MELF must, of necessity, proceed in a somewhat tentative, and eclectic manner. We intentionally set out to do what is most certainly impossible, and what is most likely very unwise: to reach beyond the immediate findings from our site of study, in order to lay preliminary groundwork for theorizing about medical ELF in general. This attempt requires tentativeness because we will propose preliminary definitions of MELF, frameworks for theorizing about MELF, and methodologies for studying MELF which will inevitably be subject to later revision. It requires an eclectic approach in that an emerging field has little of its own literature to draw from. We will therefore utilize extant research rooted in sometimes contradictory ontological positions: ranging from those more akin to the "post-modern free-fall" Baker described (2016: 446), to praxis-oriented communication analysis rooted in positivist/post-positivist biomedical models (Brown & Dueñas 2020). As our understanding of the field of MELF is exploratory and preliminary, we draw upon theoretical frames for analysis already employed by ELF researchers, such as communities of practice; propose ones not yet employed (socio-cognitive approaches; social network theory); and suggest a revisitation of discarded ones (speech communities). We feel it important to consider multiple frames for analysis, in that we observe MELF interactions in interprofessional medical communication, in intraprofessional communication, and in the type of medical communication readers will be most familiar with: the healthcare professional-patient encounter. Our methodologies, both taken up to examine our own data, and proposed for future studies of MELF, are equally diverse.

With these cautions as a backdrop, this introductory chapter will conclude by briefly touching upon the positioning of MELF within the larger field of ELF research. As such, we propose a definition of MELF for the purposes of our study and beyond.

3.1 ELF and MELF: A backdrop

The extraordinary spread of English around the world (Crystal 2003; Crystal 2008), and the scale by which non-native English speakers far outnumber native speakers (Kachru 1996), are likely unprecedented in the history of contact languages, and for better or for worse, have made English the "default mode" for international communication (McArthur 2002: 13).

The term lingua franca came into English from a Middle Ages contact language in the Mediterranean region, via an Arabic term for the language of the Francs, which was then translated into Italian as *lingua franca* (Kahane & Kahane 1976; MacKenzie 2014). In its general use in English, lingua franca describes a contact language; the Cambridge Dictionary (2021) defines the term thus: "a language used for communication between groups of people who speak different languages". In linguistics, the term lingua franca describes "any language used for communication between groups who have no other language in common" and provides as an example "Swahili in much of East and Central Africa where it is not native" (Matthews 2014). Indeed, lingua francas have doubtless been in existence since the origins of language, and are in use today in every continent, and of course in the virtual world of Internet communication. Arabic, Chinese, French, Russian, and Spanish are examples of lingua francas which have achieved wide international use, though for various reasons, English has come to occupy a dominant role in international communication.

ELF has been variously defined, with extensive discussions found elsewhere, and so in line with our purposes, we note briefly some definitions from ELF scholars which have been central to our subsequent conceptualization of MELF.

> a contact language between speakers or speaker groups when at least one of them uses it as a second language.　　　　　　　　　　　　　　　　　　　　　(Mauranen 2018: 8)

> any use of English among speakers of different first languages for whom English is the communicative medium of choice, and often the only option.　　　(Seidlhofer 2011: 7)

> "the use of English in a lingua franca language scenario".　　　　(Mortensen 2013: 42)

The notion of *similect*, as articulated by Mauranen (Mauranen 2012; Mauranen 2018) is a helpful concept in understanding ELF. Since English is in relative degrees of contact with many of the world's languages, it is reasonable to expect that observable transfer features from other L1s would be evident in the English of ELF users, in similarities such as pronunciation features and lexical usage. Names like Manglish (for "Malaysian English") are often jokingly referred to in common speech to describe this phenomenon. Similects (Mauranen 2018: 9) like "Manglish" or "Chinglish", develop in a parallel fashion, and when they come into a state of contiguity with one another, represent a sort of "second-order language contact" (Mauranen 2012: 29–30).

It bears repeating at the outset that ELF is not understood by its exponents as a deviation from English as a Native Language (ENL) norms, and thus identification of so-called error has no role. Any modifications made from ENL norms in ELF should rather, in the words of Widdowson "be recognized as a legitimate development of English as an international means of communication" (Widdowson 2004: 361). To Widdowson, the range of English is not restricted by ELF communication, but "on the contrary, enhanced, for it enables its users to express themselves more freely without having to conform to norms which represent the sociocultural identify of other people" (2004: 361). ELF users are therefore not considered "learners", and so there are some elements of Second Language Acquisition theory which are said not to intersect with ELF, such as language errors, interlanguage, L1 interference, fossilization and so on. Jenkins stresses that "the ability to accommodate to interlocutors with other first languages than one's own (regardless of whether the result is an 'error' in ENL) is a far more important skill than the ability to imitate the English of a native speaker" (Jenkins 2007: 238).

Jenkins (2015) traces an evolution in the field of ELF. In the earliest days of ELF's conceptualisation, researchers drew heavily upon a World Englishes (WE) paradigm, which advocated for acceptance and recognition of new varieties of English, emerging outside of the inner circle (Kachru 1985) of English language users. The influence of the WE paradigm may explain, at least in part, the early focus of ELF research on identification of linguistic features. The Lingua Franca Core (Jenkins 2000), for example, identified potential areas of phonological unintelligibility for ELF users, and proposed features of English deemed important or unimportant for comprehensibility. The assemblage of ELF corpora such as the Vienna-Oxford International Corpus of English (Seidlhofer 2001); the Corpus of English as a Lingua Franca in Academic Settings (Mauranen 2003), and the Asian Corpus of English (Kirkpatrick 2010b), further assisted ELF researchers in their early emphases on codifying features.

However, the focus of research and theorization in ELF began to shift away from identifying codified patterns, and toward considerations of variability and fluidity, in a phase of development for the field Jenkins calls "ELF 2" (Jenkins

2015: 55). This new emphasis on the emergent and ad hoc nature of ELF communication underscored the field's distinctiveness from a WE paradigm, where Englishes tend to be described by identifiable features, with geographically bounded patterns.

In "ELF 3", the compass moved again, this time in the direction of various multilingual perspectives on language use, particularly translanguaging (García 2009; García & Wei 2014) which may hold particular promise for further understanding of ELF. While earlier conceptualizations of ELF emphasized how L1s impacted the use of English, translanguaging perspectives enable a more complete understanding of the mutual interchange and interconnectedness of users' multilingual repertoire (Jenkins 2015).

The origins of English as a lingua franca for medical communication can be understood in a larger context of the vernacularization of scientific and medical literature (Taavitsainen & Pahta 2004). Sanskrit, Chinese, and Greek were among the earlier languages for international medical communication (Maher 1986), but in a European context Latin played a dominant role as the lingua franca of medicine prior to the 16th century, in the scholastic tradition, prior to the modern scientific approach we associate with medicine today (French 2003). By the 17th century however, the replacement of Latin in medical writing was well underway: 207 of 238 medical books in the twenty years between 1640 and 1660, for example, were written in English (Gotti 2016: 10). The 17th through 19th centuries saw expansive growth in the written publication of medical literature in English, including a multiplication of new genres, and medical writers introduced to the English language an increasing amount of specialized terminologies (Gotti 2011). From the 17th century, English, German and French all functioned as international languages for medical literature (Ferguson 2013), but for various reasons, English rose to prominence, accounting for 72% of all medical journal articles in an influential database by 1980 (Maher 1986). Between 1986 and 2005, using the extensive PubMed database as a measuring stick, while the overall number of medical publications had doubled, the number of those written in languages other than English fell from 23% to 10% (Giannoni 2008). Italian, for example, while in considerable use in the humanities and social sciences, accounted for less than 1% of all scientific publications by Italian researchers, compared to the 99.7% of their colleagues whose work was written in English (Giannoni 2008: 100). Similar trends have been observed for medical and scientific publications in Scandinavian contexts (Gunnarsson 2009), and Chinese scholars exhibit a preference for English publication in disciplines of the sciences in general (Mu & Jun Zhang 2018).

The above description speaks specifically to international medical English communication in its written form. As discussed elsewhere in this volume (see

Chapter 1), the trans-border flow of medical professionals also serves to heighten the use of MELF in spoken contexts, as ELF users from different lingua-cultural backgrounds encounter one another in healthcare settings.

3.2 Toward a definition of medical English as a lingua franca

Broadly speaking, medical English as a lingua franca (MELF) can be defined as any use of ELF in a healthcare setting. *Healthcare* is most often associated with the biomedical model, i.e., the conflation of modern scientific methods with Western medicine (Wolpe 1994), but we see no need to limit the definition of MELF to biomedical contexts alone. The approaches to healthcare encompassed in traditional Chinese (Chow 1984) and Indian (Goldman 1991) medical practices, for example, both draw to a considerable degree upon ELF as a vehicle when international, interlingual healthcare communication is required. An Indonesian businesswoman who travels to Shanghai for a medical consultation with a practitioner of traditional Chinese medicine may be a MELF encounter. Similarly, a practitioner of traditional Arabic and Islamic medicine (Azaizeh et al. 2010) in Kuwait, treating a migrant worker (L1 Gujarati), may have ELF as the only available communicative option; in our view this instance of language contact could also be considered a MELF interaction. The World Health Organization (2020a) affirms the important role of traditional, complementary and alternative medicine in healthcare, and increasingly, various practices of healthcare described as complementary and alternative medicine (CAM) feature in journals traditionally focused on biomedicine, such as *The British Medical Journal* and *The Journal of the American Medical Association* (Brodin Danell & Danell 2007). Where such practices involve ELF communication, we consider them as potential fields of study for MELF.

In the same way, a definition of MELF need not be limited to interactions specific to doctors, nurses and their patients, though certainly theirs are the most frequently discussed in research literature in healthcare communication. MELF could also include the communication of physiotherapists, dieticians, midwives, speech pathologists, radiographers, pharmacists, chiropractors, dentists and other paramedical, allied health professionals (Law & Martin 2020) who deliver healthcare services.

Because our definition of MELF has at its centre professional communication with the goal of health, rather than a focus on a specific model of *how* that is done (e.g., the biomedical model versus CAM), the categories of literature and methodological approaches upon which we draw are diverse. Healthcare communication research is abundant in publications for medical professionals, such as *The British Medical Journal* or *The International Journal of Nursing Practice*, where the focus of research is typically oriented to praxis, with the aim of strengthening communication for improved clinical outcomes. Healthcare communication is also examined through the lenses of various disciplines in linguistics, and so methodologies such as conversation analysis, interactional sociolinguistics, and sociopragmatics have yielded rich data for our exploration of MELF. Pedagogy-oriented research, aimed at improving teaching in communication for healthcare personnel, can be found in both medical education literature (e.g., Kurtz, Draper & Silverman 2005), and in applied linguistics research, in sub-fields such as English for Medical Purposes (e.g., Ferguson 2013).

In clarifying the distinction between English as a business lingua franca (BELF) and ELF in general, Kankaanranta and Louhiala-Salminen (2018: 309) identify three distinctives: the domain use of BELF; the professional role of its users, and the overall goal of the interaction. We follow this helpful frame for conceptualizing MELF. The domain use of MELF is the delivery of healthcare, whether it be through practices and beliefs underpinned by Western biomedicine, CAM, traditional Chinese medicine, Ayurvedic medicine, Arabic and Islamic medicine, or others. The role of users is less clear-cut however; in BELF, users are business professionals, and presumably, non-professionals, by definition, are excluded. MELF use extends beyond the healthcare professional and her specialized body of technical knowledge, to the patient. Kankaanranta and Louhiala-Salminen summarize the overall goal of business ELF interaction as "getting the job done and creating rapport" (2018: 309). We look to healthcare communication literature in conceptualizing the overall goal of MELF interactions: the improvement of patients' health and of medical care (Ha and Longnecker 2010: 38).

4 Conclusion

This introductory chapter has attempted to lay the groundwork for conceptualizing our approach to examining medical English as a lingua franca, to preliminarily situate MELF within ELF, and to suggest a definition of the term. At the risk of being misunderstood, we have asserted that MELF differs from ELF in several important areas, points which will be taken up in detail in subsequent sections of this book. One of those key differences – the abundance of literature available to ELF researchers from the field of healthcare communication itself – is the subject of the next chapter.

4 Conclusion

We close this introductory portion of the book with a word of explanation. The reader will note that throughout the book, we have placed snippets of information, which may appear at first glance to be somewhat extraneous to the main body of text in which they occur. These may be extracts from our data, selections from our case study descriptions, or salient points from the reviewed literature. As authors, we undertake this practice for three primary reasons. First, our personal preference as *readers* is for less "dense" text: both of us find it easier to engage with a textual viewpoint if the messages are chunked into more digestible portions. Second, we wish to honour the ELF users who graciously consented to having their words used as data for our study. The volume of MELF interactions recorded – and still being recorded – for our research far exceeds the analytical categories presented in this book. In some small way, the inclusion of at least some of their words in this volume, even when they did not neatly fit within our analytical categories, allows these ELF users a voice. Finally, as researchers we readily acknowledge our own limitations. It is our hope that by including such seemingly extraneous snippets, other reader-researchers will be sparked to uncover what we have not.

Chapter 1
Healthcare communication and MELF

Chapter key points:
- The migration of healthcare professionals is a growing phenomenon which affects health systems around the world.
- Research indicates that effective communication in healthcare contexts positively impacts patient outcomes; conversely, ineffective communication has the potential to threaten patient safety.
- The addition of linguistic and cultural factors, associated with the migration of healthcare professionals, likely contributes yet another layer of complexity to effective medical communication.
- Characteristics of medical English as a lingua franca both converge with and diverge from ELF in its primary domains of study thus far. As such, MELF holds the potential to deepen our understanding of ELF.

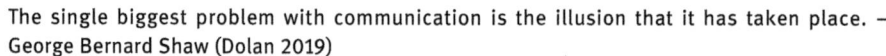
The single biggest problem with communication is the illusion that it has taken place. – George Bernard Shaw (Dolan 2019)

1.1 Healthcare professional migration

We live in an era of unprecedented labour migration, where workers across the spectrum of employment sectors, from unskilled farm labourers to university research professors, seek better opportunities abroad. Healthcare labour is no exception: the World Health Organization avers a 60% decadal increase of migrant healthcare professionals to Organisation for Economic Co-operation and Development (OECD) countries (World Health Organization 2020b). In fact, healthcare professionals account for the lion's share of all educated migrants. The number of foreign-born doctors in OECD countries, for example, typically exceeds the number of foreign-born highly educated professionals in general (OECD 2019). In many countries, foreign-trained healthcare professionals account for significant numbers of the total healthcare workforce: in 2017, foreign-trained doctors made up 42% of New Zealand's doctors, 40% of Norway's, 32% of Australia's, and 24% of Canada's. Israel topped this list with 57.9% (OECD 2019: 1.4). Foreign-trained nurses accounted for 7% of the total nursing workforce in OECD countries, with Australia, Canada, Norway, New Zealand, Switzerland and the UK all exceeding that OECD average. In New Zealand, for instance, foreign-trained professionals made up 26% of all nurses in 2017, reflecting a steady increase through the previous decade (OECD, 2019:1.4).

Another indication of the prevalence of global healthcare worker migration was the development of a Code of Practice by the World Health Organization (2010) to discourage active recruitment of healthcare professionals, in order to prevent critical shortages in migrant-sending countries. Some estimates suggest African countries, for example, may lose as much as 70% of their healthcare system workforce to high-income countries (Aluttis, Bishaw & Frank 2014), a reality which raises unsettling ethical questions for nations engaged in direct recruitment. Yet, the migration of healthcare professionals cannot be understood only in terms of traditional patterns of mobility. Delegates to the 2018 *International Platform on Health Worker Mobility* at the World Health Organization's Geneva headquarters were presented with the increasingly blurred patterns of migration source and destination, such as South to South and North to South. For example, doctors from Nigeria represented the top source of doctors entering South Africa between 2011 and 2015 (Cuba and the Democratic Republic of Congo were the third and fourth sources). The second most common source of South African doctors during this time period? The United Kingdom. In another example of the complexity surrounding source and destination for healthcare professionals, one-third of doctors registering in Uganda from 2011–2015 held nationality in North America or Europe. One-half of practicing doctors in the Caribbean country of Trinidad and Tobago in 2014 were trained in India, Nigeria or Jamaica (Health Workforce Department 2018).

In actual fact, the scale of healthcare workforce migration may well be underestimated by the numbers presented above. First, while data are more readily available on the cross-border movement of physicians and nurses, far less can be found on the migration of other types of healthcare professionals, such as radiologists, pharmacists, physiotherapists, and so on. Second, the number of available migratory pathways may further mask the actual extent of migration. A healthcare professional may migrate to a new country for the purposes of study, then join her new country's healthcare workforce at a later date. Or, recently arrived immigrants may enrol in healthcare education in their new country, and thus be excluded from counts of foreign-trained professionals. The OECD therefore recognizes the distinction between foreign-*trained* and foreign-*born* healthcare professionals: the number of foreign-born doctors in 18 OECD countries increased by more than 20% from 2010–2016, with nurses reflecting a similar trend. In Australia, foreign-born physicians account for over half of the total doctor workforce, and in Canada, nearly 40% (OECD 2019: 1.3)

> The case for distributive justice and global accountability around international recruitment [of healthcare professionals] was strengthened by Mills et al's 2011 paper, which estimated the costs to 9 SSA [sub-Saharan African] countries from the loss of locally trained medical doctors who were working in the four main destination countries: United States, United Kingdom, Canada and Australia. Estimates of losses ranged from $2.16 million for Malawi to $1.41 billion for South Africa, resulting in cost savings to destination countries that did not need to train the doctors they recruited internationally: $2.7 billion for the United Kingdom and $846 million for the United States (Brugha & Crowe 2015: 335).

Perhaps not unexpectedly, the global movement of healthcare workers has raised concerns over the impact such migratory flows may have on accurate communication in medical contexts, an observation routinely discussed in popular media (BBC News 2015; BBC News 2016). But what impact do these shifting workforce numbers have upon communication in healthcare? This is the subject of the next section.

1.2 Medical communication and migration of healthcare professionals

> Language is medicine's most essential technology, its principal instrument for conducting its work (Jackson 1998: 65).

The notion that the "most essential technology" of medicine is language is supported by a multitude of studies identifying the benefits of effective medical communication for patients. Besides improved overall health status and psychological well-being (Chou & Cooley 2018), elements of effective medical communication have been found to positively impact patient outcomes in illnesses such as blood pressure (Schoenthaler et al. 2009); diabetes (Greenfield et al. 1988); coronary heart disease (Benner et al. 2008); mortality rates from heart attacks (Meterko et al. 2010); cancer (Mustafa et al. 2013; Arora et al. 2009); and HIV (Flickinger et al. 2016). Effective communication has been shown to reduce negative post-surgery outcomes (Trummer et al. 2006; Lee et al. 2013), and positively impact pain control (Oliveira et al. 2015). As a potential remedy to today's soaring healthcare costs, effective communication also saves money (Chou & Cooley 2018; Epstein et al. 2005; Zhang et al. 2009).

Given the weight of the empirical evidence about its benefits to health, one would assume effective medical communication is widely prioritized and practiced. However, despite over 200,000 patient interactions during a typical physician's career (Chou & Cooley 2018), in the words of three MDs summarizing the literature, "We [physicians] do not seem to be very good communicators" (Tongue, Epps & Forese 2005: 652). Research suggests physicians typically select a patient problem to explore before fully hearing her or his concerns, with one study indicating doctors listen to patients for only 18–23 seconds before redirecting the conversation (Marvel et al. 1999). There may also be a wide gap between physicians' perception of themselves as communicators and the perceptions of patients. 75% of 700 orthopaedic surgeons surveyed perceived themselves as having satisfactorily communicated with their patients, while only 21% of patients perceived the communication as satisfactory (Tongue, Epps & Forese 2005). Research has uncovered multiple other factors hindering doctor-patient communication, including: excessive medical jargon (Deuster et al. 2008); a disproportionate emphasis on biomedical talk (Kain et al. 2009); ineffective questioning techniques (Roter et al. 1999); unequal power relations between physicians and patients (Todd 1984); doctors' avoidance of emotional issues due to time pressures (Maguire & Pitceathly 2002); and physicians' burden of work and fear of litigation, among others (Ha & Longnecker 2010).

ELF healthcare interaction: End-of-shift patient handover simulation
Nurse B (first language: Arabic): *Why you . . . take the blood sugar? The blood sugar, it's high?*
Nurse A (first language: Tamil): *Blood sugar, not take.*
Nurse B: *You not take blood sugar?*
Nurse A: *No. Not diabetic, not diabetes.*
(M. Gregory Tweedie & Robert C. Johnson 2018a)

The above barriers to healthcare communication describe only physician-patient interactions, and in settings in which language differences are not predominant. In many contexts, healthcare is delivered by a complex array of interactions between many medical specialties: one estimate suggests an involvement of more than 50 specialties and subspecialties (Leape & Berwick 2005). This complexity doubtless impacts effective interprofessional communication, as does hierarchical structure, a culture of individual autonomy, and dispersed accountability (Leape & Berwick 2005). In describing physician-nurse communication in the context of maternity care, Lyndon et al (2011) detail hindrances to communication such as face-saving; relational preservation; fear of negative repercussions; deference to hierarchy; and conflict avoidance. The effectiveness of pharmacist-physician communication is said to be impacted upon by several factors, including the tendency to work in silos; conflicting understandings on the role of pharmacists; a lack of time on both sides; and an overreliance on oral rather than the precision of written communication (Kelly et al. 2013; Coomber et al. 2018).

Given these complexities, it is not unwarranted to assume medical migration and attendant language differences will add yet another layer of convolution to healthcare communication (see Figure 1.1).

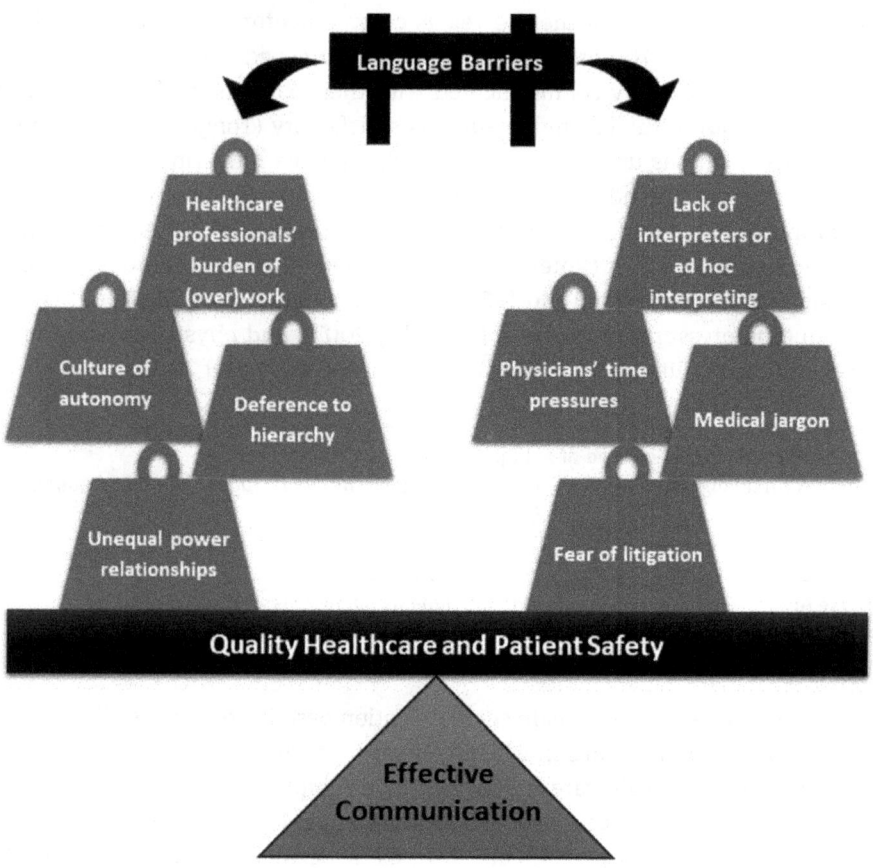

Figure 1.1: Layers of complexity in healthcare communication: a delicate balancing act.

If medical migration and differing linguacultures impact healthcare communication, it may be a case of making an already bad situation worse. Miscommunication is understood to be the main reason for medical mishaps (Khairat & Yang 2010). In an integrative review, Foronda and colleagues paint a bleak picture: "Ineffective communication in healthcare results in delayed treatment, misdiagnosis, medication errors, patient injury, or death" (2016: 36). Considerable data exists to quantify this blunt assessment. CRICO Strategies, a division of Harvard Medical Institutions, maintains a large database of malpractice cases in the United States. Their analysis of more than 23,000 cases in which patients suffered harm indicated three in ten involved a breakdown of communication (CRICO Strategies 2015: 1). CRICO's *2015 Annual Benchmarking Report* highlights 7,149 cases where communication contributed directly to patient harm, both healthcare provider-to-provider communication, and provider-to-patient. Of those 7,149 cases, failures in communication led to medium- or high-severity patient injury (including death) 88% of the time. Twenty-six per cent of all surgery cases analysed involved a communication failure, as did thirty-eight per cent of all general medicine cases, with miscommunication regarding the patient's condition cited as the dominant cause of communication breakdown.

Failures in communication have been shown to link directly to "sentinel events" in healthcare organizations. Sentinel events in medical care refer to negative outcomes "not primarily related to the natural course of the patient's illness or underlying condition" and that result in severe and/or permanent harm, or death (The Joint Commission 2016: 2).

From a patient's perspective, the Joint Commission's list of most-reported sentinel events makes for unpleasant reading. In 2015, the euphemistically-termed URFOs (Unintended Retention of Foreign Objects, e.g., sponges, catheters or needles) topped the list, and the causes for URFOs included "failure in communication with physicians:"; "failure of staff to communicate relevant patient information" and "problems with hierarchy and intimidation" (2015, p. 8). "Wrong-patient, wrong-site, wrong-procedure" sentinel events are disquietingly self-explanatory, and their causes include ineffective "hand-off communication" (p. 10). "Patient falls" are also attributed in part to "communication failures" (p. 12), as are "Delay(s) in treatment" (p. 12). A decidedly unsettling disclaimer at the beginning of the sentinel event list hints at the extent of the problem: "The reporting of most sentinel events to the Joint Commission is *voluntary* and *represents only a small proportion of actual events*" (p. 6; emphasis ours).

However, there is nothing in the Joint Commission's documentation of sentinel events to suggest that these communication failures were caused by language or cultural differences brought on *specifically* by the migration of healthcare professionals. CRICO's 2015 analysis of 7,149 malpractice cases attributes 4% of these to language barriers in provider-patient communication, but this does not necessarily point directly to healthcare migration. Yet, given the pervasiveness of medical communication problems, it is difficult to see how adding linguistic and cultural differences to the mix would not exacerbate existing challenges. Indeed, there is growing recognition of this reality by health researchers (Meuter et al. 2015).

> The ultimate objective of any doctor-patient communication is to improve the patient's health and medical care (Ha & Longnecker 2010: 38).

The term "language barriers", though imprecise from an applied linguistics perspective, is widely used in healthcare communication literature, as is the equally imprecise "limited English proficiency" (LEP). Medical literature on language barriers has tended to obscure shades of proficiency. As stated by Roberts and colleagues in their study of misunderstandings in primary healthcare care, "the issue of language ability has been treated as an either/or matter, i.e. you either speak English or you do not" (2005: 466). More fine-grained analyses, which consider language ability along continua, or according to function (e.g., ability to explain presentation of symptoms; see Ali 2003) are far less prevalent.

Typically, studies on language barriers in medicine consider healthcare contexts where English is widely spoken as a native language (ENL), such as the USA and Australia. In a cross-sectional review of 426 studies on language barriers in healthcare, Schwei et al (2016) found that the United States, United Kingdom, Australia and Canada accounted for 86% of the geographic locations studied. In these settings, language barriers tend to mean access to communication in English. Studies considering language barriers in other contexts (such as Alshammari, Duff & Guilhermino 2019; Paulino, Vázquez & Bolúmar 2019; Tay, Ang & Hegney 2012; Fassaert et al. 2010; Green 2017) are increasing in number, but much rarer. In ENL settings, language barriers are said to, among other negative outcomes, inhibit understanding and use of medications (Wilson et al. 2005); increase the length of hospital stays (John-Baptiste et al. 2004) and the use of diagnostic testing (Hampers et al. 1999); increase the risk of hospital readmission (Karliner et al. 2010); result in critical communication inaccuracies and omissions (Flores et al. 2003); elevate hospitalization rates (Hampers et al, 1999); disproportionately impact resource utilization (Hampers & McNulty 2002); increase the risk of serious medical events (Cohen et al. 2005); and, overall, limit optimal care (Nielsen-Bohlman, Panzer & Kindig 2004), with heightened risks to patient safety (Divi et al. 2007).

The use of interpreters also figures centrally in healthcare communication literature, and would seem to further affirm that language adds to the communicative strains already evident. Again, research sites are almost exclusively ENL contexts, but the evidence suggests (quality) interpreters very positively impact healthcare outcomes. In a systematic review of the literature, Karliner et al (2007) found that professional interpretation in healthcare, among other benefits, reduced communication errors, improved clinical outcomes, and increased patient satisfaction.

Clearly, readily available and quality interpreting would contribute greatly to raising the standard of healthcare in multilingual environments (CHIA 2002), and an ideal to strive toward is that access to interpreters would make it possible for all patients to receive healthcare services in the language of their choice. However, several realities make that desirable aim impractical in many contexts. First, the number of different languages encountered daily by healthcare institutions in many large cities already stretch thin existing interpreting resources (Karliner, Pérez-Stable & Gildengorin 2004). And language interpretation is not needed only in the hospital or clinic: many countries do not utilize a "one-stop" healthcare delivery system, but require patients to attend multiple appointments and locales for various outpatient services such as diagnostic imaging, specialist doctor visits, etc., unfortunately often rendering impractical the use of interpreters. Finally, critical care situations often demand on-call interpreters, a further challenge among the linguistic diversity of many population centres. In one overwhelmed New York City hospital, for example, half of patients requiring treatment during the height of the COVID-19 pandemic did not speak English (Sopel 2020); the sheer number of patients involved and the infectious nature of this particular disease would make interpreters largely nonviable in this situation. In lieu of trained and qualified interpreters, family members (including children), friends or other patients are often utilized by physicians and nurses, and one study noted that professional interpreters were actually used quite infrequently, raising concerns about the quality of care (Schenker et al. 2011). Patients reported "getting by" in communication with nurses, or "barely speaking at all" (2011: 712). While such ad hoc interpreting heightens the potential of medical error, a large-scale survey indicated it may be common practice among physicians (Lee et al. 2006). Diamond and Jacobs (2010), in proposing interventions for physicians to overcome language barriers in a USA context, describe one remedy, with typically less than satisfactory results: English-speaking physicians attempting to communicate with patients using other languages in which the doctor has limited proficiency. Cox and Li (2020) suggest that language be coupled with social interaction skills in clinical preparation to strengthen effective communication where physicians and patients speak different languages.

Remedies to the imprecise description of "limited English proficiency" have been attempted in the healthcare communication literature. Roberts et al (2005) for example, categorized sources of misunderstanding between physicians and patients as due to pronunciation and word stress; intonation and speech delivery; grammar, vocabulary and lack of contextual information; and style of presentation. Under the category of style of presentation, Roberts and colleagues identify sub-categories of low self-display; different ways of structuring information;

topic overload and recycling; and overlapping/interrupting talk. The researchers suggest that style of presentation and its sub-categories caused "more protracted, general and unresolved misunderstandings than the other three because it was more difficult for the participants to assess where the problem lay. Patients and GPs ended up talking past each other but not knowing quite why" (2005: 470). In the framework of Roberts and colleagues, low self-display encompassed patient behaviours such as showing the physician an empty medication bottle without explanation, relying on physician inference to interpret meaning. Information structuring involved preferences for topic presentation, where an explicit statement of the consultation's purpose may be structured later in the visit depending on the speaker's linguaculture. The authors observed that topic overload and recycling, where the patient introduced multiple topics seemingly unrelated to the consultation, was more common among less proficient speakers of English. Overlapping or interrupting talk was also observed as a source of misunderstanding, and like topic overload/recycling, may be attributed to talk features in differing linguacultures. While frequent overlapping of speech during conversation may be considered inattentive listening in some cultural contexts, in others it may represent high engagement with the speaker (Tannen 2005).

> Medicine is an art whose magic and creative ability have long been recognized as residing in the interpersonal aspects of patient-physician relationship (Hall, Roter & Rand 1981: 18).

Presumably, the movement of healthcare professionals across borders would also introduce cultural differences into the complex milieu of factors impacting healthcare communication. The United States Department of Health (2013) recognizes the importance of culture in healthcare, and affirms the importance of providing culturally and linguistically appropriate services, setting forth a blueprint for national standards in the provision of those. The field of nursing, where our study focuses, has been at the forefront in asserting the importance of cultural considerations in the delivery of quality care, with its models being utilized by other healthcare professions (Sagar 2012). While the necessity of cross-cultural awareness training for doctors who practice in the United States has been affirmed by the American Medical Association (AMA 2020) and the accrediting authorities for Graduate Medical Education (Goroll et al. 2004), actual practice may lag behind policy. In a survey of over 2000 American physicians, 25% felt inadequately prepared to care for patients with differing beliefs on Western medicine, to assist new immigrants (25%), or identify relevant cultural customs impacting healthcare (24%) (Weissman et al. 2005). Given the reality that multiple interprofessional interactions are the normal means of healthcare delivery in many contexts (Leape & Berwick 2005), the importance of interprofessional training in cross-cultural communication is receiving growing recognition (Liu et al. 2015). Adding to complexity in cross-cultural communication within interprofessional interactions are paraprofessionals, who may be part of the delivery of healthcare in manycultural contexts (Oelke, Thurston & Arthur 2013; Purden 2005), including the context of our research.

1.3 Interprofessional communication and medical migration

Interprofessional education in healthcare: "occasions when two or more professionals learn with, from and about each other to improve collaboration and the quality of care" (Centre for the Advancement of Interprofessional Education 2020: para. 1).

In general, it can be said that the healthcare communication literature tends to assume as a reference point an imagined, near-monolithic cultural and linguistic context in which medical professionals perform their work. The overarching aim in such circumstances is the development of competencies in cross-linguistic and cross-cultural communication that are generally *outward*-focused, toward the "other", the cultural and linguistic outsider patient seeking medical treatment. The realities of multilingual and multicultural societies are well acknowledged in the literature, but typically from the perspective of "us-them" interactions. Far less considered in the literature are the cross-cultural and cross-linguistic encounters *interprofessionally* (Oelke, Thurston & Arthur 2013): the foreign-born and foreign-trained nurse interacting with a physician born and trained in the host culture, or the foreign-born/-trained physician interacting with a host culture administrator, for example.

Several factors may account for the literature's overall lack of attention to interprofessional communication that is cross-linguistic and cross-cultural in nature. First – and positively, from a patient's point of view – is the move of modern medical systems toward a patient-centred care (PCC) orientation (Pelzang 2010). PCC moves away from what has been characterized as a solely biomedical model (Mead & Bower 2000) and places the patient in the central position in healthcare systems. This sweeping reorientation may explain in part the emphasis on research which focuses primarily on linguistic barriers in clinician-patient communication at the expense of consideration of the same barriers among healthcare providers themselves.

Second, as noted previously, the research context for the majority of studies are settings where English is spoken as a native language. In these settings, research positioning typically assumes one of two scenarios. First, the presumption is of a common level of linguistic proficiency and core of cultural similarity among healthcare providers, delivering care to patients with limited English proficiency. The "problem to be solved" in research studies with these orientations is providing effective healthcare across the linguistic divide. A second common scenario in healthcare communication research assumes the reverse of the previous: patients assumed to have a common level of "native" linguistic proficiency and cultural similarity, encountering foreign-born/-trained healthcare providers. These monolithic perspectives of course mask the range of language proficiency and communicative competence among individual speakers, and underscore a point we will take up later: the role applied linguistics can play in contributing to interdisciplinary health communication research.

Finally, cross-linguistic and cross-cultural interaction among healthcare professionals may be underrepresented in research due to a prevailing work culture existent in the field of medicine, a reality identified by clinicians themselves. Reflecting on an influential report on patient safety from the Institute of Medicine (Kohn, Corrigan & Donaldson 2000), Leape and Berwick (2005: 2387) describe "medicine's tenacious commitment to individual, professional autonomy"; "antipathy toward attempts by others outside the profession to improve practice"; and "a well-entrenched hierarchical authority structure". Though evolving with the emergence of PCC, paternalistic models are said to dominate medical culture, with information dispensed to patients only in the amounts needed to secure consent (Kaba & Sooriakumaran 2007). In this work culture environment, it is not difficult to surmise that investigations of clinician-patient, and especially clinician-clinician interactions would be less than welcome.

Nevertheless, interprofessional delivery of medical services has been recognized by the World Health Organization as an essential component of primary healthcare (WHO 1988). Interprofessional training has become increasingly characteristic of healthcare education (Thistlethwaite & Moran 2010); and its various features therefore have received considerable treatment (e.g., Slusser et al. 2018; Forman, Jones & Thistlethwaite 2016). While attention to cultural differences is discussed as an important feature of interprofessional education in healthcare (De Oliveira et al. 2015; Liu et al. 2015), these also tend to be outward-oriented, to medical professionals preparing to encounter patients from another culture, rather than preparation for interactions within the profession. Linguistic barriers in interprofessional interactions receive even less consideration.

Studies of language barriers in interprofessional interactions, where existing, often draw from data on "international medical graduates" (IMGs), typically defined as practicing doctors with medical diplomas obtained from a country other than that of their current practice (Herfs 2014; Skjeggestad, Gerwing & Gulbrandsen 2017). Consistent with the focus of the healthcare communication literature in general, discussions of language barriers for IMGs emphasize interaction with patients, likely for the reasons discussed previously. However, though not receiving the same emphasis, interprofessional communication is noted in the IMG literature. Michalski et al (2017), for example, in a systematic review of intercultural challenges faced by IMGs, described difficulties with accents, with different dialects, with medical terminology, and with general language proficiency. Pilotto et al (2007) discusses the sheer range of registers for interprofessional interactions IMGs must learn in order to communicate effectively, including other medical practitioners, diagnostic professionals, hospital medical officers, nursing staff and allied health practitioners, among others. Each group in this list requires differing communication in choice of medical terminology, and the amount and type of medical information to be given. In a Norweigan context, Skjeggestad and colleagues (2017) found IMGs' language barriers to be multifaceted in nature. Semantic communication barriers encompassed terminology (biomedical; discipline-specific; health and welfare system-specific), as well other vocabulary generally related to low proficiency in Norwegian. Matters of pragmatics were encountered in interprofessional interaction, where gaps in sociocultural understanding hindered communication with other medical professionals. Gasiorek et al (2012), using the term language-discordant mobile medical professionals (MMPs), studied colleague-to-colleague interactions in a Western European setting. MMPs identified the need for further strengthening of both medical language and nonmedical language (including idioms, dialects, humour, pronunciation and fluency), all factors confirmed by their local colleagues.

1.4 Medical communication and English as a lingua franca

English as a lingua franca: "any use of English among speakers of different first languages for whom English is the communicative medium of choice, and often the only option" (Seidlhofer 2011: 7).

We have thus far established that the literature on healthcare communication shows – rather convincingly – that medical communication on the whole, both between medical professionals and their patients, as well as interprofessionally, has much room for improvement. And we have also summarized the extensive evidence from healthcare literature which shows that ineffective communication has dramatic consequences for the quality of healthcare delivery and for the safety of patients. We asserted that while the literature touches only slightly on the relationship between medical migration and healthcare communication, it is likely that the cross-border movement of medical professionals serves to add yet another layer of complexity to healthcare communication. But this book is about English as a lingua franca (ELF). What intersections can be found between ELF and its use in healthcare communication and how might ELF inform studies of healthcare communication, and *vice versa*? In what areas do other domains for ELF and its use in healthcare communication seem to diverge?

1.4.1 Social and individual dimensions of MELF

While the earliest conceptualizations of ELF devoted attention to language form, researchers have since shifted focus to an emphasis on its social dimensions, with the aim of understanding the broader social context – "what is going on" among ELF interactants (Seidlhofer 2009a: 56). More recent ELF research has therefore drawn upon frames of reference such as the community of practice (e.g., Kalocsai 2014; Ehrenreich 2018) or imagined communities (Wang 2018) as a means of considering the social setting for understanding ELF communication. Healthcare communication research includes a similar orientation. From descriptions of asymmetrical power relationships between physicians and patients or physicians and other medical professionals (e.g., Lyndon, Zlatnik & Wachter 2011; Leape & Berwick 2005) to studies of medical interactions as institutional talk (e.g., Drew & Heritage 1992a), social-contextual features prominently in medical communication literature. Healthcare researchers, for instance, have long recognized the utility of Lave and Wenger's (1991) notion of community of practice to describe medical practice, particularly the process of medical education (e.g., Cruess, Cruess & Steinert 2018); indeed, Wenger originally used medicine as a sort of prototypical illustration of the community of practice framework (1998). As we will assert in subsequent chapters, social context is crucial to conceptualizing medical communication in general, and thus to MELF specifically. The affordances and constraints of institutional talk (Drew & Heritage 1992), for example, significantly impact MELF interactions, as do the socio-cultural expectations for clinician-patient encounters, framed within the expectations of a particular "activity type" (Levinson 1992).

Yet, paradoxically, healthcare communication research also reflects the culture of autonomy inherent in the medical profession (Leape & Berwick 2005). Despite the reality that healthcare is increasingly delivered through multidisciplinary teams – which are heavily reliant on effective communication for success (Hall 2005) – the physician-patient encounter remains the dominant site for medical communication research. The search for theoretical lenses through which to conceptualize MELF therefore must encompass both the social context in which MELF takes place, and this preeminent one-to-one setting in which much medical communication research has been undertaken. We therefore follow the lead of other ELF researchers in utilizing a community of practice framework, but also propose the use of a socio-cognitive approach (Kecskes 2010) to bridge the gap between healthcare communication as an inherently communal practice, and the one-to-one encounters which constitute its primary site of inquiry. As will be seen later, a socio-cognitive approach effectively frames the search for common ground inherent in multilingual clinician-patient interactions, accounting for both individual, pre-existing reference points, and the convergent meaning negotiated by the interlocutors.

1.4.2 ELF and norm-development

From an earlier focus on form, ELF research has shifted away from attempts to identify particular features which could in turn be taught to learners. As Baker puts it: "there is an increasing consensus that what is characteristic of ELF communication, and thus of interest to research, is *variety* rather than a *variety*" (2011: 201; emphasis in original), and ELF research has subsequently, by and large, affirmed this claim (Widdowson 2015). In summarizing ELF researchers' turn away from particular features, Pitzl asserts, "ELF is *essentially characterized* by its variability, flexibility and linguistic creativity (2018: 15; emphasis ours). Pitzl goes on to propose a number of sociolinguistic conditions which contribute to the uniqueness of ELF, including "a high degree of situational adaptability of ELF that leads to its linguistic forms being locally (re)coined and (re)adapted" (2018: 19). As such, "an *essential feature* of these sociolinguistic conditions is the fact that ELF does not take place within a speech community" (2018: 19; emphasis ours). Yet, as will be touched upon later, we observe external pressures brought to bear on ELF in the medical domain which challenge Pitzl's assertions that ELF is *essentially characterized* by its flexibility, and that an *essential feature* is its occurrence outside a speech community.

First, while there may well be a considerable degree of situational adaptability in MELF, we observe opposing forces which to a considerable extent serve to mitigate local recoining and readaptation. Consider, for example, the following

ELF extract from our data, where Nurse Johild[1] (L1 Malayalam) is performing a neurological assessment on a stroke patient.

NE-SIM6B

27 Nurse Johild (L1 Malayalam): Okay. So you are sixty-year-old female patient I can see that your um, skin color is appropriate to the ethnicity and uh, your facial symmetry is appropriate to the moment when you're talking. And you're awake and alert and uh nutrition-wise it looks fine and uh, your posture is um, posture is erect. Okay? And you are comfortable and cooperative. Your facial expression and uh, just is appropriate of the situation and the speech is clear and understandable to me. Um, [name of patient] I need to check you how you are walking. Can you please walk for me few steps?

Within this conversational turn, an example of what we have come to describe as a "biomedical think aloud", we can see features of Nurse Johild's utterance which are consistent with those of other ELF users: for instance, the flexible use of determiners (*can you please walk for me few steps*). The Nurse in this extract is not bound by "native speaker" norms and expectations for including the article *a* before *few steps*, or before *sixty-year-old female*, nor should she be, and as an ELF user she is vested with full authority to include or omit determiners as it serves her communicative purposes.

Yet, within this turn we note the use of medical assessment formulaic language, over which, we expect, Nurse Johild is afforded less freedom to innovate: *facial symmetry is appropriate to the moment*; *posture is erect*; *awake and alert*; *comfortable and cooperative*. An innovation such as *today no more sad mouth* may well be an instance of ELF innovation and creativity to describe improvement in a stroke patient's facial symmetry, but it is unlikely to be considered acceptable by her charge nurse who must sign off on the patient's discharge; the hospital administrator who sends a report to the insurance company; her preceptor; the examiner for the English-medium nursing licensure exam she must sit for; or Nurse Johild's own sense of identity as a healthcare professional in a multilingual, but ELF clinical environment such as that in which our data occurs. These, and other external factors, act to constrain the flexibility and variability in MELF which may be evident in other ELF contexts. For this reason, we suggest qualification to Pitzl's claim of ELF's *essential* variability.

---

[1] All research participant names used in the book are pseudonyms, either participant- or research team-chosen, depending on the participant's indicated preference.

Second, while we are sympathetic to the objections raised by ELF researchers to the notion of *speech community*, we find elusive the search for a more accurate term when it comes to portraying Nurse Johild's social/linguistic context. Researchers such as Seidlhofer object to the utility of the notion of speech community for describing ELF in that "speakers do not usually live in immediate physical proximity with each other and do not constitute a speech community in this sense" (Seidlhofer 2011: 83). Seidlhofer finds globalization and technological innovation responsible for making the notion of the speech community irrelevant as a lens for describing ELF, noting that ELF users "tend to spend more time communicating with people via email and Skype than in direct conversations with partners in the same physical space" (2011: 87). As a result of her own experience as an ELF user with electronic communication, Seidlhofer is convinced that "the old notion of community", involving "frequent local, non-mediated contact among people living in close proximity to each other cannot be upheld any more" (2011: 86–87). However, the experience of community by ELF users who are Western academics may be considerably different than the nature of community experienced by migrant workers such as Johild, who leave country and family to ply their skills and ELF abilities in search of employment abroad. For Johild, who is housed in cramped conditions in a GCC country with other expatriate nurse colleagues from across South and Southeast Asia, "frequent local, non-mediated contact" in (very) "close proximity" is an everyday reality. Language contact among ELF users is daily (hourly?) as lines separating work and home are blurred, if not erased altogether: Johild shares meals, laundry, household chores, Uber rides, and a small bedroom with a nurse colleague from the Philippines, who also works in the same ward at the hospital which provides their accommodation. Johild and her Tagalog-speaking colleague are two of six other healthcare professionals residing in the same villa, and ELF serves as the main vehicle for the frequent and non-mediated close proximity contact of the other residents: L1s Indonesian, Swahili, Nepali and Malayalam. In what are typically two-year contracts, and the intensified proximal contact, it is difficult for us to conceive of the absence of at least some degree of linguistic norm development.

Clearly, the situation in which Johild finds herself as an ELF user is more akin to the description posed by Mauranen (2018: 12) of multilingual communities where the relative stability results in norms, conventions and other regulatory practices.

1.4.3 ELF and centrist perspectives

The historically unprecedented spread of English across the globe has given rise to equally unprecedented language change, and new varieties of English. Linguistic features of these new varieties came to be understood not as errors, as deviations from standard norms, but rather appropriation, as English was adapted, modified and created to meet local multilingual realities and express localized culture and tradition (Kachru 1991). Although scholars originally drew heavily upon a World Englishes paradigm (McArthur 1998) in conceptualizing ELF, earlier proponents began to advocate a shift (e.g., Jenkins 2011) toward a Global Englishes framework (Pennycook 2007; Pennycook 2009). To Pennycook, the notion of Global Englishes accounted for a "gap" in a World Englishes paradigm, through addressing the question of "[h]ow to come to grips with a noncentrist understanding of English as an international language that is dependent neither on hegemonic versions of central English nor on nationally defined new Englishes, but rather attempts to account for the ever-changing negotiated spaces of current language use" (2009: 195). As informed by a Global Englishes paradigm, ELF is described as "emergent and situated with common features, frames of reference and meanings negotiated by the participants on the spot" (Kalocsai 2014: 20).

It is our assertion in this volume that Medical ELF is neither characterized *fully* by "hegemonic versions of central English", nor accurately depicted as a series of "ever-changing negotiated spaces". MELF is not easily placed at either end of this continuum; it aligns fully with neither perspective, but encompasses elements of both.

Elements of how the English language is employed and administered for medical purposes can indeed be characterized as "hegemonic" and "centrist". Consider assessment, for example. English language proficiency tests with specific medical content are used widely to assess the suitability of internationally educated healthcare professionals to practice within national jurisdictions, such as the Occupational English Test (OET 2020) or the Canadian English Language Benchmarks Assessment for Nurses (CELBAN 2020); such assessments of medical language proficiency are seen as central to the delivery of safe and effective healthcare (Carnet & Charpy 2017). General tests of academic English such as the PTE Academic and IELTS Academic are also accepted as proof of English language proficiency for healthcare professional licensure (e.g., see NAPRA 2014; Ahpra 2020). It is difficult to underestimate the impact of assessment washback (Cheng 2013) on the language use of healthcare professionals for whom English is an additional language; the influence of international language proficiency tests on linguistic skill development have been demonstrated (e.g., Allen 2016).

Active recruitment of healthcare professionals across international borders can be seen as another illustration of hegemonic and centrist practices related to language (among others). The "brain drain" (Nguyen et al. 2008) of healthcare professionals from lower- to higher-income countries is of global concern, and as noted previously in this chapter, may leave African nations with critical shortages of healthcare workers (Aluttis, Bishaw & Frank 2014). Countries where English is spoken widely as a native language may be particular beneficiaries of this unequal South-North flow of healthcare professionals (Brugha & Crowe 2015), but the formal adoption of English for medical purposes in countries where English is spoken as an additional language (e.g., see Tayem et al. 2020; Carnet & Charpy 2017) facilitates this disparate flow elsewhere. The international English language proficiency tests for healthcare professionals spoken of previously, while certainly not directly responsible for such uneven transnational flows, in one sense can be seen as "aiding and abetting" these recruitment practices.

We can also observe in MELF interactions the "ever-changing negotiated spaces" of which Pennycook's (2009: 195) plurilithic model speaks, where interlocutors mold, adapt and shape language in real-time to their communicative purposes. The following MELF interaction from our data set, between two nurses (both L1 Malayalam) and their patients (M and P, both L1 Arabic, along with P's infant) serves as an illustration.

IM-SIM3
65 Nurse B (L1 Malayalam): Is boy or girl?
66 [speaker unclear]: Boy.
67 Nurse A (L1 Malayalam): So how you feel today?
68 Patient P (L1 Arabic): Um, I'm okay.
69 Nurse A: You're okay.
70 Patient P: Yah.
71 Patient M (L1 Arabic): She's in here, my sister is having some problems sleeping so she's hoping that she can get some uh sleeping tablets. Not sure if that's I don't think that's going to help her particularly but
72 Nurse A: It started after the delivery of (all this) or it already started
73 Patient M: She's just not sleeping
74 Nurse A: Okay
75 Patient P: Um, no, not after the delivery. It was after the accident of my my husband.
    He died a year ago in a car accident.

76 Nurse A: Okay. When it happened?
77 Patient P: He died about a year ago.
78 Nurse A: A year ago.
79 Patient P: Yah.

In this simulation scenario, set at a vaccination unit of a primary healthcare centre, Nurse A is attempting to determine the onset of Patient P's sleeping difficulties. While a World Englishes perspective might theorize on the lack of do-support in Nurse A's question forms (*how you feel today*; *when it happened*) as evidence of a particular "variety" of English, either relative to a national standard form (e.g., Indian English; Sailaja 2009) or an Inner Circle one (Kachru 1985), Patient P seems to accommodate without reference to either, and the question regarding symptom onset is resolved (turn 75).

In our goal of understanding medical English as a lingua franca, we find it unhelpful to conceive of language practices in either/or categories: *either* centrally imposed hegemony *or* free-flowing negotiated meaning. Our data would suggest the reality as more nuanced. On the one hand, to fulfil her plan of practicing nursing in New Zealand, Nurse A will likely need to align the grammar of her question forms with that of Inner Circle varieties, if she is to be awarded a band 7 for Grammatical Range and Accuracy on the IELTS Academic test (IELTS 2020), requisite for licensure in her desired location (NCNZ 2020). On the other hand, Nurse A achieved her communicative intent (identifying the onset of her patient's sleeping problems) with these very same question forms. Throughout our data, we see similar patterns, with imposed structures operating alongside innovative forms, seemingly in non-contradictory coexistence. While critical applied linguists might be uneasy straddling the contradiction, MELF users in our data appear unbothered. As we will point out, medical English is replete with formulaic terminology, acronyms, and specialized lexicogrammatical structures which are taught and tested in medical training; evaluated by preceptors; required for practice by local health jurisdictions; reinforced by electronic record-keeping for data standardization; and vigorously promoted by various international healthcare organizations. The use of these language features, and the *requirement* that they be used, impose a regulatory and codification function on medical ELF users which acts to restrict – but definitely not eliminate – the emergent and real-time negotiated meaning present in some other domains for ELF.

1.5 Summary

We thus assert that medical English as a lingua franca, with its divergence in essence from ELF contexts most studied to date, represents the potential to deepen our understanding of ELF. This chapter has shown that MELF encompasses elements said to be by nature uncharacteristic of ELF – at least as presently understood – and it is this apparent contradiction that begs a revisit of what have been considered essential features of ELF. A better understanding of MELF also holds out the possibility of enhancing healthcare communication, which, by the admission of its own researchers, is in need of some improvement. In the following chapter, we consider suitable lenses through which to examine ELF in medical contexts.

Chapter 2
Tools for analysis: Framing MELF

Chapter key points:
- Defining and understanding community, a key feature of the sociocultural backdrop to the language use in this study, is central to conceptualizing ELF and MELF.
- The community of practice framework, the utility of which is well established in ELF research, is particularly apropos to researching MELF.
- A socio-cognitive approach, with its harmonization of speakers' common ground and egocentrism, provides an especially useful framework for considering the healthcare professional-patient interactions which account for a considerable portion of MELF encounters.
- Characteristics of medical English as a lingua franca both converge with and diverge from ELF in the primary domains of study. As such, MELF holds the potential to deepen our understanding of ELF.

2.1 Introduction

As we search for an analytical lens through which to investigate MELF, we consider in this chapter a number of theoretical frameworks, tools not only which enable understanding of our own data, but which might inform the study of MELF going forward. In that sense, we aim to make preliminary contributions to a theory of healthcare ELF.

For some time, ELF researchers have affirmed the value of the community of practice (CoP) framework in understanding lingua franca communication, and it is asserted here that the notion of CoP is particularly suited to the study of healthcare ELF. However, a lens through which to view MELF must be wide enough to include the activity which for many of us, represents our primary association with healthcare: the physician-patient or nurse-patient interaction. It will be argued that as an activity in which common ground is sought between healthcare professional and patient in negotiated meaning of the specialized language of medicine, MELF healthcare professional-patient encounters may be best understood through a socio-cognitive approach (SCA). We also assert that the phenomenon of MELF, though occurring in diverse healthcare contexts throughout the world, is unusually prominent in migrant destinations, and we therefore in this chapter suggest another framework for investigating medical ELF: social network theory. Preliminary to consideration of these three theoretical frameworks, however, is a brief discussion of the notion of community, and its relationship to both our present research, and the study of MELF in general.

https://doi.org/10.1515/9783110697025-003

> ...we propose an approach [to medical education] built around the theory of communities of practice, since we believe that medicine is, and has always been, a community of practice (Cruess, Cruess & Steinert 2018: 185).

2.2 Community and medical English as a lingua franca

Studying how language is used in social contexts, the chief aim of sociolinguistics, offers understanding into the nature of language, the relationships within a community, and how social identity is constructed through language use (Holmes & Wilson 2017). Understanding what is meant by *community*, then, is central to understanding the phenomena of ELF, and by extension, MELF. The notion of *speech community* (e.g., Gumperz 1968; Labov 1972; Hymes 1974), while routinely contested, is still employed broadly in linguistics to describe a social grouping sharing commonalities in linguistic norms. While critiqued for its imprecise definitions, its idealised view of homogeneity, and its overextension, among other weaknesses, it retains at least general conceptual utility for describing language in bounded social groupings (for an extended survey of the critiques of the concept of speech community, and yet its inescapability, see Patrick 2004). The speech community as a frame of analysis has been largely discarded in ELF research (e.g., Wang 2018; Seidlhofer 2011; House 2003), seemingly due to the assumption that speech communities necessarily imply physical proximity of social groupings.

Wang, for example, asserts that "speech communities are irrelevant for the research into ELF and unable to capture ELF as a phenomenon in intercultural settings that go beyond locally or physically defined boundaries" (Wang 2018: 154). Seidlhofer also argues, categorically, that the nature of ELF cannot be captured by reference to geographical or physical proximity:

> a time when many of us, and particularly those who are regular users of ELF, tend to spend more time communicating with people via email and Skype than in direct conversations with partners in the same physical space, the old notion of community based purely on frequent local, non-mediated contact among people living in close proximity to each other clearly cannot be upheld any more. (2011: 86–87)

Similarly, Seidlhofer elsewhere contends that in the "contemporary world", shaped by globalizing forces like electronic communication and air travel, "the old notion of community based purely on frequent face-to-face contact among people living in close proximity to each other clearly does not hold anymore" (2009b: 238).

But what if the forces of globalization *do* create circumstances of "frequent", "local", "face-to-face contact" among "regular users of ELF", "living in close proximity to each other"? Such conditions portray, with uncanny precision, the environment in which our investigation of MELF takes place. Consider, for example, the following extract from a case description.

Saju (L1 Malayalam), Kenny (L1 Tagalog), and Dhonu (L1 Nepali) are surgical technicians at a large teaching hospital in a country within the Gulf Cooperation Council (GCC). As is the case across the GCC generally, this country's economy is heavily reliant upon expatriate migrant labour, a reality reflected in the composition of the multinational and multilingual workforce of the hospital. The hospital's official communication channels assertively market its use of English in patient care, and consider English proficiency a requirement for staff employment. Saju, Kenny and Dhonu, as surgical technicians, are responsible for carrying out preoperative sterilization procedures in the operating theatre; assembling and preparing surgical instruments; occasionally administering medications, suturing incisions, or applying dressings under the supervision of the surgical team; and providing other assistance to the surgeon as required. Dhonu and Kenny are in their fourth year of employment at this hospital; Dhonu has worked in the GCC region for six years in total, and Kenny for five. Saju has lived in the GCC for three years, of which the entirety has been spent at this institution. While Saju and Dhonu share a functional knowledge of Hindi, their communication with each other during the course of their daily work is almost exclusively in English, which is the only language in common for speaking with Kenny.

The clear division between home and work, a feature of "work-life balance" prized in Western economies, is not an option for workers in this context. As part of their expatriate employment package, and as is typical in the GCC region, these three surgical technicians live in accommodation provided by the hospital: a five-bedroom villa, which they share with seven other male hospital staff of various nationalities. Shared rooms for sleeping, shared cooking and laundry facilities, and shared transportation to and from the hospital blur the line between home and work. While some intralingual communication takes place at the villa (Kenny shares Tagalog as an L1 with two other Filipino housemates), English is used almost exclusively as a communicative vehicle across nationalities.

This account illustrates the particular conditions of migrant destinations, such as the countries of the GCC, which serve to develop, for lack of a more precise term, "speech communities" of ELF users. Language contact is typically intensified in migrant destinations (Boyle 2012), and as demonstrated in the above description, ELF use often takes place in frequent (daily), face-to-face contact by users living in (extremely) close proximity to one another, typically for at least two years at a time.

We have no desire to reopen a discussion about the relative utility of the notion of speech community as a tool for sociolinguistic analysis, which has been discussed extensively elsewhere (see Patrick 2004). We do however wish to draw readers' attention again to how MELF, taking place as it often does in migrant destinations, presents new possibilities for deepening our understanding of the complexities of ELF. Seidlhofer's dismissal of the notion of speech community is understandable if one's data on ELF use is drawn primarily from more economically privileged users. Migrant destinations, where labour is most often supplied by decidedly less privileged ELF users, create conditions of intensified, daily, face-to-face, close proximity contact, but have been to date underrepresented in ELF research. To cite another example, English often functions as an important vehicle for interlingual communication among residents of refugee camps. Extending the scope of future ELF research to include these less economically privileged populations of ELF users promises to extend knowledge in new ways.

2.3 Communities of practice and medical English as a lingua franca

Learning in communities of practice, while said to be going on since humans' earliest existence (Wenger 1998), found its modern articulation as Western societies began a rethink of learning, driven by the economic transformation from manufacturing models to knowledge creation (Squires & Van De Vanter 2012). In the context of this broader discussion of how education might be reformed, Jean Lave and Etienne Wenger questioned the very nature of learning as it had been previously expressed. They contrasted the idea of learning as a largely individual activity, with fixed beginning and end points, separated from other activities, with the idea of an "encompassing practice of being active participants in the practices of social communities and constructing identities in relation to these communities" (Wenger 1998: 4).

Lave and Wenger put a name to a model of teaching and learning which was actually millenia-old, and one that until the industrial age probably described how most learning was carried out in human groups: learning-by-doing, with older and more experienced group members passing on knowledge to younger members through explanation and modelling. We understand this today as an apprenticeship model of learning, but our modern definition carries with it a structure and formality that belies the original notion of transferring knowledge through learning-by-doing, through instruction and demonstration, through show-and-tell.

Lave and Wenger described this phenomenon as a *community of practice* (CoP), and framed their explanation within a common group interest or profession (1991). Through sharing common experiences, and built around domain-specific information, group members develop personally or professionally, and move from relative outsiders to group insiders through an apprenticeship process. Knowledge specific to the domain is passed along in a context of community fostering exchange of ideas, which are then put into practice through continual learning experiences. Through a process of "legitimate peripheral participation" apprentices are allowed to remain as relative outsiders, while existing group members gradually introduce them to the requisite skills and knowledge through highly contextual "situated learning" processes.

Wenger (1998) elaborated further on this process, by explaining three apparatuses central to building and maintaining communities of practice. A "mutual engagement" in the particular group focus serves to solidify and support the social nature of the group, while the particular domain of knowledge or activity, negotiated and shaped by the group members, is described as the group's "joint enterprise". The resources developed by the group over the time constitute a "shared repertoire" of knowledge, skills, insider stories and jokes, specialized vocabulary, and so on.

Identify formation is a central feature of a CoP, which Wenger (1998) understood to be shaped primarily in communities of practice, and emphasized these as the central unit of analysis for understanding identity. Through the processes of mutual engagement, joint enterprise and shared repertoire, group members construct individual identity, and take on the identity of the community.

There are at least two compelling reasons for utilizing Lave and Wenger's (1991) notion of community of practice as a framework with which to analyze MELF: its prior use in ELF research generally, and the application of the CoP to healthcare as described by medical researchers themselves.

2.3.1 Communities of practice and ELF

The usefulness of the concept of CoP for understanding ELF interactions has long been recognized by ELF researchers. Juliane House (2003) first proposed the notion of a community of practice to describe ELF, in a discussion of the limitations of speech communities as a referential frame. To House, despite its many incarnations, the notion of speech community represented an inadequate analytical perspective for ELF because of its "way of being" (Holmes & Meyerhoff 1999: 178), its "dependence on essential social and/or behavioural properties which speakers can be said to possess in a *relatively stable or homogeneous way*" (House 2003: 572; emphasis ours). House contrasts this relatively fixed essence with ELF, "whose characteristic it is that each individual moves in and out of a variety of contexts" (572).

As a conceptual framework, communities of practice have been taken up in a number of ELF studies, and have found to be particularly useful in understanding ELF interactions in higher education (e.g., Kalocsai 2014; Cogo & Dewey 2012; Smit 2010). Susanne Ehrenreich (2009; 2010; 2011) has taken up CoPs as a means of analysis in international business contexts, and has offered further exploration of their utility of CoPs in understanding ELF in general (2018). Ehrenreich suggests the particular utility of CoPs for ELF may lie in understanding the social complexity of communication strategies, conception of the role multilingualism resources play, and deeper apprehension of the trajectory ELF users take in evolving identification with the linguistic resources of a CoP (2018).

2.3.2 Communities of practice and medicine

As professions, the various disciplines of healthcare provide potent examples of communities of practice, and CoPs have been used widely to conceptualize the work and training of physicians (e.g., Cruess, Cruess & Steinert, 2018); nursing (e.g., Andrew, Tolson & Ferguson 2008; Gullick & West 2016); pharmacists (e.g., Duncan-Hewitt & Austin 2005; ElShaer et al. 2016); and other medical professionals (e.g., Engel-Hills & Chhem 2012). The description of a community of practice and its link to the healthcare professions should be immediately clear: a novice student physician or nurse enters the profession as a peripheral participant, observing the expertise of more experienced practitioners while learning highly specialized professional vocabulary and insider ways of doing and being. Formal transmission of knowledge combines with the social nature of learning in internships, practicums and the like, gradually crystallizing both explicit and tacit knowledge (Cruess, Cruess & Steinert 2018). Formal and informal assessments at various points serve as markers of competency, which in turn lead to tasks of greater complexity requiring further expertise, and finally full recognition as a member of the profession. Specialization in healthcare represents another milestone of formal recognition for professional competency.

Cruess and colleagues (2018), drawing upon Snyder and Wenger's (2004) extension, observe several features of the medical profession which are readily identifiable in the CoP framework, namely *domain*, *community*, and *practice*. A specific domain with established boundaries demarcates a CoP, and provides members and the larger society with identity, purpose and significance. To Cruess et al, medicine's domain involves "the prevention and treatment of human disease and the promotion of the public good" (2018: 186). The element of community in the CoP framework includes mutuality of trust, esteem, and pride in accomplishment (Snyder & Wenger 2004; Wenger-Trayner & Wenger-Trayner 2015), and for physicians, such community is often experienced through interactions in multiple professional associations and medical specializations. Wenger (1998) referenced medicine specifically to illustrate the dimension of practice in a seminal explanation of the CoP framework, with its wealth of specific knowledge and skills, both explicit and implied, as enacted through clinical practice, medical education and research.

2.3.3 MELF as a community of practice

We have to this point demonstrated the use of a CoP framework as a tool for analysis in ELF research in general, and its ready application to the field of medicine. But what of MELF specifically? How might communities of practice aid in conceptualizing MELF?

To answer this, it is important to first underscore the pivotal role played by language in understanding the functioning of a CoP. Eckert and McConnell-Ginet (1992) were perhaps the earliest authors to highlight the importance of language in defining a community of practice as ". . . an aggregate of people who come together around mutual engagement in an endeavor. *Ways of doing things, ways of talking, beliefs, values, power relations* – in short practices – emerge in the course of this mutual endeavor" (1992: 464; emphasis ours). The role of sociolinguistic competence as a key feature of moving from peripheral participant to core member has also been recognized (Holmes & Meyerhoff 1999).

Ehrenreich (2018) draws attention to the centrality of language in communities of practice by reproducing Wenger's (1998: 125–126) summary of indicators that a CoP has been established, and we list these features again here, as further evidence that language has a focal role in Lave and Wenger's framework.
1) sustained mutual relationships – harmonious or conflictual
2) shared ways of engaging in doing things together
3) the rapid flow of information and propagation of innovation
4) absence of introductory preambles, as if conversations and interactions were merely the continuation of an ongoing process
5) very quick setup of a problem to be discussed
6) substantial overlap in participants' descriptions of who belongs

7) knowing what others know, what they can do, and how they can contribute to an enterprise
8) mutually defining identities
9) the ability to assess the appropriateness of actions and products
10) specific tools, representations, and other artifacts
11) local lore, shared stories, inside jokes, knowing laughter
12) jargon and shortcuts to communication as well as the ease of producing new ones
13) certain styles less recognized as displaying membership
14) a shared discourse reflecting a certain perspective on the world

Clearly, even a cursory consideration of this list of features highlights how language is crucial to the mutual engagement characteristic of a CoP, and how readily it can be applied to describing the work of healthcare professionals. Imagine, for example, a group of nurses in a busy paediatric ward. Patient information shared between colleagues during a passing exchange in the hallway is likely to include "jargon and shortcuts to communication". In an end-of-shift patient handover procedure "introductory preambles" are most probably unnecessary. Lunchroom conversations may well include "local lore, shared stories, inside jokes, knowing laughter". A "rapid flow of information" is likely to characterize the most busy moments at the ward, and the "ability to assess the appropriateness of actions" is an essential requirement for all members of this professional community.

So given the centrality of language in defining a community of practice, and as a tool for conceptualizing medical ELF, we take the lead of Ehrenreich (2018) in considering how MELF in particular might fulfil the three key dimensions of the CoP framework: *mutual engagement, joint enterprise*, and *shared repertoire*.

The profession of medicine is a culture into which medical learners are being socialised as they learn (Mann 2011: 64).

Mutual engagement
In discussing the nature of mutual engagement in CoP, Wenger explains that "being included in *what matters* is a requirement for being engaged in a community's practice, just as engagement is what defines belonging" (1998: 74; emphasis ours). Clearly, if involvement in "what matters" constitutes a CoP, healthcare professions are among those claiming the most lofty of aims. Callahan (1998: 385), for example, proposes the following noble goals of medicine:

the prevention of disease and injury and the promotion and maintenance of health; the relief of pain and suffering caused by maladies; the care and cure of those with a malady, and the care of those who cannot be cured; the avoidance of premature death and the pursuit of a peaceful death.

Nursing students, in one foundational textbook, learn that the primary goals of nursing include "responses to health problems, level of wellness, and need for assistance"; provision of "physical care, emotional care, teaching, guidance and counselling"; and the implementation of "interventions aimed at promoting health, preventing illness/complications, and assisting patients to meet their own needs" (Harding & Barry 2018: 7). At core then, the healthcare professions aspire to "what matters" to most of humanity, and in their mutual engagement of these aims, help to establish the sense of belonging necessary for the formation of a CoP.

Though critics have questioned idealistic depictions of CoP, as though they were free from clashes, and unencumbered by matters of power and privilege (e.g., Hughes, Jewson & Unwin 2007), a closer reading of Wenger may have pre-empted such concerns. Wenger understood sustained mutuality in relationships to be a defining feature of mutual engagement in a CoP, whether those relationships were "harmonious or conflictual" (1998: 125). Ehrenreich (2018) asserts that the broad contextuality of interactions which communities of practice encompasses hold particular promise for ELF research. This is an especially salient point, given that ELF has been criticized in the past for an overdependence on data from sources where exchanges are limited in their potential for the full range of pragmatic strategies, particularly uncooperative, non-consensual exchanges (MacKenzie 2014), a point which we take up further in Chapter 6. Uncooperative, conflictual exchanges, unfortunately, the medical communication literature shows us, are legion (e.g., Almost et al. 2010; Fassier & Azoulay 2010; Cullati et al. 2019), and therefore provide rich data for enlarging our understanding of ELF interactions.

The reality of interprofessional delivery of healthcare in many contexts both enlarges, and challenges, the fixed boundaries of communities of practice. Consider, for example, a general surgical team, perhaps consisting of one or two senior surgeons; an anaesthetist; two or three nurses working directly in the surgical task; one or two nurses assisting but not directly involved in the surgery itself; theatre support workers who perform transport patients or remove soiled materials; a cardiographer who monitors an electrocardiograph machine; and medical students observing the procedure. Except for the observing students, and although rostered, the individuals work together regularly. The complexity of the task at hand requires highly specialized knowledge and skills, and contributions from each group member are required for successful task completion. A strong sense of professional identity characterizes the individuals in the group. All of these make the mutual engagement element of a CoP readily identifiable.

However, within what would be considered an interprofessional team engaged in a mutual enterprise, several smaller communities of practice may exist. Hierarchical relationships, with asymmetrical power dynamics, and clearly demarcated professional boundaries are not unfamiliar to surgical teams (Jayasuriya-Illesinghe et al. 2016). Nurses may be considered part of the "team", but perceived by surgeons primarily in assistant roles, or the surgeon may in practice interact much more with the medical students observing the procedure. The hierarchy may make for limited interaction between the support workers and the rest of the team. The larger CoP in this example, the surgical team, may be more accurately viewed as a number of smaller CoPs: the nurses who are regularly rostered together, share meals in the cafeteria, and who may have a strong professional identity as surgical nurses; the cohort of medical students who study, work and socialize together; the support workers who share with each other "war stories" from their outlying but essential roles in surgical procedures. These smaller, "sub-" communities of practice illustrate mutuality in enterprise; regular and sustained interaction; evidence direct involvement in "what matters"; and foster a strong sense of identity among group members, yet are anything but free from conflict, hierarchy or power relationships. Wenger (1998) acknowledged that we are often part of several CoPs, with a distinction between those in which we are primarily core or peripheral members; the surgical team illustrates this reality, as do many interprofessional interactions in the delivery of healthcare.

Wenger is keen to stress that single interactions or one-off activities present inadequate lenses through which to view communities of practice. He warns against ascribing ". . . too much importance to the moment. Interactions and activities take place in the service of *enterprises and identities* whose definition is *not confined to single events*" (1998: 125; emphasis ours). In this regard, we return here to the point that MELF represents an especially rich context for examining ELF interactions. The combination of medical migration, and the extensive use of English in medicine has created conditions in which ELF interactions are increasingly common. Add to this mix the delivery of healthcare in interprofessional teams, composed of several small communities of practice, characterized by regular and sustained mutual engagement, and in our research context, daily, close-proximity contact of community members.

We contrast this consistent mutual engagement with a large portion of the data available to date on ELF interactions in CoPs. The lack of regular and sustained interaction is a point taken up by several researchers in their search for a suitable framework to conceptualize ELF. Jenkins, for example, noting the "transient encounters" characterizing many ELF interactions, suggests their "'shared' repertoire is particularly emergent rather than shared a priori" (Jenkins 2015: 64). Dewey (2009: 77) shares a similar concern with utilizing a CoP framework for ELF, suggesting a "still more fluid concept of community of practice, where the practice itself is modified as it is enacted" (p. 77).

Exceptions to the relatively few number of ELF studies considering lengthier duration are Kalocsai's (2014) analysis of study abroad students; Ehrenreich's (2009) description of business managers; and Smit's (2010) longitudinal consideration of postsecondary classrooms. Participants in Kalocsai's study were part of the European Commission's Erasmus program, and spent up to a full academic year together in intensive language learning and social activities. Ehrenreich's investigation of business managers presumably included long-serving employees. Smit's definition of longitudinal includes a pilot phase of fourteen months preliminary to the main data collection over four semesters of study (see 2010: 88ff). Although Ehrenreich does not specify the length of time in which the managers functioned in positions requiring ELF, in the other two instances, the duration and frequency of contact does not approximate that of the participants in our context, a setting which is not at all unique to the region in which our study occurs.

ELF researchers have long recognized the distinction between *learners* of English (who may self-assess their communications by comparison to perceived NS norms) and ELF *users*, who repurpose the language for communicative purposes. ELF users perceive success when their intended message is understood, not by the degree of alignment with native speaker models. In this way, ELF is often situationally- and context-dependent, and with fewer restrictions, in that it is heavily shaped by the communicative demands of a particular situation. Here, MELF may again uniquely enhance our understanding of ELF in that professional, prescribed models of communication may press upon the otherwise less restrictive, inventive and creative interlocutors who are in real time reinventing the language to achieve mutual intelligibility. The interaction between the creativity of real time ELF construction, and prescribed professional forms such as SBAR (Situation, Background, Assessment, Recommendation) (Pope, Rodzen & Spross 2008); the Surgical Safety Checklist (WHO 2009); or the requirement for standard language to aggregate data in medical record-keeping (Wang, Hailey & Yu 2011), promise to refract ELF in altogether new ways.

Joint enterprise

To Wenger, a joint enterprise constitutes the goal of members' participation, the decisions by the community on what is of importance and what is not (1998: 81).

In medicine, language is readily identifiable as an essential element of the joint enterprise, and it is in fact difficult to conceive of the enterprise without it. Jackson, in describing the role of interpreters in healthcare, described language as ". . . medicine's most essential technology, its principal instrument for conducting its work" (1998: 65). The relationship between language and the delivery of healthcare is ubiquitous and self-evident: for diagnosis; for a physician's assessment of a patient; for nursing shift handovers; for triage in an emergency department; to gauge the effectiveness of a patient's medications; to conduct surgery in an interprofessional team.

Among the three dimensions of a CoP, Ehrenreich (2018) finds the joint enterprise most problematic with respect to ELF research; specifically, the difficulty of making a direct connection between language and the CoP's enterprise, and the degree of particularity characteristic of a joint enterprise. We assert that neither problem pertains to MELF. First, as shown above, it is difficult to envision the delivery of healthcare being carried out without the centrality of language. While healthcare researchers continuously provide evidence in support of the need to *improve* communication (e.g., Chou & Cooley 2018), no one seems to be arguing there should be less of it. Second, it is a relatively easy task to identify a CoP in the work of professional groupings such as doctors, nurses, pharmacists and so on. Ehrenreich, echoing the concerns of sociolinguists such as Davies (2005), cautions against imprecise identification of a group as a CoP, particularly where groups are "self-constituted" (2005: 562), such as temporary online communities. In contrast, nurses, pharmacists, chiropractors, naturopaths or physicians become members of their profession through a lengthy process of formal education; conduct internship processes where a new member is socialized into the profession; and have their work governed, sanctioned, licensed, regulated and supported by formal professional bodies. Presumably, the joint enterprise of healthcare can be conceived of broadly ("to improve the health of the community"), or in more specific organizational terms ("achieve the least total time spent in an emergency department for patients"), or professionally, in more narrow terms ("to be empathetic listeners").

Shared repertoire

Shared repertoire includes the "discourse by which members create meaningful statements about the world, as well as the styles by which they express their forms of membership and their identities as members" (Wenger 1998: 83).

Wenger's conception of shared repertoire is broad, encompassing components both intricately related to language (e.g., words; terms; stories) and involving, but more loosely connected to language (e.g., tools; styles; routines). Examples of the shared repertoire of medical practitioners might include stories of the excesses of entrance exams or residency; shared understanding of behaviour for hospital rounds; the hierarchical power structure; implicit knowledge of a raft of medical abbreviations; or cognizance of societal expectations for physicians' bedside (or more commonly, office) manner.

Wenger highlighted the evolving and dynamic nature of a community's shared repertoire, rather than rigid and fixed in nature, a point taken up by Ehrenreich, who extends this "linguacultural ambiguity" to potentially "every aspect of ELF communication" (2018: 44). Here again, we suggest MELF might be different: exchanges in MELF communities of practice are certainly characterized by dynamic and open-ended negotiation of meaning, yet at the same time are exerted upon them external forces which press for precision and ambiguity reduction. Wenger recognized this tension:

> This inherent ambiguity makes processes like coordination, communication, or design on the one hand difficult, in continual need of repair, and always unpredictable; and on the other hand, dynamic, always open-ended, and generative of new meanings. The need for coordinating perspectives is a source of new meanings as much as it is a source of obstacles. (1998: 83–84)

For example, healthcare delivery is characterized by a dizzying amount of protocols, which aim to standardize medical practices for safety, repeatability and quality (Leotsakos et al.: 2014). Such procedures, intended to provide uniform care across international boundaries, invariably impact standardization of language use in MELF interactions. González–Aguña and colleagues (2021) point out that standardization of healthcare language is not only essential for guiding professional care, but in some countries, mandated by law. We have no doubt that MELF users engage in dynamic and open-ended negotiation of meaning as such standardized care protocols are linguistically enacted, yet it seems obvious that such external forces are invariably brought to bear upon the process of ELF language uniformity in MELF CoPs.

In this regard, we return the discussion to an earlier conception of ELF, and that of "variety" (we do so somewhat nervously, given the sometimes acrimonious debate, and because of our position as newcomers to the discourses of ELF). In describing the "repositioning" of ELF, Jenkins (2015) traces the evolution from earlier research influenced heavily by a World Englishes (WE) paradigm, through to a more current understanding of ELF as a multilingual practice. In its earliest phase, ELF researchers, drawing upon WE, considered the possibility of ELF "varieties", whose linguistic features might correspond with speakers' L1s, such as a "Chinese-influenced ELF", for example. As ELF research expanded, with more data available upon which to theorize, the possibility of describing codified "varieties" seemed misplaced. Rather, what was emerging from the data was the reality of real-time fluidity and variability as speakers coalesced forms to achieve understanding. ELF research shifted away from "the fatal attraction of lists" (Seidlhofer, in Jenkins 2015: 55) of linguistic features which might constitute a "variety", and toward an emphasis on emergent features.

The shift toward observations of ELF's emergent nature has resulted in definitive assertions by scholars that ELF must not be considered a language "variety". Addressing the question of whether ELF can be conceived of in this way, Jenkins, Cogo and Dewey state plainly, "We would argue that it cannot" (2011: 296). ELF scholars have objected to ELF as a variety on two primary premises: that ELF lacks a fixed and stable context to the degree necessary to achieve variety status, and that the notion of speech community is an outdated and therefore inaccurate frame for analysis (Björkman 2018).

Written comments from a practicing nurse (L1 Arabic), reflecting on her comprehension of patient information given by a nurse (L1 Tamil) in a recorded handover scenario (reproduced here as originally written): *No, only some litters that are going from nurse mouth is littel difficult to understand because all indina staff have this problem e speaking.*

But do such assertions result in an open-and-shut case? Perhaps it is time, as Jenkins (2015) asserts, to consider the question of variety finally closed, and move on? But what then to make of a setting for ELF with a relatively stable context, and strong external and internal forces for regularisation and codification?

Researchers have allowed for at least the possibility that, in theory, were a relatively fixed setting for contact to be established, norm stabilization might take place (Schneider 2012). In processes of language regulation, where "language users monitor, intervene in and manage their own and others' language use" (Hynninen & Solin 2018: 270), forces more external to ELF users, such as institutional policies, may exert further pressure for such stabilization. Prescribed language use protocols, for example, mandated by ministries of health, individual hospitals or medical training institutions, and promoted through international bodies, may wield considerable influence on language regulation in MELF. Consider, for example, the standardized language imposed upon MELF users by international frameworks such as NANDA International (NANDA-I), Nursing Outcomes Classification (NOC), and Nursing Interventions Classification (NIC), which guide nurses' diagnoses, criteria for defining patient outcomes, and labelling treatment types (Gonzá lez–Aguña et al: 2021). It follows that mandated frameworks such as these, legally required in some jurisdictions, serve as powerful forces of MELF language regulation.

We find in ELF research thus far a tendency to sharply differentiate the transient, temporary nature of encounters between ELF users, thus underscoring contextualized emergent features, from lengthier and relatively stable environments for language contact, a propensity Hynninen and Solin describe as a "dualistic model" that may overlook the interaction between the two (2018: 270). The relative transiency of much ELF communication has been well foregrounded in ELF research. Mortensen, for example, describes the *"transient* multilingual communities" of ELF (2013: 37; emphasis ours) in which ELF takes place. Jenkins, in searching for a more encompassing theoretical framework for ELF, argues that CoP "does not account well for the kinds of *transient and ad hoc* encounters that are arguably equally (or more?) common in ELF communication" (2015: 66; emphasis ours).

Transient and ad hoc encounters may well be more common in ELF communication. But consider the following case study depiction of a MELF context.

Andreea (L1 Romanian[2]) works as an operating room nurse in a large teaching hospital in a member state of the Gulf Cooperation Council (GCC). Among those staying with Andreea in her staff accommodation (provided by the hospital as part of her expatriate remuneration package) are two other members of the same surgical team: Joyce, a nurse anesthetist from the Philippines (L1 English), and operating room nurse Melati (L1 Indonesian). Andreea is now in her fourth year at this hospital, and has worked on the same team with Joyce for three of those years, and with Melati for two. Youssef (L1 Arabic) is the team's lead surgeon. His pre-medical and medical studies took place in his native Egypt, in Saudi Arabia, in the US, and most recently the UK. Yousef conducts surgeries with different teams on a rotational basis, depending on the roster, but works several times each month with Andreea, Joyce and Melati. Daoud, a Lebanese national (L1 Arabic) has worked at this hospital for two years, as a surgical assistant. Yousef and Daoud tend to speak Arabic with each other outside of work contexts, but rarely during surgical procedures. Martin, an anesthesiologist from South Africa, considers his first language Zulu, but received almost all of his education through the medium of English. A number of circulating nurses serve the team on a rotational basis, including Yulia (L1 Ukranian), Jaya (L1 Tamil), Germy (L1 Tagalog), and Ekjot (L1 English). The group of surgical technicians assist different surgical teams, but their shifts coincide regularly with

---

2 All L1s in this case study are self-reported.

Yousef's, and so are very familiar with the team members. The surgical technicians include Saju (L1 Malayalam), Kenny (L1 Tagalog), and Dhonu (L1 Nepali), and they reside together in the staff accommodation provided by the hospital.

The teaching hospital, on its website and other official communications, prides itself on its ability to offer its medical care using English, and highlights the international training and qualifications of its staff. The "ability to communicate in English" is listed as a key qualification on the hospital's recruitment website, and all job interviews with non-Arabic speaking staff are conducted in English. The surgical team exchanges English email communications with hospital administration, and attends various meetings conducted in English. Yousef highly values adherence to what he views as "proper English" for written communication, and often comments disparagingly to his team on non-standard grammar and spelling he identifies in hospital missives. Both the surgical nurses and the circulating nurses are enrolled in a compulsory monthly professional development session organized by the national health authority, conducted by nursing researchers from a partner teaching hospital in the United States, and delivered using English. The present focus of the sessions is on NANDA, an international framework for nursing diagnoses (Herdman & Kamitsuru 2017). The hospital encourages the use of several medical communication frameworks, including SBAR (Pope et al, 2008), and SPLINTS for surgical nursing (Flin, Mitchell & McLeod 2014), and the WHO Surgical Safety Checklist (2009). Andreea is hoping to work as a nurse in Canada, and so has been reading extensively for an English-medium licensure process, and has recently hired a private tutor to prepare for an upcoming IELTS test, as has Melati. Although there are various linguistic subgroups at the staff's accommodation, English serves as the default lingua franca, and functional communication in English characterizes the hospital staff's daily interactions outside of work contexts: in shops, in restaurants, at banks, or in taxis.

The circumstances above, not at all atypical of healthcare delivery in the countries of the Gulf Cooperation Council, illustrate clearly several distinctives of MELF as a site of study for ELF. First, we note the relative stability of many of the communicative settings. Andreea and her colleagues typically receive two-year contracts with the teaching hospital, allowing sufficient time for the mutual engagement, joint enterprise and shared repertoire characteristic of a community of practice. Sharing the same staff accommodation, with common areas for cooking, and shared sleeping quarters, intensifies the frequency and range of ELF interaction among colleagues. Such circumstances differ considerably from the "transient and ad hoc encounters" described by Jenkins (2015: 66).

Second, while acknowledging the rich and varied multilingual resources at work in this setting which would foster communicative innovation, we note as well the pressures, both formal and informal, brought to bear on processes of norm regulation. We may envision a continuum of relative regulation pressures for Andreea and her colleagues of ELF use: a visit by Andreea and Melati to their neighbourhood fruit and vegetable grocer, where they interact in English with an L1 Nepali clerk, represents one end of the continuum. This interaction between Andreea and the grocery clerk, though it may occur almost daily, is likely to be short in duration, of a casual nature, possesses a relatively restricted range of communicative demands, and particularly on those occasions where the clerk's workload permits a discussion of broader topics (life as expatriate workers in a GCC country; family at home; comparisons of the conditions of provided staff accommodation; etc.) allow greater opportunity for ELF innovation. On the other end of the continuum are found instances where Andreea's ELF interactions are permitted much less opportunity for communicative innovation: the composition of an email to the hospital's human resources manager; a phone call to a hospital pharmacist regarding a particular surgical drug; a question to the surgeon regarding patient plan of care notes; her initial job interview with the hospital; or giving assertive demands to team members during surgery. Between these two ends of the continuum might be plotted various interactions which require relatively greater or lesser room for innovation: a follow-up call with a charge nurse; preoperative teaching with a patient; an oral presentation assignment for her professional development course; or a surgical unit shift report. Variables impacting the degree of innovation permitted along the points of the continuum might include the degree of power distance between Andreea and her interlocutors in a given situation; the English proficiency of the other speakers and Andreea's perception of their proficiency; the degree of risk inherent in the situation if a communication error were to occur; externally imposed communication frameworks such as SBAR and NANDA; Andree's own relative linguistic (in)security as an English user; the mode of communication (written or spoken; in-person, by phone or by email); the duration and frequency of the communication; and so on.

In considering this continuum of Andreea's interactions, Pitzl's notion of Transient International Groups (TIGs) provides a helpful frame: "groups comprised of multilingual ELF users who interact for a particular purpose at a particular location for a certain amount of time" (Pitzl 2018: 21). TIGs are inter-national, in that their interactants are composed of at least two different countries of origin, and two different L1s. Such groupings are proposed as a complementary feature to CoP, in that they are of shorter duration, even consisting of a single speech event (2018: 24). Some of Andreea's ELF interactions in her GCC environment are best understood in terms of a TIG (the L1 Nepali grocery clerk, for example), while others would most certainly meet the criteria for a fully developed CoP.

Third, we take note of the role of written communication among ELF users in this case study. Members of the team are responsible for producing a number of written items surrounding the surgeries themselves, ranging from the highly prescribed and very brief (labelling specimen samples; documenting surgical equipment used) to lengthier, much less structured (plan of care notes; notes on untoward events), and other tasks in between these two ends of the spectrum (nurse-to-nurse shift reports; patient's position and condition documentation). Some of these items are written by hand, while others are composed electronically on tablets or desktop computers. Increasingly, the demands for research data aggregation in healthcare auto-feed standard written language for many of these tasks. In the course of their work outside the specific documentation of surgery, team members produce various other written documents, including emails; various types of reports; charts; presentations; medical research articles; literature reviews; and assigned written tasks for professional development courses.

Since expedient and thorough communication among medical professionals is considered central to patient care, writing forms an important part of their work. In the words of one group of practitioner-researchers: "Much clinician time is spent writing or dictating letters to other doctors" (Tattersall et al. 2002: 516). The referral letter from a general practitioner to a specialist is perhaps the most well-known to the public, and most widely-researched (e.g., Dupont 2002), but written communication flows back from specialists, surgeons or hospital physicians to the general practitioner, and these exchanges have also been the subject of research (e.g., Lloyd & Barnett 1993; Thong et al. 2010). Expectations for the content of written documentation from nurses are high, given the legal status of the documentation in some jurisdictions (Stevens & Pickering 2010), so accuracy, completeness, and adherence to standards are highly valued (Ahn et al. 2016). The formulaic language of "form letters" figure heavily in medical written communication, and increasingly computer-generated material is utilized (Tattersall et al. 2002; N. Wang et al., 2011).

Nurses A and B try to convince an overworked Charge Nurse to observe their documentation of a patient discharge
128   Nurse B (L1 Tamil): We will do that initial assessment but just observe us, Miss
129   Nurse A (L1 Malayalam): Just come and with us the patient=
130   Nurse B: Check our work and see how we are doing the uh the way of the information taking and everything, managing the cases
131   Nurse A: Finish together very hard
132   Nurse B: It's very, very important Miss, your ah, opinion, your ah I need that =
133   Charge Nurse: I'm asking you to please go and do what you have to do and I will come. Please go.

Written communication in MELF contexts presents a fascinating and largely unexplored area of research, and one that may, again, extend our understanding of written ELF. Horner (2018) suggests that the dynamic and emergent nature of spoken ELF, with features such as repair, rephrasing, accommodation, and negotiation, may also be reflected in its written forms as well. We anticipate this to be true of MELF writers also, but a number of variables impact upon their agency and negotiation which may exert more pressure than in the ELF academic writing context which Horner describes. Notes used to inform treatment plans or postoperative care, for example, demand an exactitude and timeliness which impact considerably upon the writer's agency. Written language requiring a high degree of compliance to prescribed forms are also brought to bear on the relative dynamism of MELF writing in a manner that is lesser so in non-MELF writing contexts. Nursing records, for instance, are evaluated in terms of their factual accuracy, comprehensiveness, timeliness and compliance with standards, among others (Ahn, Choi & Kim 2016).

All told, MELF presents a rich research site to consider the claim that ELF communication is of necessity thoroughly emergent and locally contextualized. As Baker allows, in a discussion of ELF in transcultural university settings, there are still in existence "identifiable communities and cultures and associated communicative practices", and not "some sort of post-modern 'free-fall' where nothing is predictable or established" (2016: 446). We argue that MELF serves to bring Baker's assertion into especially sharp relief.

2.4 A socio-cognitive approach to MELF

However, not all medical encounters can be placed within the relatively lengthy interaction that forms within a professional CoP. Arguably, the most familiar medical encounters to many readers will be the one-to-one doctor-patient consultation, or the hospital room nurse-patient interaction. Frames through which to examine MELF must account for the joint professional enterprise of medicine, which exerts pressure on language regulation (arguably more than any other site of ELF study thus far), but also these individual, very personal interactions at the point of "end user" of healthcare services – the patient. Through the dynamics of medical migration, and geopolitical circumstances which forge large-scale migrational patterns, these familiar one-to-one medical encounters are increasingly characterized by MELF, whether a Pakistani doctor's consultation with a Syrian patient in a Norwegian medical clinic, or a Malaysian nurse's triage assessment of a Nepali patient in Singapore.

To consider these more emergent and transitory medical encounters, we follow Bigi and Rossi (2020) in drawing upon a socio-cognitive approach (Kecskes 2008; 2010; Kecskes & Zhang 2009), with particular attention to the notion of activity type (Levinson 1992). Examining the more one-off example of MELF encounter from the perspective of a socio-cognitive approach (SCA) allows us to account for the interplay between individual situational factors brought to the interaction (prior experiences, first language, cultural background, etc.) and broader social ones (institutional requirements, social roles, etc.). This complex interplay both constrains productive language forms, and purposes emergent ones.

Kecskes' socio-cognitive approach portrays communication as a "paradox", a "bumpy road" in which interlocutors both fail and succeed (2010: 50). SCA presents an alternative to existing theories of pragmatics, which Kecskes argues are either overly idealistic, or overly focused on the situational context, with either emphasis at the expense of the importance of individual factors. In both of these models, the speaker is thought to draw upon contextual clues to form a schema of the listener's presumed knowledge. Beginning with this construct as a starting point, it is perhaps not surprising that research has persistently identified positive communicative processes, like cooperation, as outcomes; nor is it surprising that with a focus on contextual, socio-cultural elements, individual factors may be overlooked. SCA offers, then, a theoretical model for considering how an individual's previous experience and knowledge, along with egocentric perspectives, impact upon communication. Communication in SCA is characterized by a dynamic interplay between societal and individual factors, and a "trial-and-error process" of meaning co-construction (Kecskes 2010: 69).

An SCA perspective brings together and harmonizes two potentially contradictory features of communication: its intention to find common ground among interlocutors, and its egocentrism, in which individuals' intentions are inevitably rooted. The coexistence and interaction between these mutually opposing forces in communication is a delineating feature of SCA, which labels them *intention* and *attention* (Kecskes & Zhang 2009: 338). Efforts made to construct and interpret meaning among interlocutors are described in either category: communicative behaviours of *intention* are those which are cooperative in nature, while egocentric *attention* behaviours hold the potential to limit (or possibly, though perhaps less likely, enhance) meaning-making.

What Kecskes and Zhang describe as the "private context encoded in words" (2009: 345), the prior experience brought to the exchange, is illustrated in the following example (Tweedie & Johnson 2018a).

Nurse B (first language: Arabic); Why you . . . take the blood sugar? The blood sugar, it's high?

Nurse A (first language: Tamil); Blood sugar, not take.

Nurse B: You not take blood sugar?

Nurse A: No. Not diabetic, not diabetes.

During this patient handover simulation, the two nurses are discussing the conditions of a male patient, 84 years of age, admitted with congestive heart failure, whose irregular heartbeat, increasing potassium levels and intensifying disorientation are of particular worry. Nurse B works in a context where rates of diabetes are flagged as a particular public health concern, and she regularly encounters diabetic patients in the course of her work. Given the patient's profile (male, elderly, irregular heartbeat), Nurse B's go-to assumption, based on prior knowledge, is that blood sugar levels would have been taken in the course of patient evaluation. In the subsequent exchange, Nurse A clarifies that they had not been taken, as the patient was not diabetic.

Kecskes and Zhang use the term *salience* to assess these inner, private contexts which are brought to bear on communicative exchanges (called *attention*), contrasted with *relevance*, the measure of communicative behaviours of *intention*. Together, intention and attention function as "mechanisms that guide the production and interpretation of meaning" (Bigi & Rossi 2020: 22). Information deemed by speakers as *relevant* tends to result in cooperative efforts to negotiate meaning, while salient processing may impede its attainment.

Kecskes' Dynamic Model of Meaning (DMM; Kecskes 2003; 2008), central to an SCA perspective, distinguishes between dual contexts: a *prior context* "tied to the values of lexical units constituting utterances" and the *actual situational context*, the present setting and circumstances "in which communication takes place, and which is interpreted (often differently) by interlocutors" (Kecskes 2014: 129). When an interaction begins, speakers select words shaped and defined by their prior context, which are in turn interpreted by the prior context of the hearer. In the DMM, the hearer draws upon salience processes first: the private context and its egocentric focus accesses the most readily available information, that which is most familiar or easily recalled. Where misalignment between interlocutors' private contexts occurs, they then draw upon the actual situational context to render understanding. In this sense, words have a "frame-activating power" in that they may "elicit conceptual structures, frames or schemas, which are rooted in the cultural, social and personal context of each individual" (Bigi & Rossi 2020: 24–25).

In an interaction between a patient and a healthcare professional, the prior contexts of the two speakers are often differentiated by a vast difference in the lexis of medicine. Doctors have been described as "bilingual" (Ong et al. 1995: 910): fluent in the specialized language of medicine in addition to their mother tongue. The conceptual structures therefore activated for a physician during a consultative interaction may be considerably different than those activated for her patient. Since salient behaviours serve as the default for initial meaning-making in the Dynamic Meaning Model, medical terminology used by the physician which the patient has not previously encountered will inevitably impact upon communicative effect. We anticipate a MELF context to further widen this already significant variance in the conceptual schemas between healthcare professional and patient.

Also central to an SCA framework is the notion of common ground, and its subdivision into the categories of *core common ground* and *emergent common ground* among interlocutors. At least some degree of common ground between speakers is a necessary prerequisite for any communicative success (Clark 1996), and it follows that the degree of common ground correlates with "economy of expression" (Enfield 2008: 223): the more commonality two speakers share, the less effort will be expended in making meaning. Kecske's core common ground refers to the "relatively static (diachronically changing), generalized, common knowledge and beliefs that usually belong to a certain speech community as a result of prior interactions and experience" (Kecskes 2014: 161). Core common ground is composed of *common sense* (speakers' general knowledge of the world); general knowledge about community and society (*culture sense*); and *formal sense*, the understanding of the language systems speakers utilize in interactions (Kecskes & Zhang 2009).

In contrast, *emergent common ground* is actualized in the real-time setting of the interaction, and is subcategorized into *shared sense* and *current sense*. *Shared sense* refers to the personalized knowledge which a speaker holds in common with another communicant. This personalized knowledge is distinct from community knowledge, such as medical English terminology. *Current sense* describes the emergent awareness and understanding in the current communicative situation.

The following example between a nurse and a patient in a health assessment simulation illustrates these two senses as the interactants seek common ground. The patient, a male of 52 years, was admitted to hospital for complaints of a severe cough.

RE-SIM2
65   Nurse (L1 Malayalam): Okay. May I ask you a few more questions related to cough?
66   Patient (L1 English): Yes.
67   Nurse: Okay, when did you start it?

68 Patient: The cough, it started about a week ago.
69 Nurse: Yah.
70 Patient: But it's kind of been, um, on and off for a while.
71 Nurse: Okay.
72 Patient: Yes.
73 Nurse: So, uh, but you took medical treatment, maybe after uh, two three days?
74 Patient Yes.
75 Nurse: Once it started.
76 Patient: Yes, once it started I came here and they gave me some medical treatment and it seems to be getting a little bit better.
77 Nurse: Okay. So, is there any provocative part related to that uh like uh if you are taking less the the cough is subsided or if you are doing some activities, is it increasing? Do you feel a lot like that?
78 Patient: Yes, I have (0.5) Excuse me ((PATIENT COUGHS))
79 Nurse: It's okay.
80 Patient: I have some puffers at home that they the doctor's given me. So uh they help my cough. I'm a smoker, so (.) I've tried to quit before but I just can't quit, so I smoke every day.
81 Nurse: Every day.
82 Patient: And sometimes that makes me cough.
83 Nurse: Okay, so it's like uh it's irritating you by your smoking, the cough is increasing you mean.
84 Patient: Yes.
85 Nurse: Okay. So (.) while coughing do you have any pain like any chest pain, or abdominal pain? You ever find=
86 Patient: It's (.) when I start coughing it's yes it's in my chest and in my throat it's uh like a tickle in my throat that makes me keep coughing.
87 Nurse: Okay. So, you throat irritation but you don't have any pain?
88 Patient: Yes it's it's a little irritating but no pain.
89 Nurse: Okay uh so how uh you are a cough looks like it's like irritating of (0.5) are you bringing any sputum? Uh, can you just explain your cough?
90 Patient: Uh it was pretty severe the last couple of days.
91 Nurse: Yes.
92 Patient: But it's a lot better now so it's mostly just uh a bit of a cough yes.
93 Nurse: But no you are not bringing up any sputum.
94 Patient: No.
95 Nurse: Okay so it's like a dry cough.
96 Patient: Yeah it's a dry cough.

97	Nurse: What is the severity of the uh cough? How can you say it's like a mild cough or a more severe uh more=
98	Patient: Yes it was quite severe but it's a lot better now it's just mild.
99	Nurse: It was quite severe but now it's reduced.
100	Patient: Yes.
101	Nurse: Because of the medications.
102	Patient: Yes.
103	Nurse: Okay. Have you taken any, uh, treatment like you have puffer at home. Am I right?
104	Patient: Puffer, yes.
105	Nurse: Yes, so the puffer you are taking every day, or when you heard the cough early?
106	Patient: Uh mostly every day.
107	Nurse: Mostly every day.
108	Patient: Yes.
109	Nurse: So this since one week or uh before also you are taking?
110	Patient: Uh, I've was diagnosed with chronic bronchitis about ten years ago.
111	Nurse: Yes, okay.
112	Patient: So I've got the puffers for about ten years.
113	Nurse: Ten years.
114	Patient: Yes.
115	Nurse: So every day you are taking.
116	Patient: Yes. Most days. Sometimes I forget.
117	Nurse: Yes. Do you know the name of the puff?
118	Patient: No I I couldn't tell you I'm not sure.
119	Nurse: That's okay no problem. Uh do you felt this puff is uh effective for you?
120	Patient: Yeah I think they're quite effective.
121	Nurse: Effective.
122	Patient: Yes.
123	Nurse: What is your understanding about your cough? What makes you more cough, uh, or uh, is there any reason other than the smoking, do you felt any other reason?
124	Patient: Uh maybe like when I'm exercising or something I get a little bit short of breath.
125	Nurse: Oh.
126	Patient: And I'll start coughing.
127	Nurse: Okay.

128 Patient: But I think it's just a medical thing, like I've had bronchitis for, you know, ten years, and it just, the cough it'll come and it'll go away, and it'll come back bad and then=
129 Nurse: Hmm. Okay, do you exercise every day?
130 Patient: Not every day but I like to go for walks.
131 Nurse: Hmm, so like mild exercise all day.
132 Patient: Yes.
133 Nurse: But still you feel the cough.
134 Patient: Yes.
135 Nurse: Okay. Is the cough affected your family, like you are able to work uh=
136 Patient: I'm retired, so I just kind of casually work part-time.
137 Nurse: Yes. Uh, so it's not affecting that much in your family.
138 Patient: No.
139 Nurse: Okay. Um. Uh, so what is uh, do you have any past uh, history other than the bronchitis?
140 Patient: No, I've never had surgery, or, or I don't think I have any medical, medical
history=
141 Nurse: Nothing. Do you have any allergies, uh for any medicine or uh, medication or uh, for any, any allergic? You are not, uh=
142 Patient: No, nothing.
143 Nurse: Any family history of, uh, any family history of asthma, bronchitis, anything?
144 Patient: Uh, no, nothing like that.
145 Nurse: No family history.
146 Patient: No family history, no.

The emergent common ground in this extract is developing around the nature of the patient's cough. Both the nurse and the patient have a shared sense around their understanding of the notion of *cough* and its potential causes, from common, everyday experience. However, both the nurse and the patient have particularized knowledge about *cough*. Without being asked, for example, the patient brings up the fact that he is a smoker (turn 80), presumably because he felt the point was relevant to the nurse's questions on the nature and causes of his cough. The nurse may have particularized knowledge about the effects of different types of puffer, which might have caused her to ask for the specific name. In Kecskes' framework, emergent common ground develops as interlocutors communicate their understanding about the core idea (in this extract, *cough*).

To Kecskes, emergent common ground is "assumptive in that it is contingent on the actual situation, which reflects a *synchronic* change between common grounds in different circumstances" (2014: 163; emphasis in original). While the patient and nurse have common ground in their understanding of *cough*, within this shared understanding will also be experiential variation. The nurse's comments indicate her experience with different types of cough (coughs with or without *sputum*; *mild* or *severe* coughs), while the patient's experience in technical classification of cough severity is likely more limited. There is no "perfect match" in shared understanding between any two interlocutors, and "shared sense is achieved only after their joint effort to construct it" (2014: 163).

Kecskes' describes the relationship between core common ground and emergent common ground as dialectical in nature. Together, core and emergent common grounds work "as a dynamically changing background on which the interplay of intention and attention occurs and communication takes place" (Kecskes 2014: 164). Intention and attention are said to impact common ground in three ways: the activation of prior shared mental information; information seeking; and the introduction of private knowledge to the interaction (Kecskes & Zhang 2009). The nurse in this extract begins with a question which activates prior shared mental information: *May I ask you a few more questions related to [your] cough?* Within this question, she activates the shared part of the two interlocutors' experience: the knowledge that the patient has a cough for which he has been admitted to hospital. The shared information includes common sense (the basic understanding of what constitutes a *cough*); cultural sense (a shared social expectation of nurse-patient interactions); and a formal sense (their use of a common language). The question is presumptive, in that the nurse begins the utterance with an underlying assumption (likely unconsciously), that the patient shares these aspects of common ground, and that communication will therefore be possible.

Common ground is also constructed through information seeking, when information known to both interlocutors is not yet salient in the conversation. After her initial question regarding the patient's cough, the nurse asks: *Okay, when did you start it* (turn 67)? The patient replies in a way that brings salience: *The cough, it started about a week ago*. Perhaps the nurse's use of the pronoun *it* introduced to the patient the possibility that something other than the cough would be the topic of questioning, like the use of medication, or the use of a puffer. The patient deduced that among potential alternatives, the most likely subject for questioning would be his cough, and so utilizes pronoun copying (*The cough, it . . .*), a grammatical feature less typical of Inner Circle English speakers (Kachru 1985) such as the patient, in order to bring salience.

The sharing of private knowledge also assists in creating common ground. Unsolicited, the patient shares details of his smoking habit: *I'm a smoker, so I've tried to quit before but I just can't quit, so I smoke every day* (turn 80). The admission of this private knowledge is provided by the patient in an attempt to offer relevant knowledge to the conversation's perceived intention: identifying the nature of *cough*.

Kecskes sees the negotiation of common ground, realized through the above three processes, and interacted through the interplay of bringing relevance to intention and salience to attention, as central to the socio-cognitive framework of communication. It should be noted that in extending the SCA to communication between speakers from different cultures, Kecskes rejects what he deems a "problem approach", where interlocutors are "multiply handicapped" through the addition of cultural difference to the process of negotiating common ground (2014: 166). Rather, interactants are "normal communicators" who have the same challenges in constructing common ground, albeit different ones from those of speakers in intracultural interactions.

In drawing upon a socio-cognitive approach to consider physician-patient interactions, Bigi and Rossi (2020) suggest that core common ground may present the greatest potential for misunderstanding. In particular, the authors assert that it is the subcategories of cultural sense and formal sense which hold out special challenges for multilingual interactions (and therefore, by extension, ELF ones): cultural sense referring to prevalent knowledge of norms, beliefs, practices, etc.; and formal sense pertaining to the relative understanding of the language system in use in the interlocutors' exchange. The authors highlight the importance of emergent common ground in making up for the communicative gaps in cultural and formal senses. Whereas in a monolingual exchange, speakers are able to rely to a significant degree on the shared implicit meaning of core common ground, lingua franca interactions draw proportionately more upon the explicit understanding of an utterance generated by emergent common ground.

> in monolingual settings, where at least the language used is shared, the parties' attention should be brought to the implicit part of meaning, which is likely to be taken for granted, albeit not being shared. In multilingual settings, instead, the first difficulty to solve is related to the explicit meaning, which is encoded in a language that is not shared (or not perfectly known) by all the participants. Through a clarification of the explicit meanings it will be possible to access also the implicit ones. (Bigi & Rossi 2020: 29)

Even monolingual medical encounters do possess an element of "cross-cultural" communication, a point made in the medical literature. For example, in describing patient-centered medical practice, Stewart et al (2014) describe a process where "the clinician actively seeks to *enter into the patient's world* to understand both the perceptions of health (its meaning to the patient and his or her aspirations or life goals) and the unique experience of illness . . . " (2014: 7; emphasis ours). This "cultural gap" between clinicians and patients, interpreted through the lens of a sociocognitive approach, can be understood as an attempt by the physician to draw initially upon the egocentric processes of salience, the most familiar lexical usage: a "myocardial infarction" is used instead of a "heart attack", or a "thrombus" is substituted for the more familiar "blood clot". Another example of this process of salience in medical communication is evident in the previous extract, where the nurse makes use of a specialized medical use of the word *provocative*.

76   Patient: Yes, once it started I came here and they gave me some medical treatment and it seems to be getting a little bit better.
77   Nurse: Okay. So, is there any provocative part related to that uh like uh if you are taking less the the cough is subsided or if you are doing some activities, is it increasing? Do you feel a lot like that?
78   Patient: Yes, I have (0.5) Excuse me ((PATIENT COUGHS))

The use of the phrase *provocative part*, perhaps an unusual lexical choice for everyday speech, may have been informed by *PQRST*, a mnemonic common for patient assessment in nursing, where the *P* indicates *Provocation* or *Palliation* – a line of questioning surrounding the causes of the condition (Ferrell & Paice 2019). The nurse appears to recognize almost immediately that she is making use of a specialized medical term which may be unfamiliar to the patient, and attempts a paraphrase.

2.4.1 Medical consultation as an activity type

Medical consultations, whether taking the form of physician-patient, nurse-patient, pharmacist-patient, chiropractor-patient or other similar clinician-patient discussions, illustrate interactions which Levinson (1992) described as *activity types*. We assert that viewing MELF interactions through the lens of activity type provides an especially useful means of understanding the role which settings play in the inferential strategies of negotiated meaning.

Levinson defined activity type as "a fuzzy category whose focal members are goal-defined, socially constituted, bounded events with *constraints* on participants, setting, and so on, but above all on the kind of allowable contributions" (1992: 69; emphasis in original). These interactions could range from a "totally pre-packaged activity" to "a largely unscripted event" (thus the use of the term "fuzzy"), but the key focus is on the ways in which the particular "structural properties of an activity constrain . . . the verbal contributions that can be made toward it" (1992: 71). Examples of activity types provided by Levinson include a job interview, a basketball game, a university lecture, and a court case: in each of these, the attributes of the particular activity type constrain and oblige the nature of the language employed by participants, whether by elaborate prescriptions for turn-taking (a court case), or to very limited and restricted use (a basketball game). As with all activity types, in each of these examples "there are constraints on what will count as allowable contributions to them" (1992: 72).

Of particular interest for MELF interactions is that of inference. According to Levinson, "to each and every clearly demarcated activity there is a corresponding set of *inferential schemata*" (1992: 72; emphasis in original). Levinson illustrates this with a dialogue between a customer and a shop assistant: by pointing at a head of lettuce while saying, "That's a nice one", the customer had in fact directed the shop assistant to wrap the lettuce and begin the payment process. The customer's utterance had the result or "force" it did because of being governed by the inferential expectations of a particular activity type: customer-shopkeeper interactions when shopping in stores.

NE-SIM3B
Nurse assessing a patient admitted for stroke.
122   Nurse (L1 Malayalam): *I am not able to check for the right side, uh, so. Anyway. Uh, can you just, uh, sleep for me? I will check your your lower extremities. . .*

Comment: Nurse asks the patient to "sleep" for her. Patient apparently understood this to mean, "lie down" in order to proceed with the examination, and complied. (Researcher field notes)

Clinician-patient consultations, as an activity type, similarly inform, shape and constrain the language employed throughout the interaction. A doctor, beginning a consultation by asking "How are you today?" activates inferential schemata in the patient, who will very likely interpret this question differently than if asked by a friend in a casual encounter (Bigi & Rossi, 2020). Similarly, in our data, a nurse begins a hospital bedside assessment with a patient as follows:

RE-SIM8
10   Nurse (L1 Malayalam): Let me wash my hands and close the curtains. So to protect the privacy, I'm closing the curtains.

This utterance is framed by a particular activity type, a nurse-patient interaction in a hospital. The patient will interpret the nurse's words and accompanying actions (hand-washing, drawing curtains) through prior experience and societal-cultural knowledge, and will therefore expect certain types of language and behaviours from the nurse in this setting. The nurse will in turn expect certain responses and behaviours from the patient, also informed by prior experience and socio-cultural knowledge of this activity type. The notion of "activity-specific rules of inference" (Levinson 1992: 97) helps to explain how language is constrained by the activity in which it occurs, and researchers have considered medical interaction from this perspective (Bowles 2006; Lehtinen 2007).

From either patient or clinician perspective, the activity type is influenced strongly by the *institutional setting* in which it takes place (cf. Drew & Heritage 1992a), a point we consider especially germane to the study of MELF. As "goal-defined, socially constituted, bounded events with constraints on participants" (Levinson 1992: 69) clinician-patient interactions follow certain discernible, predictable patterns (Roter & Hall 2006). These patterns, and their accompanying constraints, can in part be understood by attention to the institutional contexts in which they occur.

Medical schools thus become the guardians of the values basic to the effective practice of medicine. It is within this broad institutional setting that the medical schools find their place. It is their function to transmit the culture of medicine and to advance that culture. It is their task to shape the novice into the effective practitioner of medicine, to give him the best available knowledge and skills, and to provide him with a professional identity so that he comes to think, act, and feel like a physician (Merton 1957: 7).

Institutional talk is distinguished from normal conversation in at least three broad ways: its particular orientation (toward institutional goals and function); restrictions on the kinds of contributions each party can make toward the discussion; and the distinctive type of inferences utilized (Drew and Heritage 1992a: 25). Researchers have noted that institutional talk is often characterized by a number of defining features, including distinctive lexical choices (for example, the use of *we*, as if speaking on behalf of the institution, rather than *I*), and distinct structures for participants' turn-taking (e.g., question-and-answer exchanges, rather than conversational approaches, tend to dominate physician-patient interactions); and overall task – as opposed to relational – orientation. Zimmerman's (1992) analysis of 9-1-1 emergency calls for example, shows how every aspect of the call is managed toward the fastest completion possible. Pilnick (2001) identifies a recurring structure in pharmacist-client interactions, and shows how pharmacists attempt to impose an advisory role in their encounters with patients, and how patients may resist this advice-giving role.

The clinician-patient medical encounter, as a type of institutional talk, consists of highly ritualized interactions (Helman 1984). In fact, pre-service medical training directly instructs its future clinicians in the use of various formulaic means of conducting doctor-patient interviews, a feature Ainsworth-Vaugh calls "discourse planning" (2005: 455). Medical encounters typically include distinct sequential phases, often even guided by written questionnaires (Shuy 1983); restricted turn-taking; and a lack of parity, in that the physician holds unequal rights to ask and answer questions and to both start and terminate the encounter (Ainsworth-Vaughn 2005). As a *genre*, while elements of conversation do take place in medical encounters (typically at the beginning), studies across cultures have shown the doctor-patient visit to be more like an interview, consisting largely of the healthcare professional asking questions, and the patient responding. Goffman's (1974; 1981) notion of frame, describing the means by which the self is presented and constituted within social interaction, is informative in understanding medical encounters: the healthcare professional, as part of the institution, is "framed" as doctor, nurse or pharmacist, with accompanying institutional and social expectations.

In brief, these various external factors – the nature of institutional talk; the interview genre; the medical consultation as activity type; the institutional framing of the participants – serve as powerful forces impacting processes of language regulation, and offer the distinct possibility of norm stabilization, countering strictly emergent-focused conceptualizations of ELF.

2.5 Social network theory and MELF

At the risk of overkill, we propose in passing another theoretical framework which serves as particularly useful for the contextual study of MELF: social network theory in language change and variation (Milroy 2004). We have elsewhere claimed that migrant destinations are particularly useful for the study of MELF (Tweedie & Johnson 2019), in that the intensified language contact brought about in such environments increases the likelihood of (sustained) MELF encounters. However, because there are evident parallels between communities of practice and social network theory (Meyerhoff 2004), and because the relevance of social network theory may relate primarily to a particular contextual analysis of MELF, its treatment here will be of a brief nature.

Networks are developed as people attempt to create solutions for everyday problems (Mitchell 1986), and in social network theory, these relationships constitute varying degrees of strengths, are composed of various kinds, and are of utility for understanding language change and variation. Milroy (2004: 55), as a point of analytical reference, uses the term "ego" to describe the "anchor" of the network, and the relative ties of ego to others is conceived of in degree of density and multiplexity, which serve to impact language use. To the degree that the ego's ties are strong (e.g., frequent, recurring, complex) and dense (ego's ties are networked with one another), the social network is empowered to foster linguistic norms. As those ties are loosened or restructured, as is often the case in migrant destinations, new norms stand a greater chance of being adopted. To Illustrate, we return to the example of Andreea, cited earlier in this chapter. In learning English as a secondary school subject in Romania, (perceived) Inner Circle norms, as mediated through "correct" answers to classroom and examination questions, served as powerful regulators in her understanding and practice of English language use. In her professional and personal life as a migrant worker in a GCC country, colleagues such as Joyce and Melati, with whom she both works and shares accommodation, illustrate the strong and dense ties of the social network impinging upon her language use, as they accommodate to one another's speech. The Nepali grocer, with whom Andreea chats briefly on several occasions a week, is an example of a relatively weaker and less dense tie, but which still impacts how she communicates in English.

On the one hand, the linguistic environment of the GCC would seem to loosen restrictions on Andreea's English language use, particularly when compared to her childhood experiences, and provide new opportunities for linguistic innovation and creativity. On the other hand, some features of her present environment may add further constraints. Her interactions with colleagues are "framed" (Goffman 1974) within the representation of her, and their, professional self. Andreea's discussions with patients take place within the structure of an activity type (Levinson, 1992), that of nurse-patient assessment, and its attendant expectations. Formal, institutionally-mandated safety protocols for pre-surgery communication with patients constrain her English use in that context. To be sure, emergent communication, with negotiated meaning, and accompanying opportunities for linguistic innovation, also occur within these constraining contexts. But we caution against understanding all ELF communication as *strictly* emergent in nature; doing so ignores the considerable regulatory forces at work in MELF settings.

2.6 Conclusion

This chapter has suggested several theoretical frameworks of utility for the study of MELF. The notion of community of practice has proven to be useful for understanding ELF in general, and we have made the case that it is particularly relevant to examining MELF, especially given that medical research literature itself identifies the healthcare profession as inherently oriented to the concept of CoP. However, as useful as Wenger and Lave's framework is for MELF, this chapter asserts that a predominant feature of medical communication, the clinician-patient encounter, is served well by examination through the lens of a sociocognitive approach. MELF interactions lack the shared implicit meaning in core common ground, and therefore likely depend more on the emergent common ground in the search for meaning. The SCA framework helps us understand how in the multilingual milieu of MELF, both the cultural sense and formal sense of core common ground challenge understanding, and how emergent communication is used in substitution. The medical encounter as an activity type illustrates the strength of impact upon institutional pressures to regulate norms of MELF communication, perhaps more than any other ELF context. We also submit social network theory as a helpful option for studying MELF. Given its extensive use by researchers studying questions related to migration, and medical migration in particular, social network theory may be especially appropriate for MELF, a linguistic phenomenon readily apparent in the intensified language contact of migrant destinations.

Chapter 3
The researchers, the research, and the research setting

Chapter key points:
- The exceptionally diverse linguistic context of the Arabian Peninsula in general, and the State of Qatar in particular, provide a unique window for examining MELF.
- The researchers' process of conceptualizing MELF is not confined to a single research event, but has been an emergent, non-linear and ongoing process, continuing to arise out of sustained, intentional and multi-faceted *in situ* engagement.
- The researchers employ a multi-framework perspective, and accompanying methodological pluralism, in the service of understanding MELF.
- While acknowledging the limitations inherent in simulation, there are several compelling reasons for medical simulation data as a valid means of understanding MELF communication.

3.1 Introduction

As teacher-researchers, we did not set out to investigate (medical) English as a lingua franca as such, and as such consider ourselves outsiders to this particular academic space and field of study (De Four-Babb, Pegg & Beck 2015). Both of our doctoral research studies, carried out in the early 2000s, were in areas of study only indirectly connected to ELF, and neither of us recall consulting ELF literature to any significant degree in the writing of our dissertations. I (Gregory) focused on Colloquial Singapore English and how "native-speakerist" attitudes (Holliday 2005) toward this local language variety influenced its classroom use. My understanding of Singapore English drew heavily upon a World Englishes paradigm at that time, and I was largely unaware of the potential ELF might have played in informing my research. I (Robert) conducted an *in situ*, argument- and evidence-based test validation for a standardized English language test used to make high stakes placement and admissions decisions at a higher education institution in an English as a Foreign Language context. Models investigating test score interpretation (e.g., Kane 1992) and test utility and impact (e.g., Bachman 2005) were foundational sources, but nothing which overlapped the realm of ELF. Both of us expatriate language teachers, we had worked in various contexts where English served as a lingua franca: alongside a single dominant language (e.g., China; Mexico); in multilingual environments where English was an important (but not the only) lingua franca (e.g., Malaysia); in bilingual contexts where English served primarily as a vehicle for intercultural communication (e.g., Marshall Islands). Perhaps because of the specialized foci of our respective graduate research, English as a lingua franca for international communication seemed more like a fact of life where we lived and worked, rather than a phenomenon to be researched and conceptualized.

Nor did we have particular expertise or experience in English for medical purposes. Our work as language teachers had found us in a series of international employment contexts where over the years we were tasked with providing English language instruction for a wide range of professional purposes: to scientists; to diplomats; to government civil servants; to army officers; to thesis-writing graduate students; to engineers; to subject-area school teachers; to self-described "non-native speaking" teachers of English; to university students on short-term study abroad programs. Conspicuously absent from both of our teaching resumes, however, was English for medical purposes.

It was when our paths crossed in the Arabian Peninsula, both of us as language teachers preparing nursing students for work in local healthcare contexts, that we began to ever-so-slowly grasp the unique role medical English played in communication across the multicultural and multilingual environment of the Gulf Cooperation Council. The assumption of our learners in this context, by and large, was that a "standard", "correct" English (preferably British or American), would be taught to them. Our lived experiences in multilingual contexts outside of our home countries, encountering numerous varieties of Englishes, had long since caused us to discard notions of a single, standard normative English to be imitated and taught everywhere (if we had *ever* held that notion). Through our work alongside nurse-educators, practicing nurses and nursing students, and in interprofessional medical education, all set within the "linguistic superdiversity" (Nebel 2017) of the State of Qatar, we very slowly began to conceptualize our understanding of MELF. The section that follows describes the research context in which this conceptualization began to take shape.

---

5 Education and research are central to Qatar's plans to transform itself into a nation with a modern knowledge-based economy with a sustainable future for its citizens, aligning with the human development pillar of Qatar's National Vision 2030.

Qatar's goal is to develop a world-class educational system on a par with the highest international standards, which equips citizens with the knowledge, skills and capabilities to take on the world's challenges. (Government of Qatar 2020: paras 1–2).

3.2 Research context

3.2.1 Lingua francas in the State of Qatar

The Arabian Peninsula[3] State of Qatar, represents a sort of prototype of the "sociolinguistics of globalization", where features of global circumstances are enacted in local contexts (Blommaert 2010). Situated geographically along one of the world's oldest trade routes, the history of Qatar is akin to that of its Gulf neighbours: one of intersecting languages, cultures and peoples (Carter 2005). Wilson's classic description of a "medley of races and racial blends" (1928: 8) remains accurate to this day. Qatar's positioning in the strategic waters of the Gulf facilitated Indian Ocean links to centres of commerce in neighbouring Gulf states, in Persia, in Africa, in China, and on the Indian subcontinent for millennia; the subsequent exchange of goods and labour helped make her a confluence of ethnic, linguistic and cultural influences from the earliest times. This coalescent nature, present from the earliest settlement, has not abated in Qatar, and continues to expand at present.

While both bemoaned by its leaders and recognized as an economic necessity (Janardhan 2009), expatriate labour is at the heart of the economic development of nations in the Gulf Cooperation Council (GCC), and the State of Qatar is no exception: as much as 95% of Qatar's population is composed of foreign labour (Ibnouf, Dou & Knight 2014). A 2013 report listed workers from India accounting for 31% of the population, 23% from Nepal, 11% from the Philippines, 10% from neighbouring Arab countries, and 9% from Bangladesh (Barnawi 2018). This modern mix, along with historic African and Persian expatriate populations (Fromherz 2017), help facilitate a remarkable linguistic diversity.

In many fields of study, let alone applied linguistics, finding Qatar-specific research literature presents a challenge. Typically, Qatar is "lumped together" (Hillman & Ocampo Eibenschutz 2018: 229) with other Gulf states, perhaps because Qatar-specific research, while emerging rapidly, is still not as prevalent as that of its regional neighbours. In many respects, however, Qatar's present and historical circumstances differ from other Gulf states (Fromherz 2017). Pearl harvesting and export was central to Qatar's ancient settlement, with likely influences

---

[3] We acknowledge the politically contentious naming of the body of water separating Iran and the Arabian Peninsula. Unless otherwise specified, we use the general term "the Gulf" to refer to the nations of the Gulf Cooperation Council (GCC): Bahrain, Kuwait, Oman, Qatar, Saudi Arabia and the United Arab Emirates (International Relations and Security Network 2009).

from the Dilmun commercial empire in nearby Bahrain, and it was the international demand for pearls and the accompanying mercantilism which fostered a global capitalist orientation in the Gulf, well before the discovery of hydrocarbons (Carter 2005). This mercantilist economy employed various lingua francas, and in the 18th century, before the British Empire established various protectorate agreements with Gulf states, important languages for interethnic communication in Qatar included Arabic, Hindi, Urdu and Swahili. Unlike other colonial experiments of the British Empire, Qatar's experience with their British protectors was much more indirect, and the English language was largely limited to loanwords (Hillman and Ocampo Eibenschutz, 2018).

The rise of English as a lingua franca was facilitated by the discovery and development of hydrocarbons. Beginning in 1940 with the discovery of oil and then the North Field natural gas discovery in 1971 (Sorkhabi 2010), Qatar's rapid economic development through hydrocarbons has required an influx of technical and professional expertise, and with that, the increased use of English (Boyle 2014; Karmani 2005). At present, English functions as a lingua franca among Qatar's educated workforce, particularly in fields such as healthcare, engineering and education. However, as with other Gulf states, the rapid economic expansion undergirded by petro-dollars has required a large workforce of semi-skilled or unskilled manual labour, particularly from South Asia (Holes 2011), in employment sectors like construction, and heightened in infrastructure preparation for the 2022 FIFA World Cup (Barnawi 2018). Since foreign labour is typically a sensitive topic in the Gulf (Willoughby 2006), quantifying exact numbers of these workers is a challenge; however, semi- or unskilled manual labour make up a significant portion of the population (Theodoropoulou 2015). For this segment of the workforce, Gulf Pidgin Arabic, an umbrella term for a number of Asian Migrant Arabic Pidgins (Bizri 2014) has emerged as a contact language (Avram 2018). Comprised of elements of Arabic foreigner talk register, Gulf Arabic dialects, Urdu, and English (Holes 2011; Bizri 2014; Avram 2018; Dashti 2015), and widely referred to as "broken Arabic" by Arabic native speakers, this emerging contact language nevertheless serves as an important lingua franca in Qatar and across the Gulf.

Whether a particular "Gulf English" is emerging as a new variety of English is up for debate. From a World Englishes paradigm, evidence has been put forward of a linguistic nativization process underway in the region (e.g., Fussell 2011; Mahboob & Elyas 2014). Use of South Asian[4] English lexical expressions

---

4 Following Mann (2014), we take South Asia to include Bangladesh, Bhutan, India (including its union territories), Maldives, Nepal, Pakistan and Sri Lanka.

in Qatar by users across L1s, such as *same same* (Hillman and Ocampo Eibenschutz, 2018) and *good name* (Tweedie & Johnson 2018a) have been observed. Domain use and awareness also hints at a nativization process: Hillman and Ocampo Eibenschutz describe a domain awareness by Qatari students who delineate between a "university English" and the "simple English" or "broken English" used with family and friends (2018: 235–236). Other researchers such as Boyle (2014) see rather a process of koinéization at work (where a new language variety emerges from the mixing of varieties; see Siegel 2001), in dialect levelling (the process by which regional dialects become less distinct; see Crystal 2009) and simplification.

At the pharmacy, I (L1 English) asked the pharmacist for *pantozol*, one of many proton-pump inhibitors often prescribed to treat gastritis or acid-reflux. The pharmacist (L1 Arabic), looked at me, then my hands, and then asked, "Do you have a prescription?" Surprised, I tried to explain that I'd bought it at this pharmacy, before, and other pharmacies as well, and had never needed a prescription. Her eyebrow arched, she started, "Certainly not" but then stopped and asked me the name of the drug again. I said it once more, but with more conscientious enunciation this time, and she laughed. "I thought you said '*prednisone*,' a steroid." – Author's experience in a GCC pharmacy

---

A focus on Arabic and English alone, however, obscures the "linguistic superdiversity" (Nebel 2017) present in Qatar. Nebel draws upon Blommaert's (2013) notion of linguistic landscapes to describe the "sociolinguistics of mobile resources" (Blommaert, 2010: 1) evident in globalized cities such as Qatar's capital. Nebel correctly identifies the dynamic of "post-migrants" and "second generation immigrants", "master navigators of their polycentric, transnational, and translingual world" (2017: 31–32; cf. Canagarajah 2012), who make up a growing segment of Qatar's population. She provides an example to illustrate the blurred lines between traditional categories like L1 and L2: "one of my students grew up speaking French with his mother, a regional dialect of Arabic with his father and siblings, Modern Standard Arabic at grammar school, and both French and English in high school" (2017: 33). A student of ours was born in Qatar, to Pakistani parents who had resided in the State for more than 20 years.[5] She grew up speaking predominantly Urdu and English at home, attended Arabic-medium primary and secondary schools, and over her school career had received

---

5 Until recently, non-Qataris were unable to apply for permanent residency. See: "Qatar to approve permanent residency for some expats". (2017, August 3). *Al Jazeera English*. Retrieved from https://www.aljazeera.com/news/2017/08/qatar-approve-permanent-residency-expats-170803095052801.html/.

extensive private tuition in English, whether by attending after-school/weekend classes, or from a tutor engaged by her family. Like many of her friends, she has watched Turkish television extensively from childhood, and has made it her goal to develop proficiency in that language. Such translingual complexities doubtless impact upon ELF practices in Qatar, and subsequently those of MELF as she enters the nursing profession in future.

Stranger in my own land, I see that people don't understand my words. Their garments do not cover their flaws and their glances follow me like a plague. I speak to them in Arabic and they respond in a foreign tongue; English. They laugh all around me and say: uneducated, but am I not in an Arab country? To where should I turn? To the West which sees me as backwards? Or to the people who see me as a rebel? To whom, to where, my country? – Mimi, a Qatari blogger (as cited in Alkhatib 2017: 44)

Apart from the influx of expatriates, the linguistic landscape of Qatar is made additionally complex by a "zigzagging" K-12 medium-of-instruction policy enacted for locals (Barnawi 2018: 97). From the opening of the first school in 1948 until the 1990s, Qatar education was taught through the medium of Arabic, with schools "aimed at promoting social values and Islamic traditions as well as preserving local heritage among its citizens" (Barnawi 2018: 97). Major school reform initiatives post-2000 have emphasized English as a medium for scientific and technical subjects, but actual classroom use has been described as limited largely to the "3 Ts: texts, tests and terminology" (Kane 2014: 96). Continual reports of poor performance led to structural changes to education in the second decade of this century, including a shift back toward Arabic-medium instruction. As a consequence of this zigzagging medium of instruction policy, some students receiving their education during this period felt inadequately prepared for postsecondary in both Arabic and English (Hillman & Ocampo Eibenschutz 2018). Conflicting policy shifts between Arabic- and English-medium are similarly reflected at Qatar University, where Arabic is seen as an important means of preserving local identity, while the role of English in the international academy and marketplace is affirmed (Ellili-Cherif & Alkhateeb 2015).

It is in the growing number of private K-12 schools that the linguistic superdiversity of Qatar is arguably most evident. Schools for children of expatriate workers are known as "community" schools, and medium-of-instruction at these schools include Arabic, Filipino, Urdu, Farsi, Turkish, French, Japanese and German; typically English is taught in these schools as a subject. A number of schools aimed at the children of expatriate Indians prepare students for India's national examinations, and various English-medium "international" schools follow American or British curriculum.

Qatar, along with other Gulf nations, lies at the epicentre of a large-scale experiment with international branch campuses (IBCs), a relatively recent phenomenon where foreign institutions operate campuses in another country, under that country's regulatory system, while maintaining varying degrees of self-governance, and often with the aim of global brand export (Kosmützky 2018). Qatar has emerged as a leading destination not just for IBCs, but its Education City project represents an example of the "educational hub" approach, where hosting governments provide favourable conditions (economic incentives, infrastructure, centralized support services) for IBCs (Knight 2014). Education City at present hosts 8 universities from the USA, UK and France, each with its own area of specialization, with English as the medium of instruction across all campuses, and all housed under the umbrella of Hamad Bin Khalifa University (Kosmützky 2018). Despite the linguistic diversity of its student body, observers of Education City have noted a prevalence of monolingual assumptions and practices (e.g., Kane 2014).

Callers to the State of Qatar's telephone system for scheduling medical appointments, *Nesma'ak*, are greeted first in Arabic, and then in English. In both languages, they are provided with the option of continuing in one of four languages. "For service in Arabic, please press one. For service in English, Urdu, or Malayalam, please press 2."

Among the forces exerting pressure for monolingual practices among Qatar's linguistic diversity is that of a policy of Arabization (Hillman & Ocampo Eibenschutz 2018). An emphasis on increased literacy in Arabic (though usually unstated, presumably Modern Standard Arabic is implied) features regularly in political discourse as a means to counter potential identity loss in an English-dominant environment. Whether decried in speeches from political leadership, bemoaned in newspaper editorials, or reflected in zigzagging medium-of-instruction policy, a perceived decline in Arabic use is perceived as an existential threat to identity. In fact, foreign postsecondary institutions, along with medium-of-instruction policy, represent concerns over a larger reshape of culture, language and identity in the GCC states (Vora 2015), and may impact subtle and not-so-subtle decisions on institutional funding (Hillman & Ocampo Eibenschutz 2018).

3.2.2 Research context: Institutional setting

The studies were conducted at a Canadian university's transnational campus in Qatar. The only programs offered at the institution are Bachelor of Nursing (BN) and Master of Nursing. All instruction and assessment is conducted in English. With the exception of Nursing instructor participants (described later), all participants in the studies were BN students. There are two streams in the BN program at the institution, Bachelor of Nursing Regular Track (BNRT) and Post-diploma Bachelor of Nursing (PDBN). BNRT students have no previous nursing degree or diploma and complete a full, four-year Nursing program. PDBN students come to the school already possessing at least a two-year diploma in Nursing, and bring with them (in some cases quite extensive) professional nursing experience. In this track, students complete two years of further education in order to attain a full, four-year bachelor's degree. In both streams, students complete both theory (i.e., knowledge-based) courses and clinical (i.e., practice-based, healthcare context) courses. Many courses in both streams also involve practice and assessment in the university's clinical simulation center, where they complete both individual- and group-based healthcare "role-play" scenarios, both as a means of learning and practice, and as a means of assessment. The students at the university, while predominantly Arabic speakers from the Arabian gulf region, are diverse culturally and linguistically, with some 39 nationalities and multiple self-identified "strongest languages".

At the time any of the research described in this book was completed, all instructors at the university were required to be Canadian citizens or permanent residents. The Nursing instructors who participated were registered nurses in Canada; all held Masters degrees in Nursing.

3.3 Tracing MELF: An emerging understanding

To narrow our emerging conceptualization of MELF to one particular study, with a clearly marked beginning and end point, would be to oversimplify. In fact, Davis' (1995: 445) description of "prolonged engagement and persistent observation" to establish credibility in applied linguistics research aptly characterizes our multi-year, multi-faceted involvement with our learners in our role as ESP instructors; with language teaching colleagues; with nursing faculty; with various components of the healthcare system (both healthcare providers and patients) in operation around us; and with ELF users in the Gulf at large. Therefore, when we describe a "methodology", or a "study", the reader should understand this to be much broader than individual research inquiries carried out at a particular point in time (though it includes that), but a non-linear, immersive, emergent, evolving process of conceptualization. This next section attempts to contextualize some of the important milestones in the process.

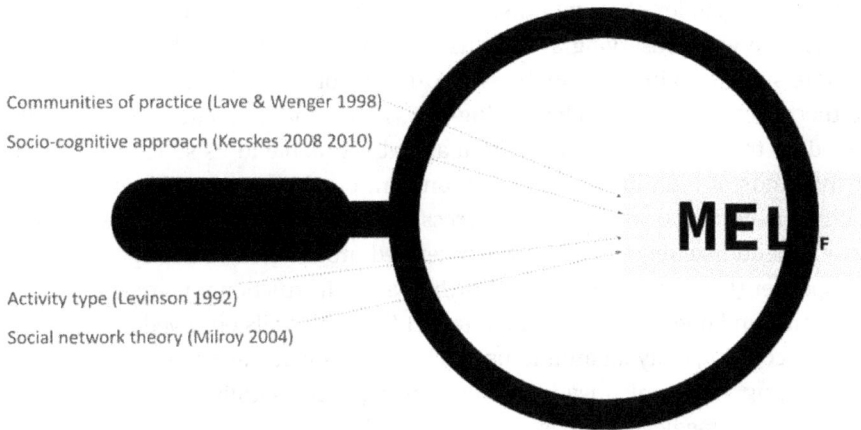

Figure 3.1: Lenses for viewing MELF.

Lying in a hospital bed, I was starting to feel the effects of the sedative the nurse (L1 Tamil) had administered in preparation for a procedure. He then checked and reported in English my blood pressure to the physician (L1 Arabic). I thought I heard "150 over 70" and became immediately concerned. I thought, "My blood pressure is never high and now it's 150. . . *after* a sedative?" but all I got out was a slightly slurred, "150?" The physician looked at me, then the nurse, and asked, "One five zero or one one five?" and the nurse responded "One one five. It's good." – Author's experience in a hospital in a Gulf Cooperation Council nation.

3.3.1 Intelligibility in MELF

An observation of ELF interprofessional collaboration in an outpatient clinic, soon after our arrival in the region, was foundational in sparking our interest in this line of inquiry: "an Indian pharmacist deciphered the instructions of a Filipino doctor to a Qatari patient mediated through a Sri Lankan nurse" (Tweedie & Johnson 2018b: 69). Our original interest was thus formed around a purely practical question: *with multiple L1s in most medical interactions in the multilingual milieu of the Gulf, was the message in English getting through?*

We therefore focused on the notion of intelligibility to frame our first inquiry[6] (see Tweedie and Johnson, 2018a). Our research at this stage was largely from the standpoint of our role as English for Specific Purposes teachers-as-researchers (see Hyland 2019); we wanted to improve our classroom teaching in order to prepare our learners for effective nursing practice in the linguistically diverse environment we were observing around us. We had not conceptualized MELF as a separate sub-discipline, and in fact were at this point largely unacquainted with the theoretical literature underpinning ELF. As language teachers, we were distressed by the dearth of instructional materials available to us suited specifically for the kinds of multilingual ELF environment our learners would work in; the teaching materials to which we had access typically portrayed ENL contexts, with speaking and listening dialogues often centred around non-native speaker – native speaker (NNS-NS) interactions. Further, aural instructional materials seemed to us static and one-way: they did not reflect listening skills observed in ELF interactions occurring daily all around us, such as repeating, clarifying, restating, and summarizing, ones which we increasingly recognized as critical to accurate communication for medical contexts.

We drew heavily upon the "Smith paradigm" (a designation by Kachru 2008) to conceptualize the interactions we saw in our English for Specific Purposes classes. Smith (1992) and Smith and Nelson (1985) identified three components of intelligibility to describe on a continuum the increasing complexity of language use: intelligibility, comprehensibility, and interpretability. In this framework, intelligibility represents our most basic understanding of language, and refers primarily to the way language sounds. A solitary individual in a coffee shop may overhear a conversation at the next table, and recognize that Chinese is being spoken. The listener may not understand Chinese, perhaps comprehending only a few isolated words in the conversation, but will recognize the sounds and rhythms as being of the Chinese language. Or, a listener encountering someone with a markedly different accent will note, consciously or unconsciously, the different sounds being used for words. Hearers expect languages to sound certain ways; when they do not, they induce reactions of some type: perhaps interest, maybe mild and temporary confusion, perhaps amusement, a quite neutral noticing, or even off-putting, to give a few possible examples.

Smith defines comprehensibility in terms of word recognition. If offered tea at a friend's house, a listener conceives of a particular thing (not coffee, a

---

[6] The content of this section summarizes and elaborates upon our original study (M. Gregory Tweedie & Robert C. Johnson 2018a; M. Gregory Tweedie & Robert C. Johnson 2018b).

hot drink served in a cup, etc.), though numerous additional conceptions may be known to the listener (a leafy plant, Masala chai, herbal tea, etc.). The particular context of the speech event helps the listener qualify the range of meanings for the word (Nelson 2011).[7]

Interpretability is the third and highest level of complexity in this framework, and refers to the intended underlying meaning: "recognition by the hearer/reader of the intent of purpose of an utterance, i.e., the perlocutionary effect the speaker/writer is aiming at" (Kachru & Smith 2008: 63). Interpreting an utterance for intelligibility necessarily requires both linguistic and extralinguistic clues such as background knowledge, attention to the setting and to body language, cultural awareness, and so on. Nelson (2011: 26) provides an example: "When I was being taught my manners, my primary caregivers made it clear to me that 'When somebody says 'Would you like to stay for supper?' it's time for you to go home". It is entirely possible that a listener would clearly comprehend the word *supper* as a meal taken later in the day (comprehensibility), but miss the cultural context in the example, where apparently an invitation to dinner is actually intended as a hint that the visit is coming to an end (interpretability). Similarly, a friend recounted to us how, as a learner of Chinese as a foreign language, her beginning vocabulary permitted comprehensibility of all the words in the question "Have you eaten yet?", and her elementary knowledge of grammar recognized the utterance as a question form. However, she had not been taught how this question functions in Chinese, as in several Asian languages, as a friendly greeting and conversation starter, usually without expectation of a factual answer, somewhat akin to "How are you?" in English (Sun 2004). Until the cultural context was explained to her, she interpreted the continual questions about her eating habits not as friendly conversation starters, but as unwanted personal intrusions.

With this tripartite understanding of intelligibility to frame our inquiry, and after receiving approval to conduct the study from the institutional research ethics authorities, we invited volunteers from students in a nursing degree program to roleplay a healthcare scenario (see Scenario 3.1) while being audio-recorded. Scenarios are used widely in healthcare education, to develop and assess clinical skills in students without the attendant risks were the training to be carried out with actual patients (Wales & Skillen 1997; Campbell & Daley 2018). We developed the scenario in consultation with a senior nursing instructor: our aim was to create a scenario with fidelity to actual clinical contexts. The scenario utilized

---

[7] We refer the reader in this regard to our discussion of activity types (Levinson 1992) in Chapter 2.

a dialogic exchange roleplay (Carter & Dickieson 2010) surrounding an end-of-shift nursing handover, an everyday process whereby patient information and nursing duties and responsibilities are transferred from one nurse to another (Kim, Hur & Kim 2018). Effective nursing handovers require strong communication skills and an ability to accurately understand patient information (Anderson et al. 2015), and are recognized as an important element in patient safety (Till, Sall & Wilkinson 2014).

Two students volunteered for the study: both were postdiploma practicing nurses who would have regularly performed nursing handovers in actual clinical settings. In terms of English language proficiency, both students had met or exceeded the institutional admission cut scores at the time (Foundation entrance: IELTS Band 4.0/TOEFL iBT 40; degree entrance: IELTS 6.0 /TOEFL iBT 80) for study at this English-medium institution. Nurse A (female) described her "strongest language" as Tamil, and Nurse B (female) as Arabic. As is often the case in multilingual interactions in Qatar's hospitals, English was the only communicative option for these two nurses to interact. Linguistic features of their discussion included lack of do support in question forms (e.g., *No any interferon?; This refer the file?*), and accent features of the interlocutors' particular English varieties (e.g., *He's also stating that he's feeling funny, feeling* /hə.ləʊs/ *around the lights; He has* /wɒm.ɪtɪd/ *twice today*).

Scenario 3.1: Dialogic exchange handover scenario

Nurse A:
Shift Change: You are giving shift report to the ongoing staff.

Mr. Saddi is an 84 year old male with congestive heart failure, who has developed pulmonary edema and has also acquired C-difficile in hospital and has become dehydrated. Medications include furosemide (Lasix) 20 mg PO qd, digoxin 125 mg PO qd, potassium chloride (K-Dur) 20 mEq PO qd. He has vomited twice today, and you are not sure he kept his pills down. He is also stating that he "feels funny and I'm seeing halos around the lights – I wonder if I am going crazy".

You report on the following:
- admitting diagnoses
- report vital signs (BP 180/82, P 92 R 26)
- urinary output hourly over the last eight hours
- auscultation: diminished air entry with inspiratory crackles throughout (review what this could be)
- cough is wet and non-productive
- tachycardic
- pulse irregular
- recent lab values show potassium level increasing
- disorientation
- patient opening eyes in response to touch

Nurse B:
Shift Change: You are the incoming nurse during shift change.

Listen to the outgoing nurse and the information they give you about a patient.

You are a participant in the conversation, so feel free to ask questions or do anything else you might want until you are comfortable you have the information necessary.

Three senior nursing instructors volunteered to participate in the study, by listening to the recorded roleplay. All three held advanced nursing degrees, indicated Canadian English (Walker 2015) as their "strongest language", and were experienced communicators in the multilingual, ELF clinical and educational research context. The instructors were asked to listen to the recording, and in a semi-structured interview with the researcher following immediately after, explore areas of communication in the recorded scenario which might impact upon quality healthcare and patient safety, either positively or negatively, were this nursing handover to occur in an actual clinical setting.

As all three instructors were experienced nurse practitioners, and accustomed to giving direct instruction to nursing students on clinical skills, we began the listening/interview session with an explanation of the study's purpose, explicitly highlighting our aim of identifying *language-based* elements impacting quality care. For example, one nursing instructor was concerned that the patient's rising potassium levels were not adequately discussed during the handover. This omission, in her view as a senior nursing instructor, was an error in *clinical practice* communication that would impinge upon patient safety, but not a *language-based* communication error per se, and therefore was outside of the scope of our study.

Bachelor of Nursing students at the same institution were then invited to participate in the study by listening to the audio-recorded handover roleplay and responding to questions gauging both actual and perceived comprehension of the content. The comprehension questions were developed by consulting with a senior nursing instructor: we wanted to highlight content for listening assessment that reflected matters of patient safety and quality delivery of healthcare – ones that would be critical for accurate understanding in an actual clinical handover. The comprehension items (Questions 1–6) were sequenced to align with their appearance in the discussion (Rost 2002), and to include processing of both explicitly stated and, where important to safe and effective patient care, implied meaning (Buck 2001). Questions 7–10 focused on participants' perceived comprehension of the discussion: misalignment between interlocutors' appraisal of interactional success has been shown to be a barrier to effective healthcare communication (Tongue, Epps & Forese 2005). Listening comprehension questions are included in the Appendix.

14 Bachelor of Nursing students participated in this phase of the research. They were asked to specify their "strongest language": five indicated Arabic; three Tagalog; two Farsi; two Malayalam; and two participants indicated Yoruba and Indonesian, respectively. While we had hoped to gather a mix of genders as participants, all those who responded to the invitation to participate indicated their gender as female, indicative of the reality that a significant majority of the institution's student body are female. All of the participants had completed the required nursing assessment course, which covers skills needed in order to construct a health history and assessment.

While the findings and their implications will be considered more fully in subsequent chapters, overall, concerns over patient safety due to language-related communication errors were not unfounded. In the view of the three nursing instructors, matters of miscommunication related to language in the roleplay scenario would have negatively impacted patient care were it to have taken place in an actual nursing handover. With regard to the nursing students who listened to the recorded scenario, perceived intelligibility generally matched what the listeners had actually understood. However, where mismatches in perceived intelligibility did occur, they were in instances where patient safety could be threatened. For example, consider the discussion regarding blood sugar levels in the roleplay scenario (also described in Chapter 1). The two nurses in the scenario were able to alleviate misunderstanding by clarification.

> Nurse B (L1 Arabic) Why you . . . take the blood sugar? The blood sugar, it's high?
>
> Nurse A (L1 Tamil) Blood sugar, not take.
>
> Nurse B You not take blood sugar?
>
> Nurse A No. Not diabetic, not diabetes.

Of the 14 nursing students listening to the scenario, 13 indicated that they had understood at least 70% of the exchange, and all 14 described as their understanding of the patient's condition and symptoms (50% said they understood "easily"). Yet, when asked about the patient's blood sugar level (which in fact had not been taken), three listeners described his level as "normal", one as "within normal" and one "good". The conclusions from this initial study fed back, in numerous ways, into our work as language instructors preparing students for admission to their nursing degree. The findings formed a part of the impetus for the development of a frequency-based nursing corpora for more targeted vocabulary instruction at the institution (Shimoda, Toriida & Kay 2016), for example. During the recorded scenario, a lack of precise expression in describing the patient's condition was flagged by the nursing instructors, who noted both Nurse A's use of the words *funny* and *crazy* as attempts to describe potentially threatening conditions, and Nurse B's failure to press for clarification on what these terms meant. The patient's high potassium levels, coupled with what may have been growing disorientation, called for much more precise description to ensure appropriate care post-handover.

However, the findings also brought to the forefront a reality we had observed previously: a clear disconnect between language instruction and the nursing content instruction it is ostensibly intended for.

Challenges in making connections between language and disciplinary content are not unusual in English for Specific Purposes contexts (e.g., Luo & Garner 2017), and may encompass assumptions of discipline incompetence by learners, isolation from other language teachers, lesser status than disciplinary specialists in the hierarchy of the academy, and lower priority in scheduling (Robinson 1991). Hyland (2014: 146) outlines the particular challenges of forging collaborative partnerships between disciplinary specialists and language instructors, noting "a range of attitudes from enthusiastic cooperation to cold indifference". The extreme version of this partnership portrays language specialists as butlers, serving at the disciplinary specialists' bidding (Raimes 1992). Even when collaborative partnerships between the two are successful, learners may struggle to reconcile the disparate discourses utilized by language and disciplinary specialists (Barron 2003). None of these challenges were outside our experiences as language teachers in the research context, but our research finding regarding patient safety made more pressing our efforts to more thoroughly integrate language support and nursing content. We thus turned our attention to the simulation laboratory.

CO-SIM4
20 Doctor (L1 English): Okay. I'm here to see the patient.
21 Nurse B (L1s Arabic / Malayalam): Excuse me doctor, uh, this patient is uh, contact isolation so we have to wear the PPE [Personal Protective Equipment]. Uh, we have to wear the PPE?
22 Doctor: No, don't have to wear that.
23 Nurse B: Um, doctor it's the policy=
24 Doctor: I've washed my hands, I always wash my hands. Touch those, how many people have touched? Nope.
25 Nurse: No, doctor.
26 Doctor: No, that spreads germs, more, germs than I would after I sanitized my hands.
27 Nurse: No doctor. You have to wear, the policy=
28 Doctor: You're telling me, that I have to?

29 Nurse: Yes, doctor, because it is the policy and the patient, it's just for the patient safety and at the same time I think it is better for you also, so that we will go outside and no one will, it will not co, uh, contaminate the other area (also). So I feel it will be better like, you will uh, wear the PPE before entering the patient so that we can see, we can prevent the cross-contamination, doctor.
30 Doctor: I have a lot of patients to see, today, I, no need for that because how many people have, got germs on it. It makes no difference after the clothes that I put on clean today. I need to go in, I need to see the patient.

3.3.2 MELF in simulation training

The desire for more integration between English for Specific Purposes (ESP) instruction and the nursing courses it was intended to support led us toward a second research study in our role as language instructor-researchers. Our intended field of investigation this time was the nursing simulation laboratory. Nursing curricula utilizes simulation training, drawn upon real-world healthcare scenarios, to develop nursing skills (Gliva-McConvey, Nicholas & Clark 2020). In "high-fidelity" simulation laboratories, through technology and the use of simulated patients, nurse trainees are exposed to conditions, medical equipment and scenarios which closely imitate an actual clinical environment (Reilly & Spratt 2007). At its best, high-fidelity simulation offers trainee nurses "the cues necessary to suspend belief during dynamic, immersive hands-on scenarios" (Yaeger et al. 2004: 328). Simulation training therefore seemed the ideal environment to provide the kinds of speaking and listening instruction required for the multilingual ELF interactions our students would encounter in future. However, ESP instruction was restricted almost exclusively to "foundation", pre-degree language preparation courses, with little direct connection to the simulation curricula or instructors. Fortunately, when we reached out to the nursing simulation lab specialists, we found a similar desire for integration of English listening and speaking instruction with simulation lab content in order to better prepare students for a multilingual nursing environment, and a fruitful collaborative research partnership was formed.

For this analysis of MELF interactions in the simulation lab, we attempted to draw upon several theoretical frameworks. Initially, we attempted to interpret the simulations largely within the notion of communities of practice (Lave & Wenger 1991; Wenger 1998). Trainee nurses in simulations, after all, are being socialized as they learned into a culture of healthcare practice (Mann 2011), absorbing, explicitly and implicitly, "ways of doing things, ways of talking, beliefs, values, power relations – in short practices" (Eckert & McConnell-Ginet 1992:

464). We were also cognizant that researchers had found considerable utility for a CoP framework to understand the work of physicians (e.g., Cruess, Cruess & Steinert, 2018), nurses (e.g., Gullick et al, 2016), and other healthcare professions (e.g., ElShaer et al, 2016), and that the framework had gained substantial currency within ELF research (e.g., Ehrenreich, 2018; Kalocsai, 2014). However, as alluded to in Chapter 2, as the process of data analysis unfolded, we became increasingly aware that the relatively broad notion of a community of practice, while of utility for framing the overall range of encounters observed in nursing simulations, did not provide us with the "zoom lens" of particular subsets of interactions. We found the need to account for language use and meaning-making processes in the simulations from both macro- and micro-conceptualization, and so searched for a theoretical undergirding to account for individual situational factors trainees brought to the interaction (such as first language, or prior healthcare experiences), as well as broader social ones (like institutional and professional requirements, or sociolinguistic factors shaped by the context of a migrant destination).

A striking feature from the outset of data analysis was the relatively uniform sociolinguistic behaviour of nurses during simulations, despite not having had explicit coaching or modelling beforehand. Patient assessment scenarios during simulations, for example, proceeded along predictable lines: clearly defined turn-taking, nurse-directed question and answer exchanges, with the nurse choosing when to open and close the discussion, and in what direction it would take. We began to understand these seemingly formulaic exchanges as "activity types" (Levinson 1992: 69): "goal-defined, socially constituted events with constraints on participants" (p. 69). We found that the field of conversation analysis was replete with examples drawn from healthcare communication. Institutional talk (Drew & Heritage, 1992) as is prevalent in healthcare communication, serves to orient discussion toward institutional objectives, and place restrictions on contributions and inferences interlocutors can make. The literature indicates that physicians are explicitly trained in the "discourse planning" of the doctor-patient interview during medical education (Ainsworth-Vaughn 2005: 55). The nurses during simulation, seemed to instinctively orient toward characteristics of institutional talk and its asymmetrical conversation features, without being explicitly directed to do so in the simulation pre-briefs. The healthcare professional-to-patient interview event is universally experienced, and nurses seemed to glide relatively smoothly, and early on, into the societally-prescribed role. The observed influence of the nurse-patient interview as societal activity type, a feature of professional socialization, alerted us to the role such constraints might play in understanding MELF communication. While we acknowledged the emergent nature of much ELF communication, where ELF users innovate and repurpose the English language for particular communicative circumstances, with our understanding of activity type came a growing recognition of some of the linguistic constraints that accompany medical ELF, and which serve to press upon it unique regulatory forces.

This theme was further developed as we considered a sociocognitive approach (SCA) in which to analyze the simulation lab data, an approach broadly introduced in Chapter 2. Critical to SCA is a Dynamic Model of Meaning (DMM; Kecskes, 2003, 2008), whereby speakers in an interaction are understood to draw both upon a prior context and the present situational context. A participant in the nursing simulation lab might draw upon *salience* first as s/he attempts to gain and assert meaning in a conversation: the private, inner, previously learned, and readily available knowledge individuals bring to the simulation scenario. This might include, among much other salient information, the societal prescriptions for a healthcare professional-patient interview. When this largely egocentric background information is confronted with a differing set of inner salient assumptions expressed through another simulation participant, the present situational context further activates the inner knowledge frames of both interlocutors, as meaning-making processes are enacted.

Simulation participants bring a degree of *core common ground* to the interaction (Kecskes, 2014; Kecskes & Zhang, 2009). The SCA framework divides core common ground into constituent parts, which includes interactants' general knowledge of the world (*common sense*), their knowledge about cultural roles and expectations (*culture sense*), and their understanding of language systems (*formal sense*). In an ELF nursing simulation, participants' culture sense might encompass elements such as societal norms for the patient interview (experienced both as patient and healthcare professional); behavioural expectations for undergraduate students (experienced in the present institution and in prior learning experiences); norms of relating within and across gender (experienced previously in the learners' country of origin and perhaps differently now in the Gulf); and the desired framing of participants' professional selves within a nursing community of practice (experienced both as neophytes and as developing healthcare professionals). In terms of the *formal sense* as articulated by Kecskes and Zhang, nurse simulation participants bring (in unequal distribution relative to one another) knowledge of their first language(s); knowledge about the forms and systems of English as taught and experienced in their country of origin; knowledge about usage particular to "Gulf English"; knowledge of specialized medical and nursing lexis, including mandated communication protocols; and the relative density of ego ties in the social network (Milroy 2004). With the exception of course of first language knowledge, all of these formal senses are brought to the simulation interaction by each participant in unequal amounts, being as they are "rooted in the cultural, social and personal context of each individual" (Bigi & Rossi 2020: 24–25).

Emergent common ground in an SCA framework encompasses a *shared sense* (personalized knowledge both communicators share) and a *current sense* (the emergent understanding drawn from the interaction). As discussed elsewhere in this volume, medical interactions between healthcare professionals and patients often exemplify emergent common ground: while both patient and nurse share an understanding of the word *cough*, a nurse may classify a cough further as *wet* or *dry*, *paroxysmal*, *croup*; or identify a cough in grades like into *mild*, *severe*, *persistent* or *debilitating*; or label the cough by its effects, such as *vomiting*, *sleeplessness* or *incontinence*. Shared sense in a conversation between a healthcare professional and a patient, as with any two interlocutors, is accomplished through mutual construction. Of course, joint construction implies contributions from both conversants, and shared understanding may not always be achieved. However helpful from a treatment standpoint it may be to identify a *cough* in precise terms, healthcare researchers have noted how excessive biomedical talk and medical jargon may serve as hindrances to successful physician-patient communication (Deuster et al. 2008; Kain et al. 2009).

In doctor-patient interactions, communication can be interpreted as a component of care. The quality of communicative interactions is indeed considered one of the factors impacting on patient understanding and adherence (or compliance) and, therefore, indirectly also on the achievement of clinical outcomes *(Bigi & Rossi 2020: 13)*.

In interactions between healthcare professionals and patients in MELF contexts, it may be that core common ground presents the greatest challenge for mutual construction of understanding. Communicators across differing first languages may rely disproportionately on emergent common ground to compensate for misunderstandings in the cultural sense of core common ground (knowledge of beliefs, norms, practices), or its formal sense (knowledge of the language system). Bigi and Rossi contrast medical interactions in monolingual settings, where in a shared first language, "the parties' attention should be brought to the implicit part of meaning, which is likely to be taken for granted", with multilingual ones, where "the first difficulty to solve is related to the explicit meaning, which is encoded in a language that is not shared (or not perfectly known) by all the participants" (2020: 29). Clarification processes to access explicit meaning can therefore ingress implicit meaning. Even so, healthcare researchers have noted the element of cross-linguistic challenges of medical communication in ENL settings, with monolingual physicians characterized as "bilinguals": the specialized speech of medicine portrayed as a sort of second language (Ong et al. 1995: 910). Adding further complexity to the task of achieving core common ground is the distinction between the "textbook language" of medical terms, and what Hull (2013; 2016) calls medical language. Hull distinguishes between medical language and medical terminology: the latter encompasses specialized technical terms, while the former "consists of words, phrases, jargon, acronyms, abbreviations, terms and expressions that are used less formally to communicate about a patient's status, to confer with peers, and to be sure that meaning is understood during interactions with patients" (Hull 2013: IX).

As this core common ground was being constructed by our participants, we were particularly interested in areas of potential or actual misunderstandings, given the importance of precise, accurate and time-sensitive communication that is required in healthcare. Bremer (1996) distinguishes between non-understandings and misunderstandings among interlocutors, with the delineating feature being the hearer's recognition. In a non-understanding, the hearer recognizes "that s/he cannot make sense of (part of) an utterance" (1996: 40), and may seek clarification from the speaker, or let it pass (Firth 1996) in anticipation that the meaning will become apparent later. In instances of misunderstanding, the hearer "achieves an interpretation which makes sense to her or him – but it wasn't the one the speaker meant" (Bremer 1996: 40). Instances of non-understanding may be relatively easier to identify, in that the listener signals non-understanding in some way, either by asking for clarification, a pause (Kaur 2009a), or other means. In the definition of Roberts et al (2005), drawn from data recorded in patients' consultations with general practitioner physicians in London, misunderstandings "occur whenever there is insufficient understanding for both parties to continue, or where there is the illusion of understanding which is only revealed later on, or where there are unresolved ambiguities" (2005: 468). Roberts and colleagues include in this definition "social discrepancies where problems of sustaining social interaction lead to uncomfortable, disruptive or confusing moments" (2005: 468; cf. Schegloff 1987). For further clarity in identifying non-signalled misunderstandings, researchers such as Deterding (2013) involved participants in a post-conversation discussion; in our case, we had the benefit of a written scenario which framed the simulation's backdrop, providing us with the "actual" patient condition.

The reality that *perceived* understanding and *actual* understanding represent two different things is well documented in healthcare research. Though physicians *explain*, what patients actually *understand* of the explanation is often overestimated: in treatment decisions (Berger, Boss & Beach 2017); in acute coronary events (Chen & McCormick 2015); and in the treatment plans to be carried out after patients have been discharged (Calkins et al. 1997). Assessment of recall on information given to patients has been shown to be as low as 50 percent (Schillinger et al. 2003). The typical yes/no question forms that characterize medical interviews are problematic as a demonstration of actual understanding: patients may be embarrassed to admit they do not understand (Heritage 2010), and low health literacy is a significant barrier to comprehension (Knighton, Brunisholz & Savitz 2017).

The discrepancy between perceived and actual understanding in healthcare interactions extends beyond physician-patient discussions. In our first study (Tweedie and Johnson, 2018a; 2018b), nursing student listeners were asked to describe to what extent they felt they had understood a recorded healthcare scenario, which involved detailed medical information on an elderly patient with pulmonary edema. 13 of 14 listeners felt they had understood 70% or more of the discussion, with half indicating they comprehended the patient's conditions and symptoms "easily". Despite listeners' self-perceived apprehension, significant differences were observed between information conveyed in the scenario and what listeners indicated they heard, including details of critical import for safe patient care. A nurse who is aware that she doesn't understand can ask for more information; a nurse who acts on information that "she doesn't understand she doesn't understand" may threaten patient safety.

Hull (2016) envisions scenarios of word-level misunderstandings in a European healthcare context, among caregivers and patients of Hungarian, Spanish and English L1s. Misunderstanding due to phonemic imprecision among healthcare providers in describing *feces* (excrement) and *facies* (the expression of the face) is entirely plausible. Similarly, in a Spanish-dominant context, an L1 English patient using the word *commode* (a chair-like toilet) may be heard by the Spanish L1 nurse as *comóda* (comfortable). In both of these examples, misunderstandings are likely to be repaired quickly, and apart from some chuckles as the story is recounted to colleagues, of little consequence. More serious though would be a misunderstanding of the English medical term *Valsalva* (a manoeuvre used to arrest supraventricular tachycardia) and the Hungarian word *válságos* (critical). In all three examples, Hull asks readers to "Imagine these same terms spoken hurriedly during a crisis" (2016: 162).

In a study of medication errors by pharmacists and nurses, Bohand et al (2009) note the dispensing challenges associated with drugs of similar names, such as CORVASAL® 2 mg (molsidomine) and COVERSYL® 2 mg (perindopril). The study in which this example is mentioned does not consider language barriers as a factor in mistaking CORVASAL and COVERSYL, so it is not difficult to imagine a heightened chance of phonemically-induced misunderstandings for these two drugs in an ELF healthcare environment.

Along with the micro-perspectives evident in activity types and an SCA framework, it also became apparent to us that analysis of the interactions would be incomplete without attention to the broader "sociolinguistics of mobile resources" (Blommaert 2010: 1) characteristic of a globalized locale such as Qatar. In the "linguistic superdiversity" of Qatar (Nebel 2017) and its GCC neighbours, at a confluence of national, migrant, post-migrant, second generation immigrant, and historical immigrant populations, the conditions are set for unprecedented language contact and change. Gulf Pidgin Arabic and an emerging Gulf English serve as important lingua francas across the region, but as noted earlier, a focus on Arabic and English masks the increasingly fuzzy lines between L1 and L2, as post-migrants and second (or third) generation immigrants hybridize their linguistic resources (Nebel 2017). In such an environment, with the intensification of language contact, the application of social network theory to language use (Milroy 2004) offers a helpful frame for analysis. Where an individual's contact with others in a social network are multiple, frequent, recurring and intertwined within the same network, linguistic norms are likely to be entrenched, upheld and reinforced. Deviation from such norms is likely to receive disapproval and social sanction in some form, from mild disapproving glances to moral disapprobation. In a migrant destination however, where social networks are abruptly unfastened, then subsequently reshaped and restructured, linguistic norms are ripe for disruption. Accommodation to differing accents, dialect simplification and new vocabulary are adopted and applied at an escalated rate, as means of social sanction toward linguistic non-compliance are no longer in play. Domain awareness and adaptation become paramount for communicative success in such an environment, and even individuals who derive a considerable sense of identity from use of a particular dialect are challenged to restyle their speech to make a transaction at a bank, describe a destination in a taxi, ask for assistance in a supermarket, or navigate the hospital admission process.

Among the 138 nurses participating in the simulation exercises that formed our data were: second generation immigrants and "post-migrants" (Nebel 2017: 31–32), young adults with blurred boundaries between their L1s and subsequent languages; diploma-prepared nurses from South Asia who had already spent several years working in Gulf clinics; native speakers of Egyptian Arabic; Qatari nationals; and English speakers from Australia, Canada, the UK and other "Inner Circle" English-using countries (Kachru 1985), among others. We recognized in this collection of dialects, languages and cultures, brought together as a cohort for study out of the linguistically superdiverse milieu of the Gulf, the possibility to directly observe these language contact processes as brought on by the dynamics of loosened social network ties.

These multiple frames of reference with which to consider our data – communities of practice, a socio-cultural approach and activity type; and social network theory – juxtaposed with the positivist/post-positivist paradigms characteristic of medical research literature – presented an additional challenge: how to simultaneously integrate observations from multiple perspectives? It is here that we drew upon the notion of the bricolage, and its application to the discipline of nursing. Patient centred care (PCC) is championed by the nursing profession (Lauver et al. 2002), as is the case with a larger shift within the healthcare profession in general (Pelzang 2010). As a holistic perspective, PCC calls for a comprehensive understanding of all those aspects of patients' lives which might impact upon health and wellbeing. Such a standpoint on care requires a "postformal" approach in which nurses are able to draw from a range of theoretical perspectives to inform clinical practice (Warne & McAndrew 2009: 855). Warne and McAndrew therefore advocate a multifaceted bricolage approach (cf. Kincheloe 2001), in which methodological pluralism is employed to colligate a range of theoretical and disciplinary perspectives, including the nurses' own personal experience, with the aim of new knowledge production. A bricolage perspective contrasts with monological knowledge (Kincheloe 2005), said to be one-dimensional and narrow in its approach, and thus arriving at limited conclusions. To Kincheloe, underlying a bricolage approach to research is the epistemological and ontological position that "the domains of the physical, the social, the cultural, the psychological, and the educational consist of the interplay of a wide variety of entities" (Kincheloe 2005: 327). The nurse-researcher/practitioner interested in PCC must therefore consider data interpreted and integrated from multiple theoretical perspectives, adding to these their own self-reflexivity and the lived experiences of the patient. In navigating the interpretation of our data, we attempt to learn from the point of view utilized by the bricoleur, to seek an understanding of the interplay (Kincheloe 2005) among the many factors that shape MELF communication.

3.4 Practical considerations for data collection: Simulation research

Ethical considerations for the conduct of simulation lab research present additional challenges. Simulations in this institutional context are routinely video-recorded for pedagogical purposes: nursing instructors often utilize the recorded proceedings to provide feedback to learners on various aspects of their clinical practice. In this sense, the data collected and analyzed for our research can be considered secondary data, in that it was originally gathered for another purpose

(Smith 2008). At the beginning of each term, nursing students are invited to sign a consent form indicating they agree to simulation video recording for the purposes of teaching and learning. As part of the research design approval from both institutional research ethics review boards under whose jurisdictions this study fell, we added to this initial consent form a separate line where students could also indicate they agreed to permit researchers access to the video recording for research purposes. Those who consented to researcher access were then asked to indicate their "strongest language". This dual consent introduced numerous ethical complexities to the research. If a student did not provide consent for the researchers to access the recording for research purposes, her or his utterances would not be considered as data. In a scenario where a simulation involved only two or three participants, one of whom withheld consent, that entire data set would need to be discarded: there would no longer be any "communication" to analyze.

A second complexity was obtaining informed consent from simulated/standardized patients, members of the community who agree to support teaching and learning by acting as patients in the simulation (Churchouse & McCafferty 2012). Logistical and administrative challenges often prevented the research team from meeting the standardized patients until the day of the simulation, and community members were understandably not always as familiar with the research consent process as students. Obtaining their consent required a separate form, accompanied by a more detailed oral explanation of the study's aims and purposes. As with student participation, we understood that withheld consent from one standardized patient would likely exclude the entire simulation from the data.

In consultation sessions with the institutional research office, course instructors, the simulation lab team, and potential student participants, it became evident that audio recording was a preferable means of data collection, given the unique challenges to participant confidentiality associated with video-recorded data (Gibson 2008). The simulation capture software allowed audio to be separated from video after recording, preserving the video for instructors' pedagogical use while providing audio-only recordings for the research team. Audio-only simulation sessions made easier the preservation of participant confidentiality and anonymity, and therefore encouraged participation from students and standardized patients, while audio-only data did not permit the analysis of non-verbal communication, posited to be an important element for achieving understanding in MELF (Ting & Cogo in press), and in ELF communication generally (Matsumoto 2018; Kaur 2018).

In all, 47 hours of simulation sessions were recorded, with an average recording length of 18 minutes per simulation. Recordings were made using

B-Line SimCapture software (B-Line Medical 2019), operated by the institution's simulation lab technician, who then prepared audio-only files for the research team. A total of 104 nursing students consented to involvement in the study: 91 women and 13 men, a gender distribution consistent with overall institutional enrolment patterns. 10 different languages were self-identified by participants as their "strongest language": Arabic; Bengali; English; Hindi; Kannada; Konkani; Malayalam; Somali; Tagalog; and Tamil. Given the linguistic diversity of Qatar, with the often blurred lines between L1 and L2 (Nebel 2017), and the limitations associated with these traditional categorizations (García & Wei 2014), we preferred to employ the term "strongest language" on the consent form. Like Pitzl (2018: 8), we acknowledge the inherent imprecision in any language labels, and affirm the unbounded and heterogenous nature of language(s); however, we sought to utilize terms and categories readily understood and regularly accessed by participants.

3.4.1 Inside simulation scenarios

A typical simulation included pre-briefing instructions for students, in both oral and written form, which involved a basic description of the healthcare scenario to be roleplayed, and any specific directions as aligned with the learning outcomes of the particular nursing course which the simulation supported. The following examples are typical of the pre-brief instructions used in the simulations which formed our data.

Pre-brief scenario instructions example A: Confidentiality and Coercion
Pre-brief for student[8]: You just finished reviewing the patient's file and you learn that your patient is an 82 year-old woman who is expected to be discharged tomorrow morning at rounds. She was hospitalized on October 3 for elective hip replacement, after which she developed a UTI [Urinary Tract Infection]. Since she has diabetes and chronic kidney disease, it took time for her to recover and stabilize. She is a pleasant patient and is very cooperative with nursing students. She is now in ultrasound but should be coming back soon.

---

8 The pre-brief instructions for this simulation noted its adaptation from National League for Nursing. (2015). *Managing incivility*. http://cms.montgomerycollege.edu/nursingsims/ and Child, Sepples, & Chambers (2007). Designing simulations for nursing education. In P.R. Jeffries (Ed.) *Simulation in nursing education: From conceptualization to evaluation* (p 42–58). New York: National League for Nursing.

She had a mammogram a few days ago to investigate a fairly large lump found in her right breast. This morning when you took her vital signs, she told you she was scared she may have cancer and results in her file show that she may have a malignant tumor but it is for biopsy at a later time (not during this hospitalization). Your primary nurse asked you to go make the bed and tidy the room while you wait for the patient. You notice that her daughter is in the room, which is a good opportunity to learn more about your patient and family.

Pre-brief scenario instructions example B: Depression with Suicidality
Pre-brief for student: You are a nurse working in the female unit at [name] Psychiatric Hospital. You will be interviewing a new patient, [patient name], who was admitted due to suicidal ideation. She has a history of depression and this is her first hospitalization. You and your nurse colleagues will be interviewing [patient name] to conduct a mental status assessment and engage in therapeutic communication.

In some cases, depending on the preference of the instructor and the particular nursing course being supported, specific learning objectives for the simulation were included, such as the following.

Learning Objectives: The students will
- Identify cause of conflict.
- Stay present/engaged in the conversation and demonstrate ability to address conflict calmly and professionally.
- Use the **DESC** tool to manage incivility.
  DESC Communication Tool
  D – Describe the behavior
  E – Explain the effect of the behavior
  S – State the desired outcome
  C – Consequence: say what will happen if the behavior continues
- Some people prefer to memorize the key words that represent this model because it gives them a consistent structure to follow:
  D – When . . .
  E – I feel . . . because . . .
  S – Therefore I want / need
  C – So that . . .

An instructor-led debriefing session followed the simulation, where the students explored their learning experience, and were provided feedback on their performance. A question guide was often (though not always) included in the simulation description for the instructor to utilize during the debriefing, as exemplified below.

Pre-brief scenario instructions example C: Grandson with Enuresis (Appointment with Grandparents)
Debriefing questions:
1) *How did you feel about this simulation?*
   e.g. nervous/anxious
   Listen for strengths in the student's answer – highlight these
   e.g. "At which point in the assessment did you feel (insert their feeling)?"
2) *What was the easiest moment for you during the interview?*
   Listen for strengths and highlight these
   Key components of a family conversation might be highlighted here, both verbal and non-verbal
3) *What was the most difficult or challenging moment for you during the interview?*
   Listen for areas that you can add in feedback around their interaction, assessment
   What did they do well – one or two things you heard them say?
   Offer ideas for development of these difficult/challenging moments.
4) *Is there one question that you wish you would have asked in this interview?*
   What do you think would have been different if you had asked that question?
   Hypothesize if there is time.
5) *What is one thing you are going to take away (learn) from this simulated interview?*
   How might you use this "take away" in clinical practice with families?
   Commend the student for this work.

Standardized patients were also provided with pre-brief instructions, in both oral and written form, which set the stage for the simulation. In keeping with the learning objectives for the particular scenario and instructor preference, pre-brief instructions for standardized patients varied in detail provided. Extracts from typical sets of pre-brief instructions are provided for illustration.

> **Pre-brief scenario instructions example D: Immunization Clinic**
> **Setting:** Outpatient Clinic; Vaccination Unit; Primary Health Care Centre
> **Standardized Patients:** Salwa, with baby and sister

Salwa: You do not smile and have limited to no facial expressions. You present as exceedingly tired. Your hair is unkempt but your clothes are clean and tidy. There are long pauses before you answer a question. You give the impression that it takes all your energy to speak. Your body posture is slumped & your eyes are cast downward most of the time. You frequently sigh. Your most common statements are: "I'm just really tired", "I have so much to do these days". You keep looking at your baby (Sari) rather than making eye contact with the nurse. You let your sister answer for you. If asked whether your sister should leave the room to give you space to talk, you say: "She can stay if she. She is my support." But you are open to coming back for another appointment alone.

Medical History: Overall the family has not had any serious health concerns, with the exception of your husband's (Adam's) accidental death.

Family History: You have two younger siblings. Your two younger siblings live in Lebanon and Kuwait. Before the accident, you used to have telephone contact with them every couple of weeks although you have not talked with them for about 6 months. They have tried to call you but you have not had the energy to talk with them. Your Mom and Dad are both healthy. Adam's mother has diabetes and his father has heart disease.

Social History: You and your husband used to visit with your families every Thursday night. One week you went to Adam's parents and the next week you went to your parents' home. Now, you make excuses even though you know that the visit would be good for the children. You also know that your parents might try to trick you and invite the family friend over so that you could meet him. When Adam was alive, you were attending night classes at [institution name] studying to be a nurse. Since his death, you have been unable to continue your studies so you have lost touch with many of your nursing student friends. You do not work outside the home.

Other: You are a non-smoker, non-drinker. You do not take any medication but lately you are thinking maybe you need some sleeping pills. You are not interested in getting married again.

Pre-brief scenario instructions example E: MD Aggression to Students
Standardized Patient/Medical Confederates: Stroke patient, physician

Physician: You are the neurological team that is examining the patient. You found out that the patient's blood sugar is very high and you are worried it will affect his healing process and put him at risk of second stroke. You are frustrated by the nurse's action and are not listening to what the nurse is saying. You keep repeating how he is at risk of stroke and questioning the type of nurse he/she is. You come across being rude and loud. You do not listen to the nurse as she/he tries to explain their actions. Asking: *what are you learning in nursing school*, you are not listening and cut the student off. If you feel the student is trying to communicate to you, you can tone down your anger and state you will communicate with the medical doctor. Let the student talk and have the problem.

3.4.2 Simulation data analysis

The recordings were transcribed using *Rev* transcription software (2020), with the transcriptions subsequently checked for accuracy by the research team. During the first round of analysis, the research team labelled the data according to two categories: instances of unimpeded communication (where there was no apparent misunderstanding between interlocutors, and the discussion proceeded unimpeded); and impeded communication (listeners halted the discussion for clarification, repeated what s/he had heard, suggested more precise vocabulary for the speaker, etc.). Instances such as the latter, where the listener recognizes apprehension is not being achieved, are sometimes labelled non-understandings in the literature (Cogo & Pitzl 2016). While more difficult to identify, the research team had also intended to note instances of perceived intelligibility (the discussion proceeded unimpeded) but with actual miscommunication (the content was inaccurate). Cogo and Pitzl deem this a misunderstanding (contrasting with a non-understanding), referring to instances where a comprehension problem "surfaces retrospectively, by accident (if at all). It cannot be indicated or negotiated immediately because no participant is aware of its existence when it happens" (2016: 340). We considered the transcripts for this misalignment between perceived and actual intelligibility because of its prevalence in healthcare communication (The Joint Commission 2016), and its potential risks for patient harm. For example, a patient handover discussion may proceed unimpeded (the incoming shift nurse thought she understood the outgoing shift nurse), but important information was actually misunderstood. Identification of perceived but inaccurate communication required input of nursing instructors to review the transcript through the lens of their medical training. The simulations had a strong pedagogical focus on soft skills (Ray & Overman 2014) such as communication, delegation and collaboration (e.g., communicating with a demanding charge nurse). As the bulk of medical errors result from miscommunication between caregivers (Pfrimmer 2009), such soft skills are central to patient safety, so provided an excellent lens through which to view medical communication.

Reports that say that something hasn't happened are always interesting to me, because as we know, there are known knowns; there are things we know we know. We also know there are known unknowns; that is to say we know there are some things we do not know. But there are also unknown unknowns – the ones we don't know we don't know.
– Donald Rumsfeld, United States Secretary of Defense. 2002.

A second round of analysis considered both categories from the standpoint of communication features, and speaker/listener strategies to remove potential or realized impediments. Some selected examples are provided in Table 3.1, below.

Observable in our second inquiry was the role that collaboration between nurse interlocutors played in both unimpeded and impeded medical ELF interactions. Researchers have previously noted such cooperative features among in ELF interactants, including strategies such as prompting, paraphrasing, repetition, lexical suggestion and anticipation, explicitation, and clarification on the part of both speakers and listener (Kirkpatrick 2010a; Mauranen 2006). The following extract from a simulation on immunization provides an example.

> Nurse A (L1 Tamil) Like, as a woman, how, what do you believe about the man?
>
> Nurse B (L1 Hindi) In your position.
>
> Patient 2 (L1 Arabic) Do you mean like about the role of the man?
>
> Nurse B (L1 Hindi) Yes.
>
> Nurse A: (L1 Tamil) The man.
>
> Patient 2: (L1 Arabic) Oh, okay.

In a simulated immunization clinic, Nurses A and B are interviewing a mother (Patient 1) and her sister (Patient 2) regarding their level of familial or community support for challenging circumstances in parenting. Nurse A is presumably attempting to query Patient 2 on her views regarding male roles in parenting. Nurse B anticipates that A's question does not provide sufficient clarity, and offers the phrase *in your position*, perhaps to specify "in your position as a mother to children". Nurse B's addition provides enough information to prompt a clarification question from Patient 2: *Do you mean like about the role of the man?* The phrase *role of the man*, and specifically the word *role*, seems to provide adequate clarity, and Nurse B confirms the clarification with *yes*, which prompts *Oh, okay* from Patient 2 indicating comprehension.

As we interacted with our data in both of the first two rounds, we looked to principles of conversational analysis (CA), specifically that of turn-taking (Sacks, Schegloff & Jefferson 1974). In the words of Hutchby and Wooffitt, the aim of CA

> is to discover how participants understand and respond to one another in their turns at talk, with a central focus on how sequences of actions are generated. To put it another way, the objective of CA is to uncover the often tacit reasoning procedures and sociolinguistic competencies underlying the production and interpretation of talk in organized sequences. (2008: 12)

CA is generally understood to part company with other linguistic analysis in that utterances are not considered in light of their linguistic features, but in terms of

Table 3.1: Selected examples of noted communication features and strategies to remove (potential) impediments.

Scenario	Extract	Noted	Result
3 nurses (A, B & C) are attempting to require a doctor to follow ward sanitization procedures before examining a patient in isolation; the doctor is resistant	Nurse C (to doctor): *Don't do like that.* Nurse B (to doctor) *For patient safety. You want for you.* Doctor: *I know about patient safety. Okay? I know about patient safety. I have been seeing patients for years.*	Semantic generality (lack of precision / clarity) *Don't do like that.* *For patient safety. You want for you.*	Communication proceeded unimpeded: listener understood by contextual clues
3 nurses (A, B & C) are speaking with the daughter of a patient. The daughter is requesting confidential information that the nurses are only permitted to share with the patient directly.	Nurse C: *So how do you think your mother, mother feeling?* Nurse A: *How's she feeling?* Daughter: *So, she just wants to get home now, you know?*	Cooperative repair *So how do you think your mother, mother feeling?* *How's she feeling?* Nurse A offers a standard question form as a summary of Nurse C's utterance.	Discussion proceeds unimpeded.

(continued)

Table 3.1 (continued)

Scenario	Extract	Noted	Result
Nurse A and B are discussing a parent's concern with his child's enuresis	Parent: *It's for the family to try and I think looking forward we're optimistic about that and I think you asked all the right questions that I know of. And hopefully we get the right answer.* Nurse B: *Okay. Uh, like, we wanted to just like, eh, the problem goes ahead him, okay? And eh, the problem, like if anyone is suffering like, the same issue comes to you, then you can address the same interventions, like you can give some type of intervention to them. Okay, any more challenges in their life, like any problems happen, you can, you can contact our family nursing [CITY NAME] unit, uh, we'll give, uh, the secretary will uh-* Nurse C: *Call you.*	Unusual expression *the problem goes ahead him* (possible meaning: *get ahead of / get on top of the problem*)	"Let it pass" strategy (Firth, 1996) Discussion proceeds unimpeded. The expression is not central to the message of the larger utterance; listener makes no comment.

their "social accomplishment" (Hutchby & Wooffitt 2008: 12). CA has been previously utilized in ELF research (e.g., Firth 1996; Firth 2009; Kaur 2011), and we drew upon such studies in attempting to understand the processes of how meaning-making was achieved. Our approach to analysis of the secondary data recorded in the simulation training contrasted with our first investigation of medical ELF. Perhaps because of our backgrounds, and our roles as teacher-researchers, our instinct was to approach the first inquiry through a primarily linguistic lens. In this first inquiry, we focused on linguistic features in the speech of the nurses, noting phonemic and lexicogrammatical elements as we considered intelligibility. While we did not exclude a consideration of such elements in our conversational analysis, we deliberately focused our attention on the social accomplishment (Hutchby and Wooffitt) of the interactions, and considered linguistic elements in light of that aim.

Yet, we were determined not to limit ourselves to CA, in that we felt that to focus *solely* on the turn-taking of our participants, without attention to the larger sociolinguistic context, would provide an incomplete picture of the factors shaping MELF communication.

In a third round of analysis therefore, we opted to deliberately "step back" from our data, and made another pass at our data from an intentionally less granular perspective. As noted previously, our conceptualization had – and continues to be – emergent in nature, and we wondered after the second round of analysis whether a more bird's-eye view of the data would provide fresh perspectives. After self-reflection, discussions with colleagues, and an expansion of the scope of our literature, our revisitation of the data in this third round was done with an eye to the larger sociocultural elements which might inform our research, a perspective which was to later prove invaluable to the conceptualization process.

Around the same period of time, the nurse-researchers in our research partnership were making us increasingly aware that interprofessional interactions are the normal means of healthcare delivery in many contexts (Oelke, Thurston & Arthur 2013; Leape & Berwick 2005), and that while language barriers are widely researched in medical communication, their effect in interprofessional healthcare delivery has been largely overlooked (Hull 2016). This led us to plan for a third inquiry: a study of ELF interaction among healthcare professionals from different disciplines.

3.5 MELF in interprofessional healthcare communication

As noted in a previous chapter, healthcare research literature on cross-cultural communication has been largely oriented toward encounters with a linguistically diverse set of patients, seemingly assuming a linguistically homogeneous group of healthcare professionals. Some of this orientation may be explained by the research context in which many studies occur: settings where English is widely spoken as a native language. Even so, this belies the reality of medical migration, where, in OECD countries, foreign-born and foreign-trained healthcare professionals account for significant percentages of the total medical workforce (OECD, 2019, 1.4). The observation therefore of Oelke et al (2013) is surprising: that crosslinguistic and cross-cultural encounters among healthcare professionals are underrepresented in the research literature, particularly so when interprofessional care has long been acknowledged as a central feature of primary healthcare delivery (WHO 1988). As discussed, what studies do exist on language barriers in interprofessional healthcare tend to consider international medical graduates (e.g., Michalski et al. 2017).

It seemed then, that a perfect opportunity had arisen to examine MELF interprofessional interactions when we encountered plans for an immunization Clinical Professional Development (CPD) program to be held in a GCC country. A prior needs assessment had uncovered knowledge gaps in the area of immunization safe practices, identified across physicians, nurses and pharmacists in primary health clinics. A three-day training program was planned by health authorities, and hosted by a training institution with which the researchers have existing research partnerships. The plan called for CPD participants, after receiving instruction on vaccination best practices, to then work through real life case study simulations in mixed interprofessional (ELF) groupings. These sessions would be audio-recorded to subsequently inform teaching and learning about clinical best practices.

For us as researchers, this represented an opportunity to consider how social dynamics of interprofessional healthcare delivery (e.g., power asymmetry; demarcated professional boundaries) were played out in the realm of ELF language use. In particular, interprofessional healthcare interactions would provide a window into MELF communication outside of the constraints of the health assessment activity type, and its structured turn-taking. We applied for, and received, approval from the requisite research ethics boards to seek consent from participants to transcribe and analyze anonymized recordings of the CPD sessions, and submitted a large-scale grant funding request to conduct the research. We looked forward to the findings from this research making significant contributions to this present volume in understanding MELF from the standpoint of interprofessional healthcare interactions.

However, it was not to be. The bulk of the preparatory work to study interprofessional MELF usage had taken place in late 2019, and early 2020, and by March of 2020 it was clear that all health research, unless directly related to the SARS-CoV-2 coronavirus, would – rightly – be postponed indefinitely. As we write this chapter in November 2020, a second wave of coronavirus infections is underway, and so our research on interprofessional healthcare interactions remains on pause.

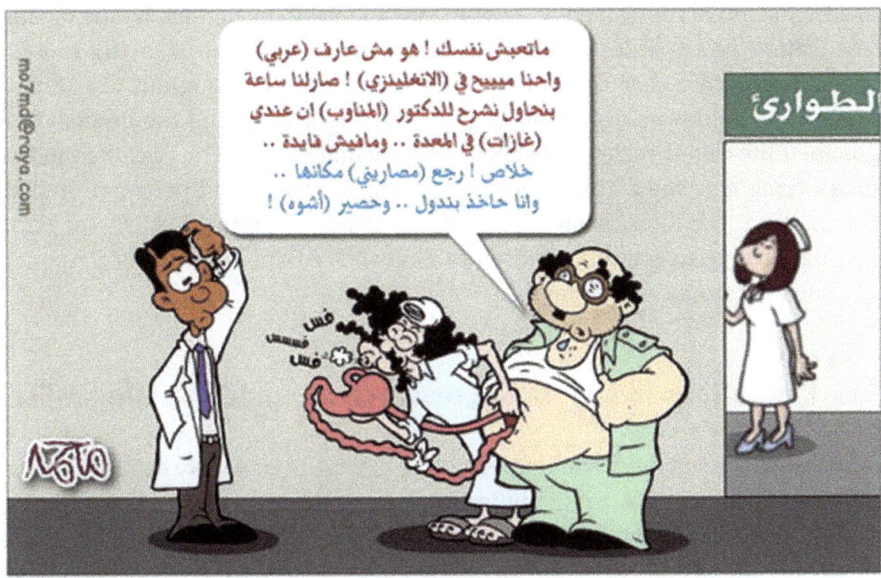

Figure 3.2: Cartoon by Mohammed Abdelatif, *Al Raya* newspaper, 4 May, 2014.

Translation and commentary (Alkhatib 2017: 61–62)

[This cartoon] portrays an Egyptian man (in the green shirt), addressing his Qatari friend in the Emergency Room of a public hospital in Doha. The Egyptian man says:
(1) Relax! Enough of explaining my problem to the doctor!
(2) The doctor does not know (Arabic) and we are 0 level in English.
(3) For the last hour we have been trying to explain to the (on duty) doctor that I have (intestinal gases). No point . . . enough . . . put my (intestines) back into my belly . . .
(4) I will take a Panadol tablet and I will be (fine)!
(5) However, the Qatari man keeps trying to imitate the sound of breaking wind to the confused doctor.

. . . The Egyptian man is using words from both Egyptian and Qatari dialects. Words such as *ashou-ah* (Arabic for "I will be fine") bear relation to the Arabic of the Gulf, while *ma ta-abeshi nafesak* (Arabic for "Relax, my friend") is derived from the Egyptian variation of the Arabic language. This suggests familiarity among Arabic speakers of the Arabic dialects, and the ability of the speakers to switch between them . . .

All the attempts by the Egyptian man to calm his Qatari friend down are met by the latter's sustained attempt to make himself understood by the doctor. The Qatari man's endeavors end with the extreme action of taking out his friend's intestines. The Qatari man's extreme action of taking out his friend's intestines could possibly resemble the pressure of acquiring the English language in the Qatari society. The pressure to acquire English has resulted in Qataris taking extreme actions, including recruiting well-paid personal English tutors, enrolling in expensive language courses, recruiting English-speaking nannies, and even sending children to English-speaking countries for a period of time, to acquire the language.

3.6 Limitations in simulation research for understanding MELF

Simulation training with standardised patients has been widely shown to be an effective means of improving clinical and communication skills of healthcare professionals, not only of student trainees (e.g., Cockbain et al. 2015) but also of already practicing clinicians including doctors (Grudzen et al. 2016), nurses (Hegland et al. 2017), and across multidisciplinary healthcare teams (e.g., Siassakos et al. 2011). While extensively used in pre-licensure healthcare education (e.g., Jeffries 2020), we note the increasing use in skills training for current practitioners (Fernando et al. 2017). The advantages of simulation training are widely known (Pilnick et al. 2018), chief among them being the ability to develop skills without risks to actual patients (Campbell & Daley 2018).

Ultimately, however, simulations are exactly that: simulations. Our data analysis was conducted on recorded interactions in a laboratory setting, designed to accomplish educational objectives, which made use of patient-actors. Though we certainly intend to do so in future, data presented in this present study is not taken from actual hospital wards. The simulated setting of this study needs to be taken into account as a limitation when we suggest broader generalizations of the characteristics of MELF in real life clinical contexts. Indeed, a guiding principle of conversation analysis is that it relies on data recorded in naturally occurring conversations (Sacks, Schegloff & Jefferson 1974). While fully acknowledging this limitation, we propose several reasons why simulation data represents a valid means of contributing to theory regarding the nature of medical ELF.

The first reason we have alluded to above: the wide recognition of simulation training within healthcare education as a means of both developing and *assessing* skills. We emphasize the role of assessment here in that healthcare educators themselves affirm the value of simulation in providing actual evidence of skills required for healthcare practice (e.g., Gude et al. 2015). In a nationwide study of nursing simulation, Hayden and colleagues (2014) found evidence to assert that up to 50% of clinical experience can be substituted with simulation training as a valid means of competency demonstration for licensure. Since healthcare educators consider simulation a valid means of evidence regarding a trainee's suitability for medical practice, we follow their lead in considering the language data generated in simulation as a meaningful representation of clinical use outside the laboratory.

A second important factor to recognize in regard to the validity of simulation data concerns the use of standardized patients. Readers new to medical simulation should not confuse "role plays" (such as those many of us use in classroom language teaching) with simulation training. Although peer role plays are used to good effect in medical education (e.g., Xu et al. 2016), including when peers play the role of patients in simulations (Miles et al. 2014), peer role play inevitably suffers from a number of limitations in its ability to recreate high fidelity to real world conditions (Nestel & Tierney 2007). The use of standardized patients therefore is seen as a more effective means of mimicking actual clinical conditions (Pilnick et al. 2018). In contrast to role plays, simulations that involve standardized patients involve extensive attention to coaching, including matters related to selection and casting; pre-simulation training, particularly on the nature of the medical case; relevant information on acting; and how the case is to be presented to trainees (Wallace 2007). Standardized patients used in simulations which form the data for this present study were recruited, trained and coached by experienced nursing educators with specialized training and qualifications in keeping with best practices for maximising the value of standardized patients in nursing simulation (Nehring & Lashley 2010; Alexander et al. 2015).

Our assertion that MELF language use in simulation may be extrapolated to actual clinical usage is strengthened by the results of empirical studies. Carvahalo and colleagues (2014), for example, compared the effects of training on healthcare professionals' communication skills delivered through standardized patients or actual patients. The effect between the two groups was non-significant, suggesting consistent transference of skills across simulation and real practice. Similarly, Quail et al (2016) considered changes in self-reported communication skills by speech pathology students who had engaged with a real patient, a trained patient-actor, or a virtual patient. Self-reported increases in communication skills were consistent across the three different scenarios.

A particular challenge faced in analysis of simulation data was the influence of what we came to call "the pedagogical effect". Consider the following extract, which begins with the nurse conducting a test for the presence of bronchophony (abnormal sound transmission from the lungs) during a respiratory exam by asking the patient to repeat the number ninety-nine (e.g., see Rosenberg, Cassese & Barbon 2018):

RE-SIM3C
181 Patient Anu (L1 not indicated): 99, 99. 99. 99. 99. 99. 99.
182 Nurse (L1 Malayalam): Wow, perfect. Okay. Now I'll be tapping your lung feel.
    Okay? If you feel, not, uh, if you're comfortable, just let me know.
183 Anu: Okay.
184 Nurse: Okay. Dull sounds is the heard over the lung field, and flat sounds are
             heard over the scapula and also on some of the visceral space. Okay?
             Now I'll be auscultating your lung. When I tell you to take a deep breath, just take a deep=
185 Anu   Mm-hmm [affirmative]

We observe in this extract Nurse using technical and formulaic biomedical language (*dull sounds . . . over the lung field*; *flat sounds are heard over the scapula*), some of which appears to be directed to Patient Anu in a communicative manner (i.e., with expectation of a response): *and also some of the visceral space. Okay?*; *Now I'll be auscultating your lung. When I tell you to take a deep breath just take a deep*). Such technical descriptions contrast with the view that plain language should be used in healthcare provider-patient communication (Warde et al. 2018), yet were found to be a consistent feature across our data. Certainly, this phenomenon can be attributed at least in part to a "pedagogical effect": a nurse being assessed during simulation on particular clinical skills will want to make the use of those skills explicit for the observing evaluator. Yet, we noted such uses of biomedical language by nurses in simulations even when factors were present which ought to mitigate this "pedagogical effect", such as: well-prepared standardized patients; experienced, already practicing nurses; simulation settings with a high degree of fidelity to actual clinical situations; and explicitly stated learning goals for the simulation which required patient-centred, therapeutic communication *as opposed to* technical language use.

What might account for biomedical descriptions as nurses' "default mode" of communication during simulations, even when these mitigating factors were present? The "pedagogical effect" certainly exerts some influence. Another might be the culture of medical jargon use observed to be pervasive in healthcare (Deuster et al. 2008). Still another reason for these biomedical descriptions may be the tendency of healthcare professionals to assert authoritative expertise through the use of technical language (Lipkin et al. 2011).

In discussing the phenomenon of biomedical language use with senior nursing instructors, a nurse educator with extensive international expertise in simulation training offered another explanation, drawn from her own experience as an ELF user (self-described L1: Tagalog). With her advanced degrees taught through the medium of English, she described her "go-to" language for nursing technical and formulaic terminology as English. Observations of hundreds of hours of nursing simulations in her professional capacity as a simulation educator have led her to surmise that the experience of many EAL nurses mirror her own: it is preferable and more natural to default to the technical, formulaic terminology they learned in English than to "translate" it into English plain language for the patient. As an example, she referred to a nurse's use of the descriptor *nasal flaring*, a potential sign of respiratory distress, in a transcript from our simulation data (see Chapter 5). She suggested that the ELF user in this instance may have defaulted to the technical term rather than "translating" *nasal flaring* into plain English, because of lexical limitations: "Many of our students know the nursing terms in English, but actually do not know how to explain them in everyday English" (Masaba, personal communication, 2020). This observation runs counterintuitive to the focus of much English for medical purposes instruction, where language research tends to emphasize specialized text genres, grammatical features prevalent in medical usage, and specialized healthcare vocabulary (Ferguson 2013). The notion that language training for MELF users may involve *less* instruction in technical usage, in favour of instruction which helps clinicians explain medical terms in plain language to patients, has implications for healthcare education.

Finally, in considering the limitations of simulations as a source of data, we note again the contextual frame in which the research continuously emerges: analysis of the simulation data should not be seen as a bounded, fixed point inquiry isolated from the context in which the researchers live and work, both professionally and personally. Rather than considered in isolation, analysis of the simulation data is understood from multiple perspectives, whether direct engagement with other MELF research and researchers internationally (see Tweedie and

Johnson, in press); through sustained interaction with teacher-researcher colleagues across the GCC region in both applied linguistics and healthcare fields; and by our own extended, immersive experiences in the local community.

3.7 Summary

This chapter has described our position as researchers, provided a backdrop to the linguistic environment in which our research takes place, and oriented the reader to considerations of methodologies utilized in our investigations of MELF, and in contributions to its emerging theoretical base. We explained that, as researchers, our process of conceptualizing MELF was not occasioned by a single research activity, but an emerging one, arising in situ from direct, intentional and sustained interaction with our participants and data, and that this is reflected in a methodological pluralism which utilizes multiple frameworks. The chapter explained the rationale for using data from medical simulations as a way to understand MELF, notwithstanding its very real limitations. With this backdrop in place, we now turn to analyses of the collected data.

Chapter 4
Strategies for MELF communication

Chapter key points:
- Our data on MELF challenges the notion that ELF communication is inherently fleeting and temporal in nature.
- The data shows MELF communicators successfully using strategies for meaning-making identified in studies of other ELF domains, but also strategies reflecting communication techniques particular to healthcare.
- Collaborative repair and cooperative pre-emption are shown as successful strategies to avoid non-understanding in instances when healthcare communication is being carried out in teams.
- Actions and other non-verbal forms of communication play an important role in successful MELF communication.
- By and large, the data evidences successful MELF communication given the aims of the particular communicative situation. As is the case with healthcare communication in general, instances of non- or misunderstanding in the data presented dire consequences for the safety of patients.

Variability, i.e. the particularity of constellations as well as their fleetingness, can be regarded as an inherent feature of ELF communication (Hülmbauer 2009: 325).

Over recent years, a number of publications have made the point that an understanding of language depends on recognizing that it is unstable, dynamic, intrinsically variable and that the way it is used simply cannot be accounted for by supposing that it is a static system of rules that users conform to. This is often presented as an innovative insight into the nature of language, revealed by postmodernist thinking about performativity, complexity theory and the socio-linguistics of globalization, and a radical departure from previous unenlightened approaches to linguistic description (Widdowson 2015: 359).

4.1 Introduction

Variability in speech is ingrained in all language use, and we would therefore expect ELF to be no exception. That ELF exhibits variation as a core feature should come as no surprise; perhaps the surprise is that we would think otherwise. However, researchers have asserted that an exceptional degree of variability is one of the features which makes ELF communication distinct. The assumption is that ELF users do not belong to a speech community (Osimk-Teasdale 2018), and therefore draw upon linguistic resources other than English in real-time to fulfil immediate communicative needs, with variability an inevitable result. A further boost to the notion of variation in ELF is the supposed fluid and temporary nature of communicative settings. Some researchers (certainly not all) are adamant about this transitory feature of ELF, and imply it is part and parcel of all ELF communication. Hülmbauer, for example, understands variable settings, which feature "temporary relationships, with speaker constellations frequently being tied and untied anew for each emerging interaction" as marking "an inherent feature of ELF communication" (2009: 325). As we noted in Chapter 2, the claim that all ELF interaction is characterized by fluid communicative settings has led researchers to dismiss the notion of the speech community as a useful frame for analysis. As Wang (2018: 154) declares categorically, "speech communities are irrelevant for the research into ELF". Similarly, Seidlhofer sees no place for understanding ELF in terms of the regular, face-to-face interaction of the speech community: "the old notion of community based purely on frequent local, non-mediated contact among people living in close proximity to each other clearly cannot be upheld any more" (2011: 86–87).

Our data on medical ELF would seem to contradict such claims. We find that MELF interactions, particularly in the nations of the Gulf Cooperation Council region but evident elsewhere in the conditions created by healthcare migration, are not, by and large, taking place in fleeting and temporal communicative constellations. Rather, local, frequent, sustained and close-proximity interactions comprising both work and home contexts, feature prominently in our research setting. Additionally, we observe that external pressures are brought to bear on medical ELF for uniformity, standardization and codification of language that in fact mitigate against the fluid and emergent nature said to characterize ELF communication in other domains. Prescribed communication protocols (see, for example, the mnemonics in this chapter), abound in healthcare education and practice, and are regularly mandated by local health ministries, as well as strenuously advocated by international professional bodies. National and international standards for medical record-keeping, particularly so now that much patient data is being stored in electronic form, require uniform vocabulary for the purposes of aggregating data (Wang, Hailey & Yu 2011; Müller-Staub et al. 2008). Similarly, healthcare-specific techniques, such as therapeutic communication (Tamparo & Lindh 2017) are widely advocated and may inform instruction in healthcare curriculum. Taken together, frequent, sustained contact along with the pervasive nature of mandated communication features help make MELF a distinctive form of ELF communication, and challenge the sometimes asserted notion that ELF interactions are *in essence* transitory, temporal and emergent.

In this chapter, we examine the data collected from healthcare simulation training, in order to understand elements of how understanding is achieved in MELF communication. The presentation of the data is organized around several key communication strategies which arose from our analysis. Where we have felt it was helpful to do so for the reader, an explanation of the simulation scenario is included, either in the form of the actual text prepared by the nursing instructor / simulation lab coordinator, or our own editorial comments where further explanation is required. Symbols in the simulation extracts are marked following conventions of conversation analysis from Jefferson (2005), and a glossary of symbols can be found in the Appendix. Participants who opted to indicate their "strongest language" on the consent form are here denoted as L1 (first language), following common usage in applied linguistics. Any identifying features were removed from the recorded simulations during the transcription process, so any names used are pseudonyms. When referring to direct words of a participant's utterance outside of its use in the extract itself, we indicate this by the use of *italics*.

For the most part, the data shows evidence of communication strategies seen in ELF usage in other domains, affirming findings of previous studies. The healthcare professionals and their patients effectively utilized repair strategies, repetition, playback, and reformulation to pre-empt potential non- or misunderstandings. MELF users, when working in intraprofessional groupings, were seen to add collaborative and cooperative dimensions to these pre-emptive strategies, particularly important given that healthcare is more often delivered in teams. The data also revealed underlying influences of communication elements specific to healthcare, which, overall, appeared to be adopted and utilized to positive communicative effect by MELF users. As was the case with our previous research, data in this present study indicates that the MELF interactions were for the most part successful in the communicative aims which the communicative situation required. However, the analysis also showed that where there were instances of non-/misunderstanding, these could have very serious consequences for patient safety – a reality not unique to MELF interactions, but well documented in healthcare communication even among speakers of the same first language.

Selected common mnemonics for healthcare professionals

FAST – for detection of, and enhanced responsiveness of strokes
Facial dropping (unequal smile; facial asymmetry)
Arm weakness (inability to raise/hold arms)
Speech difficulties (slurring; word-finding difficulties)
Time (timely response; or test)
(e.g., see Harbison et al. 2003)

OPQRST – for patient assessment in acute illnesses
Onset (sudden or insidious?)
Provocation or palliation (movement or pressure worsen/lessen symptoms?)
Quality of the pain (sharp burning, tingling, dull, etc.)
Region and radiation (area of the pain and whether pain moves to other areas)
Severity (use of a pain scale)
Time (symptom duration)
(e.g., see Thomas 2003)

SOCRATES – for assessing and evaluating pain
Site (location)
Onset (sudden or gradual)
Character (dull ache, sharp, etc.)
Radiation (movement of the pain)
Associations (other signs or symptoms)
Time course (patterns)
Exacerbating/relieving factors (things which make the pain worse or better)
Severity (pain intensity)
(e.g., see Manna, Sarkar & Khanra 2015; ; see also Epomedicine 2020)

4.2 Pre-emption strategies

4.2.1 Repetition and collaborative repair

Pre-empting strategies are used by interactants to circumvent potential non-understandings, and may include various methods of repetition (Cogo & Pitzl 2016). The interlocutors in excerpt AD-SIM1A utilize repetition effectively to define an occupation-specific term, and to clarify idiomatic usage. The two nurses also work together for collaborative repair (Hanamoto 2016) to facilitate overall interactional goals.

Excerpt AD-SIM1A – *Pre-emption*: *Repetition*
Scenario: Alcohol and drug abuse
Pre-brief instructions: You are a nurse working in the outpatient clinic at [name] Psychiatric Hospital. You will be interviewing a new patient, [name]. He is coming to the clinic because his employer requires that he get treatment for his addictions. This is his first visit. You and your nurse colleagues will be interviewing [patient name] to conduct a mental status assessment and engage in therapeutic communication.

61	Nurse B (L1 Tagalog):	Where do you live? Do you live here in [city name] or=
62	Patient (L1 English):	=Yeah, I live here. I've been working here for seven years.
63	Nurse B:	↓Seven years. ↑And may we ask your occupation?
64	Patient:	I'm in construction right here. Internal controls.
65	Nurse B:	↓Internal controls.
66	Patient:	Paperwork kind of stuff.
67	Nurse B:	↓Okay, paperwork. ↑And so do you work in an office? Do you=
68	Patient:	=I work – I have an office at the construction site too.
69	Nurse B:	Mm-hmm. Okay.
70	Nurse C (L1 Bengali):	So can we know why you're here today?
71	Patient:	I'd like to know that also. My my boss told me to go and get checked out and he's not going to let me back at work unless I get a paper that everything's okay with me.
72	Nurse C:	Oh, what do you mean?
73	Nurse B:	↑Sorry
74	Nurse C:	You can go on.
75	Patient:	I don't know why, but my boss said so, here, just get a piece of paper saying everything is alright.
76	Nurse C:	Okay. Umm, okay, so if I understand you, your boss asked you to come here to get a paper that everything is alright?[9]

Nurse B (L1 Tagalog) encounters what appears to be an unfamiliar term to her when the Patient specifies his role in the construction industry, *internal controls* (typically referring to processes and procedures in construction site management to safeguard against unauthorized use of equipment or resources). Nurse B repeats *internal controls*, which serves as a signal to the Patient to clarify further: *Paperwork kind of stuff*.

When Nurse C (L1 Bengali) directs the conversation to the main purpose of the clinic visit (*So can we know why you're here today?*), the Patient replies with

---

9 Transcription symbols following Jefferson (2005).

what appears to be sarcasm, in an expression of apparent displeasure at being forced to attend this medical evaluation: *I'd like to know that also*. After the sarcastic remark, he directly addresses the question of the visit's purpose: *My my boss told me to go and get checked out and he's not going to let me back at work unless I get a paper that everything's okay with me*.

At this point, Nurse C seems unclear and asks a probing question, *Oh, what do you mean?* The probing question may be intended to uncover the Patient's displeasure at having to attend the clinic, or perhaps to explore further why specifically he needs to *get checked out* and will not be allowed to return to work without an evaluation.

Whatever the intention of Nurse C's question, Nurse B intervenes with an apology (*Sorry*). Perhaps Nurse B perceives the question to be too direct, or inappropriately personal at this early phase of the interview. Whatever the reason, following the intervention Nurse C opts to discard the question, and directs the Patient to continue (*You can go on*). The Patient then proceeds, by clarifying with a self-paraphrase of his early utterance (*I don't know why, but my boss said so*), and with what seems to be a paraphrase of his supervisor's directive (*here, just get a piece of paper saying everything is alright*).

On the one hand, this intervention by Nurse B can be viewed as uncooperative, in that she is directly or indirectly challenging the line of questioning being pursued by Nurse A. While to date underrepresented in ELF research, we would expect uncooperative lingua franca encounters to occur as in any other communicative exchanges, as interlocutors pursue different intents and goals in the interaction (Jenks 2018). However, Nurse B's intervention can also be seen as a successful example of nursing communication: Nurse C did not challenge the intervention, subsequently withdrew her question, and the overall goal of patient assessment proceeded. Conflict among nurses is recognized as a significant issue for the delivery of effective healthcare worldwide (Vivar 2006), and an ability to manage elements of conflict such as personalization of disagreement is an important feature of quality nursing communication (Nicotera, Mahon & Wright 2014). Collaborative repair, then, would seem to be an important strategy for MELF communication in nursing teams.

As the conversation proceeds, Nurse C utilizes rephrased repetition in another attempt at meaning-making. Her use of *so if f I understand you* at the beginning of the utterance, which may indicate an active listening technique for nurse-patient communication (Klagsbrun 2001; Ali 2018), precedes a reformulation of what the Patient has said. We note with interest her slight rephrase: from the Patient's *my boss said so, here, just get a piece of paper saying everything is alright* to her restatement as *so if I understand you, your boss asked you to come here to get a paper that everything is alright*. While inconsequential to the achievement of overall meaning-making, she interprets *here* as referring to the present clinic, whereas the Patient was more likely referencing the prior conversation between himself and the boss. The use of *a paper* (countable noun) for the Patient's *a piece of paper* (uncountable) may reflect either an ELF feature of countable to uncountable shift (Jenkins 2012), or it might be that Nurse C understands the Patient's use of *paper* to be describing a piece of writing on a particular subject or an official government document (both countable; see "Paper" 2020). The Patient's intended use of *a piece of paper* in this context may have disparaging intent, to highlight its uselessness. Someone who says "marriage is just a piece of paper", for example, implies that the paper itself does not legitimize the relationship; in the same way, the Patient is expressing doubt as to whether a visit to the clinic and the resultant form will validate or invalidate his suitability for work. In any event, these differences in intended meaning are inconsequential to the overall conversational goal, and the Patient's assessment proceeds despite the non-understanding.

4.2.2 Allo-repetition and reformulation

Repetition and reformulation, specifically allo-repetition (Tannen 1987), is also used as a communication strategy in the nurse team-patient interview in the excerpt following.

Excerpt DE-SIM1B – *Pre-emption: Allo-repetition*
Scenario: Depression with suicidality
Pre-brief instructions: You are a nurse working in the female unit at [name] Psychiatric Hospital. You will be interviewing a new patient, Faiza, who was admitted due to suicidal ideation. She has a history of depression and this is her first hospitalization. You and your nurse colleagues will be interviewing Faiza to conduct a mental status assessment and engage in therapeutic communication.

50	Nurse A (L1 Arabic):	What activities? you used to do (.) before?
51	Faiza (patient):	I used to walk with friends. To socialize.
52	Nurse C (L1 Arabic):	And when was the last time you went out?
53	Faiza:	Months ago.
54	Nurse C:	Months ago. So you've been feeling like this for months ago? Yeah? Do you have a job?
55	Faiza:	Lost my job.
56	Nurse C:	You lost your job? Can you tell any more about that?

57	Nurse A:	How did you lost your ↓job.
58	Faiza:	Because the place I worked (.) they were downsizing. And they didn't need me anymore. I tried to get another one (2) It's crazy.
59	Nurse C:	(2) Did you like? your job?
60	Faiza:	I liked my job.
61	Nurse C:	↓Yeah. And how how long was ↓that. When did you lose your job?
62	Faiza:	Six weeks ago.
63	Nurse C:	°Six week ago°
64	Nurse B (L1 English):	Has your job affected you lately?
65	Faiza:	°I didn't catch what you said°
66	Nurse B:	Right (.) um (.) has your experience with losing your job affected you lately.
67	Faiza:	Yes, and since I lost my job I feel like this (3) ((coughing))
68	Nurse C:	Do you think losing your job (.) made you feel (.) tired all the time.
69	Faiza:	I just feel worthless.
70	Nurse A:	Because your work was (.) like (.) stress. a lot of stress?
71	Faiza:	()
72	Nurse B:	Why do you think you feel worthless?
73	Faiza:	(.) hh I just d:o
74	Nurse A:	(3) What about your mood. How (3)
75	Nurse C:	°How do you feel?°
76	Nurse A:	How do you how do you feel yourself. What about your feelings about yourself?
77	Faiza:	Just feel as if I'm worthless. (2) And it'd be better (2) just so so exhausted.
78	Nurse C:	You said it'd be better if if what?
79	Faiza:	If I wasn't here.
80	Nurse C:	°If I wasn't here?°
81	Nurse B:	Do you plan on harming yourself?
82	Faiza:	(2) Yes, I've thought about it.
83	Nurse A:	Why do you think?
84	Faiza:	I think (1) I think everyone would be better off if I wasn't here.

4.2 Pre-emption strategies

Allo-repetition (or other-repetition) is shown twice here as a communication strategy by Nurse C. Faiza is about to add to her statement about a feeling of worthlessness, by saying *it'd be better*, when she pauses slightly, and then seems to switch topics, by describing a feeling of worthlessness. In the next turn, Nurse C, perhaps detecting the possibility of suicidal thoughts, restates Faiza's previous utterance as a question, adding *You said* to indicate an upcoming allo-repetition, and *what* to invite further exploration: *You said it'd be better if what?* When Patient Faiza responds by saying *If I wasn't here*, Nurse C echoes Faiza's utterance verbatim.

Allo-repetition, where a speaker repeats the words of another, either the exact words, or paraphrased with a degree of reformulation such as tense switch, subject substitution, or making a statement a question, etc. is thought to be a feature of all conversation, and not unique to ELF (Tannen 2007: 85). Allo-repetition has been shown to perform a number of functions, including a means of indicating participatory listening, acceptance and familiarity; ratifying the contribution of another interlocutor; to convey humour; to stall; to request confirmation and clarification; to indicate surprise; and to mark boundaries for the beginnings and endings of conversations, among others (Tannen 2007). However, allo-repetition (or other-repetition) is said to play an enhanced role in ELF communication, to confirm an utterance's accuracy (Sawir 2004); to construct mutual understanding (Kaur 2009b); to increase comprehensibility (Murata 1995); or to create a positive environment for communication (Mauranen 2010).

With respect to healthcare ELF, Capuzzo (2015), looking specifically at the medical section of the English as a lingua franca in Academic Settings corpus (see Mauranen, Hynninen & Ranta 2010), noted that allo-repetition "showed interpersonal involvement in talk, and contributed to maintaining and/or enhancing sense-making" (2015:50), finding that complex medical terminology served as particular triggers for allo-repetitive strategies.

In this instance however, Nurse C's reformulated allo-repetition would seem more aptly classified as part of an active listening strategy for nursing communication in cases of potential suicide. Effective listening (of which allo-repetition forms a part) when discussing suicide ideation, serves to validate the perspective of the patient, allowing patients to share more fully and feel understood on her or his own terms (Murray & Hauenstein 2008). Therefore, both the first and second instance of Nurse C's allo-repetition might be seen as successful examples of effective therapeutic communication given the patient's circumstances.

This serves as another example of how MELF communication may be distinctive from ELF communication in general. The direct instruction in communication techniques received by ELF healthcare professionals, in particular that of nurses and the emphasis on therapeutic communication, may serve to in part govern the emergent and fluid nature of ELF interactions.

Reformulation is demonstrated here by Nurse A (L1 English). When the patient indicates a non-understanding (*I didn't catch what you said*), Nurse A reformulates with what appears to be an utterance of even more complexity: *has your job affected you lately* is restated in a second attempt as *has your experience with losing your job affected you lately*. The reformulation appears successful, with Faiza responding in the affirmative, and then going on to add that the job loss marked the onset of *this* (presumably the depression which has led to her hospital admission). We considered the possibility that Faiza's request for clarification was caused by inaudibility, but noted both that inaudibility among interlocutors was found nowhere else in this 26-minute discussion; and that according to both technical recording data and our perception as listeners, the audibility levels in the recording remained consistent during Nurse A's initial question. Assuming Faiza's signal of non-understanding (*I didn't catch what you said*) was not brought on by inaudibility but by non-comprehension of meaning, it is possible that Nurse A's reformulation is an example of weak ELF accommodation skills thought to be characteristic of L1 English speakers (Barančicová & Zerzová 2015; Jenkins 2011). However, it could also be understood as an instance of self-correction, and thus viewed positively in terms of communicative effectiveness, and ELF accommodation ability. Nurse A's initial utterance seems quite imprecise (*has your job affected you lately*), and so reformulates it to focus the question on Faiza's *experience* of job loss.

Cooperative pre-emption is illustrated in this exchange.

74   Nurse A: (3) What about your mood. How (3)
75   Nurse C: °How do you feel?°
76   Nurse A: How do you how do you feel yourself. What about your feelings about yourself?

After the question word *How*, a lengthy pause ensues as Nurse A presumably searches for a means to phrase a potentially personal line of questioning surrounding the patient's feelings of self-worth. Nurse C intervenes by providing the beginning of a question: *How do you feel*. Nurse A then continues, using the prompt from Nurse C, and then subsequently reformulating it more precisely within the same utterance: from *how do you feel about yourself* to *What about your feelings about yourself?* Viewed from a deficit perspective, this lack of immediacy in precise expression may be seen as a hindrance to Nurse A's ability to provide effective patient care. However, if viewed in entirety in light of

Nurse C's intervention, it may be understood as an instance of cooperative communication among ELF users, and a means of intraprofessional nursing collegialism (Miller & Kontos 2013).

Another example of repetition is seen in the following extract.

Extract: NE-SIM5B

29	Nurse Jana (L1 Malayalam):	So as um what I know that uh you came with uh some right-handed weakness due to stroke. And uh, wh- this is three days back you got admitted so- shall I know, can I know? what is uh, before? what happened. and when this pain started for you?
30	Patient (L1 undeclared):	Yeah. I us::ually I have hypertension before. uh been diagnosed hypertension fo::r twenty years now.
31	Nurse Jana:	So uh so this weakness? when it was started?
32	Patient:	It started three days ago I just had a ↑stroke. Then I have that right hand ↓weakness so that's why I'm here. So almost three days now.
33	Jana:	Ya. and um, now what'd you think >that is it radiating< pain? uh weakness for you? Or only in the [shoulder]
34	Patient:	[No.] Just here right now.
35	Jana:	Is there any pain? or something?
36	Patient:	N::ot at the moment.
37	Jana:	But on the leg [also?]
38	Patient:	[No.] I'm fine.
39	Jana:	You're fine with the [leg] only the hand you have an issue
40	Patient:	[Yes]
41	Jana:	And uh, u::h, what do you think that- u::h what will be the reason for having this uh weakness for you? [u::h do] you believe that uh, why it happened for you?
42	Patient:	[u:h I don't really] I don't know because I have history of hypertension=

43	Jana:	=You're thinking that the hypertension? may be due to you had a stroke? you get a stroke because of this weakness right?
44	Patient:	Yes.

Nurse Jana twice uses reformulated allo-repetition to positive effect in assessing this patient, who is presenting stroke symptoms. Jana preempts a potential non-understanding of the biomedical term *radiating* by self-clarification within the same turn by following the descriptor *weakness* with the question *or only in the shoulder*. The Patient then identifies the localized source of the weakness (*no just here right now*), presumably referring to her right hand (turn 29). In turn 35 Nurse Jana questions further on whether there are other symptoms in addition to the weakness (*is there any pain or something*); when Jana receives a negative reply, she explores further (*but on the leg also?*). Perhaps this is because she has observed the Patient exhibiting signs of leg pain or weakness either prior to or during the assessment, or perhaps she is drawing upon prior medical knowledge about the presentation of stroke symptoms. Whatever the cause for Jana's query, the Patient confirms that the weakness is confined, at least at present, to the right hand. Nurse Jana closes this portion of the assessment with a reformulation (*you're fine with the leg only the hand you have an issue*), which the Patient affirms (turn 40), and the assessment moves to the next phase. Turn sequence 41–44 is another instance of reformulated allo-repetition. In response to Nurse Jana's exploration of the source of the right-handed weakness, the Patient begins turn 42 by saying *I don't know* but mid-turn links it to her preexisting *hypertension*. At this, Jana reformulates in summary form: *you're thinking that the hypertension may be due to you had a stroke*, followed by the question tag *right*: the Patient confirms this reformulation with *yes*. These examples of repetition/reformulation, the accuracy of which were confirmed by the Patient, are particularly important, given the high stakes nature of the communication: inaccurate assessment of stroke symptoms can have dire consequences (Newman-Toker et al. 2014).

4.2.3 Spelling

Another strategy used by ELF communicators to pre-empt potential misunderstanding is that of spelling (Cogo and Pitzl, 2016): interlocutors may draw upon prior experience in recognizing lexical items which represent particular difficulty, and spell those to forestall miscommunication. In the excerpt below, Nurse (L1 Malayalam), reviewing a medical history with a stroke patient, anticipates a potential mishearing, and clarifies it pre-emptively through an adapted form of spelling.

Excerpt NE-SIM3B – *Pre-emption*: *Morphemic Spelling*
73	Nurse (L1-Malayalam):	Okay. Uh, what about your family? is, u:::h, suffering from any [illness]
74	Patient (L1 English):	[Yeah] my dad has a history of hypertension so:
75	Nurse:	°Father. Hypertension.° Since how many years?
76	Patient:	A::bout forty years now?
77	Nurse:	Fourty. Four zero?
78	Patient:	Yes.
79	Nurse:	Oh. (.) No one else?
80	Patient:	N::ot that I know of.
81	Nurse:	Any history of u::::h like any stroke in your family?
82	Patient:	My ↑dad
83	Nurse:	Your dad also had stroke?
84	Patient:	Yes.
85	Nurse:	°Stroke.° And mother? Anybody.
86	Patient:	N::o.

In attempting to specify the onset family illnesses, Nurse (while writing) utilizes partial repetition (*Father*; *Hypertension*) of Patient's answer in turn 74. Nurse queries further as to the duration: *Since how many years?*, to which Patient replies *About 40 years now*. To ensure clarity, Nurse reiterates the answer: *Forty. Four-zero?* The number is confirmed, and Nurse proceeds with the interview.

We cannot of course be certain about which potential area of misunderstanding Nurse was intending to prevent, but her decision to clarify through (a form of) morpheme-level spelling could be to avoid confusion brought about by stress shift in the numbers *fourteen* and *forty*. In some varieties of native speaker speech, the addition of a following noun possessing initial syllable stress can result in *fourTEEN* becoming FOURteen (Lewis & Deterding 2018: 74), blurring the distinction between the two numbers. Nurse may have encountered this communicative challenge previously, and pre-empted it through the sounding of *zero*. Whatever her motivation for this pre-emption, the strategy was successful and the Patient's family history was accurately documented.

Another example of pre-emptive clarity through sounding numbers is provided by a patient whose self-identified L1 is English. The patient, having previously given his age (turn 23), seems to assume Nurse's second inquiry (turn 26) is a result of confusion around the number's second syllable: / sti /. He articulates the word *zero*, which Nurse confirms (*Six zero okay*), after which she continues with the assessment.

20	Nurse (L1 Arabic):	hh Okay. Yes so you're in a comfortable ↑position. S::o I'::m just I want to ask you what's your ↑good name please
21	Patient (L1 English):	U::h mister Daryl?
22	Nurse:	O::kay mister ↑Dar::yl. (.) How old are you?
23	Patient:	I'm sixty years old?
24	Nurse:	Okay, I feel we good and oriented?
25	Patient:	Mm-hmm [affirmative]
26	Nurse:	Sir? (.) How old are you exactly?
27	Patient:	Six zero. Sixty.
28	Nurse:	Six zero, oka::y. Um, I can feel your hh your face is smiling. Your presence with m::e

We note here the use of this pre-emptive strategy by an interlocutor whose L1 is English. While it has been suggested that English native speakers may lack the flexibility required for effective ELF communication (Sweeney & Hua 2010), this particular native speaker adeptly recognizes a potential misunderstanding, and pre-emptively moves to address it. Such instances of linguistic accommodation (Drljača Margić 2017) by native speakers are increasingly prevalent in the context of the GCC, and in fact necessary to carry on daily activities, and it would be inaccurate to suggest accommodation skills for English communication as the preserve of non-native speakers alone.

Incidentally, we note the use of the phrase *good name* (turn 20) here as a means of asking for a patient's name, a practice we observe in several instances in our data. Since asking for one's *good name* is associated with South Asian varieties of English (Kachru 1993), its observed use by speakers of other L1s from outside of South Asia (in this extract, Arabic) has led us to speculate elsewhere, drawing upon a World Englishes perspective, that this may exemplify norm development in an emerging Gulf English variety (Tweedie and Johnson, 2018a). Readers who view this exchange from a translanguaging perspective (Kimura & Canagarajah 2018) may frame this instead as an example of translingual practice.

4.2.4 Other-initiated repair

The next excerpt shows an example of other-initiated repair (OIR), with a nurse reformulating an utterance in accommodation to a patient's query. However, despite three attempts, the repair appears unsuccessful, and the discussion proceeds without resolving misunderstanding, unfortunately leaving the potential for an adverse medical event (Divi et al. 2007).

Excerpt NE-SIM1B – *Pre-emption: Reformulation (Other-initiated Repair)*
Scenario: Depression with suicidality
Pre-brief instructions: You are a nurse working in the female unit at [name] Psychiatric Hospital. You will be interviewing a new patient, Faisa, who was admitted due to suicidal ideation. She has a history of depression and this is her first hospitalization. You and your nurse colleagues will be interviewing Faisa to conduct a mental status assessment and engage in therapeutic communication.

42	Nurse (L1 Malayalam):	°Okay° what medicine ↑you are taking
43	Patient:	I have couple of medication I=
44	Nurse:	=Oh [Okay]
45	Patient:	[Take] u::h ↑Metaprolo
46	Nurse:	Oka::y
47	Patient:	And I'm taking Novax.
48	Nurse:	Oka::y
49	Patient:	And u::h, Aspirin.
50	Nurse:	Oka::y
51	Patient:	An::d I think I'm taking als::o anti-platel::et Coumadin.
52	Nurse:	°↓Coumadin also°
53	Patient:	°Yes°
54	Nurse:	(.) This all once daily you are taking? or u::h ↑variated
55	Patient:	What?
56	Nurse:	U::h how frequent you are taking this ↑medicine
57	Patient:	U::h I take some once a day some twice a day.
58	Nurse:	Can you tell me which of medicine you are >you are taking?<
59	Patient:	N::o but I know=
60	Nurse:	=Ah it's oka::y
61	Patient:	Some of=
62	Nurse:	=It's oka::y. Any associated u::h ↓symptoms with this weakness you have any u::h numbness or u::h headache nausea
63	Patient:	N::o no

64	Nurse:	Nothing. When you started this u::h weakness ↓no associated symptoms
65	Patient:	N::o
66	Nurse:	°No° Anyone in your family have the same history?
67	Patient:	Yeah u::h my dad. My dad yea::h
68	Nurse:	°Okay° U::h he was the ↑hypertension or?
69	Patient:	Yes.
70	Nurse:	Oka::y and he also was taking the medicine
71	Patient:	Yes.

Repair refers to "the set of practices whereby a co-interactant interrupts the ongoing course of action to attend to possible trouble in speaking, hearing or understanding the talk" (Kitzinger 2013: 229), and is generally categorized into self- and other-initiated repair. An instance of other-initiated repair occurs when Nurse uses the more clinical term *variated* to question Patient with respect to medication frequency; Patient responds with a one-word question: *What?* At this signal of non-understanding, Nurse reformulates her question: *how frequent you are taking this medicine* without identifying which of the three previously mentioned medicine(s) she is referring to. Patient's answer reflects this imprecision, and seems to indicate that she understands the importance of identifying both medication and dosage frequency: *I take some once a day, some twice a day*. At this, Nurse attempts further clarity: *Can you tell me which of medicine you are you are taking?* The researchers were unclear on the intent of this question: we understood Nurse to be clarifying with her Patient which medicines were taken on which day. However, Patient's answer (*No, but I know*) would seem to indicate she interpreted Nurse's question differently. Patient had already listed four medications (*Metaprolo, Novax, Aspirin* and *Coumadin*), so it seems unusual that Patient would have answered *No* in response to a query she had just answered with an affirmative. Did Patient interpret Nurse's *which of* to mean *how much of* each medication (i.e., dosage frequency)? Whatever Patient's interpretation, her attempts to elaborate are interrupted twice by Nurse (with *Ah, it's OK* and *It's OK*), and the interview proceeds with the question unanswered.

As nurses often represent the last step in drug administration, communication at this stage of the process is deemed a high-risk activity (Bohand et al. 2009). Despite the importance of nurses in the dispensing chain, research indicates nurses may detect as few as one-third of errors in dispensed medications (Leape 1995), and since medication errors account for a significant proportion of all hospitalizations and adverse events (Beijer & de Blaey 2002), precise nurse-patient communication in drug administration is critical. Drug-drug interactions are a source of toxicity leading to adverse effects (Guchelaar et al. 2005), so the listing activity Nurse is undertaking in identifying Patient's medications represents a crucial step in ensuring patient safety. Medication errors can be classified as "wrong patient, wrong diagnosis, wrong drug, wrong dose, wrong delivery, wrong timing" (Hudson & Guchelaar 2003: 1010), and in this case, Nurse's imprecision in identifying the dosages and timing is setting the stage for potential adverse drug-to-drug interactions.

A second and third other-repair are attempted by Patient when she utters *No but I know* (interrupted by *Ah it's OK*) and then *Some of* (interrupted by *It's OK*), after which, Nurse proceeds with a different line of questioning. Three attempts at other-repair were unsuccessful, and a lack of clarity surrounding the critical questions of *how much of which medication at what time on which days* was left unresolved. This is the type of communication failure with regard to medication that has the potential to lead to serious adverse drug events (Bohand et al. 2009).

4.2.5 Playback and non-verbal communication

Another kind of reformulation is playback, where a conversation participant immediately repeats or builds upon the words of another interlocutor, either through "question intonation inviting patient repair or extension . . . or . . . a plain statement indicating attentiveness and information receipt" (Jin & Watson 2020: 718). Playback in medical contexts has been shown to assist completion of the medical interview, build rapport, and show empathy (Ting & Cogo: in press; Jin & Watson 2020). In the excerpts that follow, nurse Roxane (L1 Malayalam) makes extensive use of playback in a neurological assessment of a stroke patient.

Excerpts NE-SIML4 – *Pre-emption: Playback*
Scenario: Neurological assessment
Pre-brief instructions: Mr._, 60 year old male is admitted to the neurology medical floor for a stroke. He has been in the hospital for 3 days. He is been treated with antiplatelet agents and antihypertensive agents. He will be discharged to a rehabilitation facility tomorrow. His confusion is resolved but he continues to have right arm weakness. His speech is fluent and does not have any memory loss.

46	Patient (L1 English):	And I can't lift my my arm up.(0.5) It's very weak on this side this side's good but this side I I can barely feel my fingers.

47	Roxane (Nurse; L1 Malayalam):	O:::kay. Can you tell me exactly when it happened?
48	Patient:	U::h three days ago
49	Roxane:	Three days ↓ag:::o
50	Patient:	Three days ↑ag:o
51	Roxane:	O:kay
61	Roxane:	Okay and u:h can you tell me sir with this weakness? uh is there any factors which increases this weakness or something [that]
62	Patient:	[N:o it seems] to be constant all day all day all night. [It] doesn't get better
63	Roxane:	[O:kay] (1) just constant for all the time.
64	Patient:	Constant. yes.
131	Roxane:	U:h have you had history of smoking?
132	Patient:	I u:sed to smoke a whole bunch but I quit. My wife told me to quit smoking.
133	Roxane:	O:h so now you no more=
134	Patient:	=No more smoking.
135	Roxane:	°No smoke° A:re you working sir?
213	Roxane:	You have to do first l:ike this (.) on your knees ((patting knees with hands)) both the hands
214	Patient:	Y:eah I can't
215	Roxane:	This one you cannot do.
216	Patient:	Right.
217	Roxane:	So this one you cannot >can< d:o
218	Patient:	°Yep° ((patting knees with hands stops))
219	Roxane:	°O:kay° Can you do like this finger? to finger? (1) ba:ck. (2) O:kay This hand? (2) You ↓cannot
220	Patient:	Maybe take a little while longer hh (2) not very good
221	Roxane:	O:kay Can? you touch your nose and touch my fi:nger?
222	Patient:	O:h
223	Roxane:	(2) Okay. With the other hand?
224	Patient:	I can't lift my arm up.
225	Roxane:	You cannot do it.
226	Patient:	°No°
227	Roxane:	Can you ho:ld ↑this hand like this? And touch your n:ose. And this hand you cann:ot
228	Patient:	°No°

229	Roxane:	You cannot do this one. Oka::y. Show me your finger-hand? °Okay° So:: close your, eyes? Tell me which position I am lifting it or I am making it down.
230	Patient:	Mm-hmm (affirmative). Up?(1) Down. (0.5) Up? Down.
231	Roxane:	°Okay° And this ha::nd?
232	Patient:	Uh, I thi:nk that's up (1) I can't tell. That's up.(2) I don't know.

In turns 46–51, Nurse Roxane is attempting to determine the onset of stroke symptoms: *Can you tell me exactly when it* [the symptom Patient describes in turn 46] *happened?* The reply is *uh three days ago.* Roxane repeats Patient's utterance verbatim (less the filler word *uh*), to which he confirms *three days ago.* Following Merritt (1977), Jin and Watson (2020) distinguish between queryback playback and affirmative forms of playback: queryback requests an answer from the respondent, while affirmative playback does not. Queryback may involve a restatement to solicit repair or extension, accompanied by rising intonation, or an acknowledgement that information is received, and indicating attentiveness.

The use of queryback here in the process of confirming onset of stroke symptoms may be seen as a means of information verification, without inviting extension. Confirming the accuracy of information is an important element of patient history-taking in medical communication, and Nurse Roxane utilizes queryback effectively for this purpose. Patient's repetition (turn 50), followed by Roxane's final *okay* closes the loop for the neurological assessment to proceed, and shows complementary accommodation (Street 1991), where both patient and nurse mutually accomplish the roles of other-utterances.

A similar use of queryback is seen in turns 61–64, as Nurse Roxane seeks to identify factors which exacerbate or relieve the symptoms. Patient answers this query in the negative, stating that the *weakness* in his arms *seems to be constant all day all night.* Roxane acknowledges her understanding (*Okay*) and reformulates Patient's utterance as *just constant for all the time,* to which Patient confirms *constant yes.* Again, complementary accommodation is achieved, and the next phase of history-taking can begin. The process of queryback in complementary accommodation is seen again in the discussion of smoking cessation (turns 131–135).

The series of physical assessments performed by Nurse Roxane in turns 213–232 provides multiple examples of playback. She prompts Patient to attempt basic physical tasks as part of a stroke assessment procedure by first modelling the action herself (usually with the prompt *like this*) and then inviting Patient to follow, with verbal confirmations from both participants supplementing the information-giving process. Lines 213–217 illustrate this communication loop of nurse modelling action, patient attempt and answer, nurse confirmation, and patient's final confirmation, which closes the loop and leads to the next physical assessment in sequence.

213 Roxane: You have to do first l:ike this (.) on your knees [Nurse models and describes desired action] both the hands.
214 Patient: Y:eah I can't. [Patient attempts action unsuccessfully; verbally indicates thus]
215 Roxane: This one you cannot do. [Nurse verbally confirms]
216 Patient: Right. [Patient re-confirms]
217 Roxane: So this one you cannot >can< d:o [Nurse initiates next physical assessment: (Patient's other hand)]

With some exceptions, Matsumoto (2019: 569) finds in ELF research an orientation heavily tilted toward linguistic elements of communication, perhaps underlaid by an assumption that "embodied actions (e.g., smile, body orientation, and gaze), and non-verbal vocalizations (e.g., laughter) tend to be regarded as mere illustrative supports to speech". Drawing upon Block's (2014) challenge to Second Language Acquisition researchers, Matsumoto asserts that a widening scope of analysis which includes the simultaneous use of embodied actions and non-verbals – interlocutors' multimodal resources – represents a significant opportunity for deepening our understanding of ELF communication. If so, MELF extends this potential further. Turns 213–232 illustrate what may be common in MELF communication and generally in healthcare professional-patient interaction: the simultaneous use of embodied actions and linguistic resources in communication. Protocols for physical assessment of patients presenting stroke symptoms (e.g., FAST; Harbison et al. 2003) call for assessed performance of arm movements. Nurse Roxane communicates these skilfully, simultaneously utilizing modelling of desired actions while verbalizing either prompts or confirmations of task completion. Utilizing her "multimodal ensemble" (Bezemer & Kress 2008: 166), the nurse proceeds effectively and efficiently through the healthcare assessment, pre-empting potential non-understandings.

4.3 Summary

To summarize, the data from MELF interactions presented in this chapter both affirms and extends our understanding of ELF. The use of communicative strategies in MELF such as playback, repetition, spelling and the like are consistent with the study of ELF interaction in other domains of use. Cooperative measures to achieve understanding were used effectively by intraprofessional MELF users attempting to communicate with patients, a finding which bodes well for quality healthcare delivery in MELF contexts, as does the potent use of non-verbals. In our data, pre-emption strategies for the most part were used with good effect by MELF users to avoid non- or misunderstandings, but as is the case in healthcare communication generally, instances of unsuccessful communication represent a very real threat to patient safety.

Chapter 5
Finding common ground in MELF

Chapter key points:
- Elements of nursing health assessment, viewed through the lens of an activity type, collude to constrain, restrict and shape medical ELF conversational features.
- Within these constraints, our data shows MELF users successfully managing strategies to confirm the accuracy of patients' information.
- A "biomedical think aloud" strategy used in MELF health assessment, while perhaps serving useful functions for the healthcare professional, appears of limited value to patient comprehension.
- In using a sociocognitive approach to consider nurse-patient health assessment, biomedical language is often the healthcare professional's default starting point in the search for communicative common ground.

5.1 Introduction: Health assessment as an activity type

A basic premise underlying Levinson's (1992) description of activity types is that utterances, in order to be fully understood, must be considered within the social context in which they occur. Levinson provides an example of talk occurring within a cricket match and a basketball game (1992: 67–68) to make the case that while a hearer can comprehend the meaning of words like *tip*, *out* and *here!*, the context of the talk is an essential element of understanding. For example, an exclamatory *here* in a basketball game might be directing one player to pass the ball to another; the reader can easily envision multiple other settings where *here* might carry entirely different meanings.

What features essentially in the idea of activity type is the limits it places upon the language contributions participants may offer. In the words of Levinson, activity types are "goal-defined, socially constituted, bounded, events with *constraints* on participants, setting and so on, but above all on the kinds of available contributions" (Levinson 1992: 69; emphasis in original). Levinson conceptualizes social events along a "gradient" along two opposite poles: "the totally pre-packaged activity, on the one hand (e.g., a Roman mass) and the largely unscripted event on the other (e.g., a chance meeting on the street)" (1992: 69).

An important part of ascertaining meaning of a given utterance is an understanding of its social context, and the expectations for communication structured around the shared goals in a particular setting. Bigi and Rossi (2020: 19) give the example of a physician beginning a medical consultation with "How are you today?". The patient will likely interpret this question in light of an understanding of the kinds of contributions relevant to a medical consultation, and structure a reply accordingly. The same question asked during a chance encounter between friends at a supermarket will likely be interpreted – and therefore responded to – differently. In both cases, the activity type acts to shape and restrict the kinds of admissible contributions.

As a social event, medical encounters may be understood in light of Levinson's characterization of activity types as "fuzzy" (1992: 69), in that while there is a discernible and predictable structure to medical interactions (Roter & Hall 2006), the exact nature of allowable contributions are not always clearly defined. For example, when has a patient given enough information, and the healthcare professional should therefore interrupt and shift topics? Or is a role reversal appropriate – is it permissible for the patient to query the healthcare professional on her physical condition (Bigi & Rossi 2020)? Such decisions are informed by, among other factors, the healthcare communication paradigm being used (e.g. patient-centred care; therapeutic communication, etc.).

Plain language communication is utilized across multiple disciplines, and its value is supported by the research behind its development that draws from an equally diverse number of fields. This value is increasingly being recognized in health care applications for its role in mitigating the barriers posed by limited health literacy and enhancing patient safety. Plain language is defined as communication that can be understood the first time it is seen or heard, that uses succinct active-voiced grammatically correct complete sentences to better enable patients and caregivers to engage with information, using a more informal tone and common terms whenever possible (Warde et al. 2018: e54).

In this chapter, we view nursing health assessment through the lens of activity type, and consider how the bounded characteristics of this particular social event impact upon the language use of ELF users. Health assessment is considered a central role of nurse practitioners, and an important part of improving patient outcomes (Baid et al. 2009). While traditionally associated primarily with the work of physicians, health assessment is now internationally recognized as part of nurses' expanding role in patient care (Maejima & Ohta 2019). Baid (2006) proposes a framework which has been widely implemented for patient health assessment by nurses: after taking the patient's health history, a nurse determines whether to undertake a comprehensive (full body) assessment, or a more targeted examination of a particular area (focused assessment). This framework specifies procedures and steps for both assessments, often explained via technical, formulaic language (e.g., *ptosis*; *discoloration or discharge*; *rhythmic oscillation*; *Angle of Louis*; etc.), sometimes with accompanying mnemonic (e.g., *HEENT: head, ears, eyes, nose throat; Apple Pie Tastes Mmm Eee: aortic, pulmonic; tricuspid; mitral; Erb's point*). The assessment leads to an interpretation of findings, with the final result being a recognition of abnormality, or a different diagnosis, followed by an appropriate clinical decision in response. Other frameworks for nursing assessment adopt a broader perspective, encompassing time-lapsed evaluations (to monitor improvement or deterioration of the patient's condition) and emergency assessment (especially rapid assessment and accompanying action) (IMedPub 2020).

The following section will consider data from health assessment simulations, paying particular attention to how this particular activity type might impact interlocutors' language use.

5.2 Lexical simplification, biomedical summaries, and answer-offering

Lexical simplification as a pre-emptive strategy involves providing a simpler reformulated version of the original item (Svennevig et al. 2019; other pre-emptive strategies used in MELF communication have been described in Chapter 4). As excessive biomedical talk has been shown to hinder effective healthcare communication with patients (Kain et al. 2009), Nurse Sindi's simplification in the excerpt below of the more clinical adjective *associative* to *you have symptoms* (preceded by the filler, *you know*) within the same turn demonstrates an important element of a plain language approach to medical communication (Warde et al. 2018).

Excerpt RE-SIM1A
Scenario: Respiratory assessment
Pre-brief instructions: A 52-year-old patient is admitted for upper respiratory tract infection with severe cough. The patient has been in the hospital for two days and will be discharged home today.

137	Nurse Sindi (L1 Tamil):	Do you like? why do you think like it has caused this bronchitis, anything, do you have a, do you have any other habits? Like, do you smoke?
138	Patient Susan (L1 English):	I I do smoke, yes.
139	Sindi:	Oh, okay. So, okay. Do you have any other associative, like, you know, you have symptoms, like uh, vomiting? When you had cough?
140	Susan:	No.

141	Sindi:	Nothing. Okay. So, how does like, uh, when uh, this uh, this cough? is like, getting relieved by um, uh, like, you know, when you, if you sleep in the kind of a position like a 45 degree angle, or uh, how, how d- it was, was it relieved?
142	Sindi:	Oh.
143	Susan:	It was just, it was just=
144	Sindi:	=It is getting worsened.
145	Susan:	Yeah, it was just a bad cough.
146	Sindi:	Okay.
147	Susan:	Yeah

One type of reformulation to pre-empt misunderstanding is for an interlocutor to offer the listener answers to a question. As a communication tool, this strategy serves the useful function of guiding the respondent toward a relevant answer. However, offering an answer may also hinder accurate communication, by placing limits on the type of response that can be given (Svennevig 2013). In this extract, the nurse's attempt at offering answers to her original question appears less than successful at obtaining accurate information. In her assessment, Nurse Sindi is attempting to determine what actions provide relief for the symptoms presented, and suggests a particular sleep position as a potential example (turn 141). The patient's reply does not seem to address symptom relief directly, but the cough itself, and her repetition in turn 143 suggests some difficulty in exact expression (*it was just it was just*). Sindi provides a completion to the patient's utterance: *It is getting worsened*. However, the patient's response (*it was just a bad cough*) does not confirm Nurse Sindi's completion. We take Susan's statement that *it was just a bad cough* to mean, presumably, *there were no particular* (sleep?) *strategies that provided relief*. Susan did not affirm the nurse's suggestion that the cough is *getting worsened*. Nurse Sindi's *okay* followed by the patient's *yeah* closes this line of questioning, but an important piece of information – the question of whether the cough is getting worse – seems unresolved.

In a number of instances, this particular respiratory assessment evidenced characteristics of Levinson's (1992) conceptions of an activity type, where formulaic, goal-defined exchanges served to direct and constrain turns and contributions of both participants. Researchers have noted how doctor-patient consultations often orient toward establishing or reaffirming the physician's authority through technical and scientific expertise, yet the patient also has important insight into her own condition and treatment, and the two perspectives would ideally converge (Lipkin et al. 2011). While physicians may assert this authoritative expertise during the diagnostic consultation, patients for their part may perpetuate this orientation through subordinating responses (Heath 1992). In such instances Levinson's notion of activity type is instructive in understanding the seeming paradox. In an analysis of physician-patient communication around diagnosis, Peräkylä (2006: 218) suggests three means by which doctors orally validate the relationship between a named diagnosis and its evidence: describing the symptoms without accompanying reasoning for the diagnosis; by describing inferential references to the evidence for the diagnosis; and explicitly laying out the evidence for the diagnosis. On multiple occasions during the patient assessment, we observe Nurse Sindi orienting the discussion to an authoritative stance, through biomedical summary statements.

236	Nurse Sindi:	it's, your skin looks uh, normal to your ethnicity and then there is no lesion or mass or anything. And then it is [inaudible]. Uh, and then uh, your respiratory, uh, movement there is uh, some chest wall is uh, symmetrical and then the [inaudible] elliptical in shape and then uh, uh can you just uh, in the, it, it's fine. Can you just put this up? And then uh, your [inaudible] is elliptical in (thing), chest, your chest wall movement is equal. Equal, and then just with weight is uh, regular, and you're not having any (unclear word) now at the moment. Okay. You're having, uh, cough.
237	Susan:	Just a bit.
238	Sindi:	Yes, yeah, you're having cough.
239	Susan:	It's so much better.
240	Sindi:	And then, it's, and then your um, anterior and then the posterior diameter, we say, but it's actually lesser than the transfer for diameter, which is one [inaudible] that is also normal.
241	Susan:	Okay.
242	Sindi:	Okay. And then uh, you're uh, you're not using any accessory muscle, your respiratory effort is, yeah, effort is good. You are not using any accessory muscles, and there is no audible, like when you are uh, breathing in. And there is no nasal flaring. Uh, yeah. Okay, there is no audible that sounds, I noted. So, okay. And I will just lie down, I will just palpate you.
243	Susan:	Okay.

244	Sindi:	And I will just see if there is any, uh, lump or anything. Okay.
245	Susan:	Okay.
246	Sindi:	Okay. Um, there is no ten= do you have any pain here?
247	Susan:	No.
248	Sindi:	Nothing? Okay. There is no tenderness, no lumps. There is no swelling or anything. Okay. Can I see you on the back, please?
249	Susan:	Yeah.
250	Sindi:	Thank you. There is no uh lesions, or tenderness, or any injury. Okay. Palpation, now your skin is like, uh, palpation, you don't have any uh, skin lesion or injury or any mass of swelling I noted. And then uh, your uh, uh, the septum now I will just check for your um, har, just uh, you, I will tell you, I will touch my palm on your back.

As Nurse Sindi proceeds through the assessment, she verbalizes her observations, often utilizing technical biomedical language such as *lesion, symmetrical chest wall, palpate you, nasal flaring, anterior, posterior, accessory muscle, respiratory effort, transfer for diameter*, and *septum*. Sometimes these descriptions are accompanied by questions to the patient (*there is no ten* [-derness] – *do you have any pain here*), but some observations are uttered without inviting response (e.g., the descriptive sequence in turn 242).

In examining the patient's chest (236–238), Nurse Sindi returns to the cough, a symptom established previously in the assessment: *You're having, uh, cough*. Patient Susan clarifies the nature of the cough by specifying *just a bit*, but the clarification seems to be overridden by the nurse's subsequent restatement: *Yes, yeah, you're having cough*. Susan attempts a second clarification regarding the cough (*it's so much better*), but Sindi seems to ignore it, and moves the assessment to its next phase.

In Peräkylä's (2006) data, patient responses during diagnostic consultations were found to be minimal acknowledgements, silences, or extended responses. In some cases of extended responses, conflict resulted, where the patient either rejected the physician's diagnosis, or sought to correct it. Patient Susan here attempts to revise Nurse Sindi's assessment of the nature of the cough (*just a little bit*; *it's much better*), but the revision appears unsuccessful. Sindi's override of the patient's perspective, and the missed opportunity for an extended patient response, can be understood as a failure in therapeutic communication (Tamparo & Lindh 2017). Heath (1992) suggests that extended responses from patients are most likely to be generated through the physician's framing of diagnoses: as questions, as uncertain, or as differing from patient expectations. If the cough had actually improved significantly, but this was not taken into account in the patient's record due to the nurse's communication override, the result could be a delayed discharge and an unnecessary extension in hospital stay, with attendant costs to the patient and/or the healthcare system (John-Baptiste et al. 2004).

💬 Talk in consultations involving frequently attending patients can demonstrate equality regarding participants' claims to knowledge concerning such topics as illness management, medication and test results. However, doctor-patient consultations deal with the additional activity of interpreting patients' problems and describing patients' problems from a medical perspective. It is specifically during these interpretative activities that asymmetric claims to epistemic authority tend to remain. Despite these patients having experience of chronic, recurrent or long-term illnesses and frequent contact with health care professionals, discussion or debate around these issues was strongly avoided. Even if overt disagreement occurs, resolution is quickly established as both parties 'retreat' to their realms of epistemic authority (Ariss 2009: 918).

5.3 Playback, queryback and recipient design

The next simulation scenario further underscores the role of activity type in shaping interlocutor discourse in MELF interactions. As an activity type, the format of the medical interview serves to place limits on the types of contributions participants make, facilitated through features like allocated turn-taking and question forms. Within these constraints, however, we see a number of ELF communication strategies. The setting for the simulation is unique in that it occurs outside of a clinical setting in a home visit.

Excerpt ST-SIM1
Scenario: Cerebrovascular Accident (CVA; stroke) home visit
Pre-brief instructions: Ragia is a 45 year old woman who was discharged from the rehab hospital at [clinic name] two days ago. After experiencing a CVA 2 months ago, she spent two weeks in the ICU, followed by a 6-week stay in the rehab hospital. She continues to have significant residual left-sided weakness. She is to visit her physician every 2 weeks; is scheduled for weekly blood work; has a follow up CT Scan in one month; and is to attend physiotherapy every other day. She is on anticoagulants [blood thinners] and hypertensive [blood pressure] medications. She currently requires a walker to mobilize safely. Her speech and memory have improved greatly, though there is some residual slurring, especially when she is fatigued. She is left-handed so completing her

ADLs [Activities of Daily Living] is difficult. Ragia lives with her older sister, Roz. This is your first visit to her home. You have been assigned to work with this family for two months.

The learning objectives underlying this particular scenario center on family assessment and intervention, which provides a framework for helping nurses understand patient needs and treatment within the context of familial dynamics (Shajani & Snell 2019).

23	Nurse B (L1 Arabic):	Your name?
24	Patient Ragia (L1 Arabic):	Ragia.
25	Nurse B:	Ragia. Okay. What bring you today here?
26	Ragia:	I have a stroke.
27	Nurse B:	Stroke. You have stroke. Okay. Uh. You have a stroke before?
28	Ragia:	No.
29	Nurse B:	This is first time.
30	Ragia:	Yeah.
31	Nurse B:	Okay. How old are you.
32	Ragia:	45
33	Nurse B:	45 years. Okay. Uh. You have any blood pressure or, you have blood pressure?
34	Ragia:	Yeah.
35	Nurse B:	Okay. You are on medication?
36	Ragia:	Yeah.
37	Nurse B:	Uh, okay. You take your medication daily?
38	Ragia:	Oh, no.
39	Nurse B:	Okay, you should take your medication, as [inaudible].
40	Ragia:	Okay.
41	Nurse B:	Okay. And uh, and your family, anybody have blood pressure, or any disease?
42	Ragia:	Mm-hmm. Mother, father.
43	Roz (L1 Arabic):	Father, mother, they have diabetes and arthritis.
44	Nurse B:	Father, mother have diabetes?
45	Ragia:	Mm-hmm.
46	Roz:	And arthritis.
47	Nurse B:	Arthritis. Okay. Uh, your father and mother, they are alive?
48	Roz:	No.
49	Nurse B:	Okay. Okay. Which age they are died?

50	Roz:	Father was 70.
51	Nurse B:	70
52	Roz:	Mother was 65.
53	Nurse B:	60?
54	Ragia:	65
55	Nurse B:	65, mother. Okay. And (.) you have any sister, or this one? what's the relationship between you and?
56	Roz:	Sister.
57	Nurse B:	Your sister?
58	Roz:	Yeah.
59	Nurse B:	Okay. Uh, you have any brother or sister? Only this one?
60	Roz:	Mm-hmm.
61	Nurse B:	Only this one. You are married?
62	Ragia:	No.
63	Nurse B:	No married. Okay, uh, how old she is?
64	Roz:	I'm 50.
65	Nurse B:	50 years. Okay. She's 45.
66	Roz:	Yeah.
67	Nurse B:	Okay.
68	Nurse A (L1 Arabic):	Who's taking care of you in the house?
69:	Ragia:	My sister.
70:	Roz:	↓Sister.
71	Nurse B:	You are working?
72	Roz:	Yes.
73	Nurse B:	What you're working?
74	Roz:	Teacher.
75	Nurse B:	↓Teacher. Okay.
76	Ragia:	Me also.
77	Nurse B:	Both of you are teachers?
78	Roz:	Teachers for [institution, jurisdiction name].
79	Nurse B:	Teachers for [institution, jurisdiction name], okay. You have any any allergy for any medication or food?
80	Ragia: No.	No allergies.

Nurse B makes effective use of queryback for clarification in the process of taking a family history. An initial question about parents (*which age they are died*) begins a sequence of playback and queryback. In turns 52–54, Nurse B is unsure she heard correctly the age at which the mother died, and seeks confirmation with rising intonation (*60?*), to which Patient Ragia supplies a corrective response (*65*). Nurse B then effectively uses a type of playback strategy, plain statements to indicate information receipt (Jin & Watson, 2020), to gather further information as the interview moves along. To her question *only this one* (i.e., is the sister here with us at present your only sibling?), Nurse B receives an affirmative interjection (*mm-hmm*), to which she indicates receipt by repeating *only this one* without rising intonation. This form of playback is utilized again in the question utterance immediately following: *you are married*; Ragia replies in the negative, and Nurse B confirms receipt by reframing her previous question as a statement (*no married*). The same strategy is used to confirm information on the patients' occupations, and allergies.

In terms of confirming the accuracy of information, a critical element in the process of medical history-taking (Hogan-Quigley, Palm & Bickley 2017), Nurse B's strategy proves effective. Her use of intonation to indicate either question or receipt of information in playback sequences represents a skilful tool for ensuring information is transferred with precision. As we will note later, language instruction intended to prepare healthcare professionals for MELF environments would benefit from awareness-raising activities (Zhang 2004) which highlight the role of intonation in questioning and confirming important information.

At the same time, we note the constraints which the medical interview activity type places upon participants, both healthcare professional and patient. Upon first read, the information exchange sequence between Nurse B and her two patients is reminiscent of the caricature described by Heritage and Boyd (2006: 163): the mechanical healthcare professional embodying a sort of "living questionnaire" as in in social research, "neutral and consistent across patients" (see also Cassell 1985).

The "living questionnaire" analogy, where the healthcare professional ensures standardized responses with framed questions, contrasts sharply with the type of holistic assessment advocated in contemporary healthcare training textbooks. For example, Hogan-Quigley et al (2017) speak of health assessment practices which attend to the "7 Facets" of health: encompassing not just the physical, but emotional, social, cultural, spiritual, environmental and developmental elements (2017: 3). Healthcare educators assert that gaining meaningful information from patients on all such facets of health is unlikely to be accomplished through a highly structured "Q & A" format. Patients' extended responses obtained through open-ended questions, while espoused by healthcare educators, are apparently less so taken up at bedsides or clinics.

It is important to note that the routine, almost checklist-like nature of medical history-taking is not brought on by the mandates of the healthcare professional alone. The format is in fact "*co-constructed* as routine (or not) through the actions of *both* doctors and patients" (Boyd & Heritage 2006: 169; emphasis in original). Presumably, a patient being asked a question preferentially requesting a restricted range of answers *could* provide an extended response, yet patients typically do not do so. Rather, patients comply with the brief, often one-word answer requested via the structure of the healthcare professional's question, and the history-taking proceeds quickly. "In this sense, doctor and patient progressively co-construct and realize this sequence of questions as embodying a "checklist" of routine questions dealing with background or "face-sheet" data" (Boyd & Heritage 2006: 170). With these widely utilized social conventions for medical communication evident as well in our data, we cannot ignore the impact such conventions have on the nature of MELF communication, and in particular the role they play in pushing back against the transitory features said to characterize ELF interaction.

While the constraints of the structured interview orientation serve to introduce another regulatory process into the variable and emergent nature of ELF in other domains, this orientation of medical communication is of course not unique to MELF contexts.

Boyd and Heritage (2006: 164) identify two primary features of medical history-taking question sequences which enable a particular kind of social relationship between healthcare professional and patient. In the principle of optimization, physician questions orient toward "best case" or "no problem" answers. When Nurse B asks Ragia and Roz about their parents (turn 47), she does so in a way that is preferential toward a positive answer: *your father and mother, they are alive*? Presumably, she could also have posed the question as: *your father and mother, they are dead*? Structuring questions in a manner that presupposes a positive outcome has been observed to be characteristic of physicians' history-taking procedures in ENL contexts, and it is noteworthy that Nurse B, an ELF user, does so as well. This observation points again toward the important role that constraints of a socially prescribed activity type play in regulating the features of MELF communication.

The principle of recipient design, seminally articulated by Sacks and colleagues (1974: 727) describes the "multitude of respects in which the talk by a party in a conversation is constructed or designed in ways which display and orientation and sensitivity to the particular other(s) who are the coparticipants". In a different simulation session of the same Cerebrovascular Accident home visit scenario, a nurse with L1 Malayalam directs an opening question about the patient to the patient's sister.

Excerpt ST-SIM2
21   Nurse (L1 Malayalam):   She can talk
22   Patient's sister (L1 Arabic): She can talk slowly yes

| 23 | Nurse: | Slowly |
| 24 | Patient (L1 Arabic): | I can talk |

Given the context of the home visit (a stroke), it might have been seen as rude, insensitive or even mildly confrontive to ask the patient directly whether she was able to talk. Nurse attempts to navigate this potentially awkward situation by instead directing her question to the patient's sister. Nurse's use of reformulated playback (*slowly*) then leads to a contribution from the patient herself (*I can talk*). In addition to the principle of recipient design evidenced here, we also note the optimization orientation of the question: *she can talk* structures the query toward a "best case" scenario, rather than the alternative (*she cannot talk*). In considering the claim that ELF is in essence emergent and transitory, it is of salience that both features of a medical history-taking, previously identified in ENL settings, occur in MELF contexts as well.

Application of plain language in patient self-monitoring instructions

Before plain language review	After plain language review
You can self-monitor by observing any of the following signs that persist for 2 weeks or more: - Unintentional weight loss - Persistent cough - Hematochezia - Hematuria - Profound fatigue	Report these signs to your oncologist (cancer doctor) if they last 2 weeks or more: - Unplanned weight loss of more than 10 pounds - Cough that won't go away - Blood in urine (pee) or stool (poo) - New fatigue (feeling very tired)

Adapted from Warde et al, 2018, p. e54.

5.4 Sociocognitive approach (SCA)

In Kecskes' (2003; 2008) sociocognitive approach (SCA), the Dynamic Model of Meaning (DMM) posits that interlocutors draw upon both prior and current contexts for communicative understanding (see the extended discussion of SCA in Chapter 2). The prior context utilizes inner, private, previously acquired knowledge (termed *salience*) to put forward and grasp meaning as the conversation unfolds. Consider the following exchange, an opening to a health assessment, between Nurse Silke and her patient.

Excerpt RE-SIM2
11 Nurse Silke (L1 Malayalam): Okay. I am Silke? I am your assigned nurse today, I would like to take, uh, some history about you like your uh, related to your health? and uh, ah, your day to day activities in [inaudible] care in the hospital. Okay?
12 Patient: (L1 English): Okay
13 Silke: So, I'm here, going to do some investigation so I'm just gonna um, take an examinations and, uh, assessment as well. Is it fine with you
14 Patient: Yes please
15 Silke: Okay. The door is closed to maintain the privacy. Okay? Let's start. [inaudible] to document or as something in between
16 Patient: Okay

A patient admitted to the hospital, as is the context of this extract, likely fully expects to be examined and assessed by a nurse. Nurse Silke initially identifies the purpose of the discussion (*take some history about you related to your health and your day to day activities*), and then specifies her planned activities (*take an examinations*; *assessment as well*); after which, she requests the Patient's consent (*is it fine with you*). The Patient's addition of *please* to his affirmative response to the response to the query regarding consent is interesting: he could have opted to simply reply in the affirmative as was the case in turn 12. *Yes please* may indicate an urgency to be examined; perhaps expressing irony, as in *What else would I expect when in a hospital?*; or may be voicing annoyance for a long wait to see the nurse, as in <u>Finally</u> *you're beginning the examination! I've had to wait so long!*; or perhaps connotes cynicism about the nurse's competency; or may be expressing politeness. We note also Silke's statement that *the door is closed to maintain the privacy* before proceeding with the assessment.

Whatever the reason for the Patient's choice of *yes please* (turn 14), or for Nurse Silke's question regarding consent (turn 13), or her remark regarding the reason for a closed door (turn 15), we see here the inner, private worlds of both interlocutors brought to bear in the opening moments of the encounter. Nurse Silke may be asking for permission to perform the examination, and explaining that *the door is closed to maintain the privacy* because these preliminaries are hospital policy; or because she believes they are central to patient-centred care; or because she has had negative prior experiences on matters of consent and privacy with patients; or any number of other reasons unknown to us as listeners. The Patient's addition of *please* to his affirmative consent similarly draws upon an inner world to which we are not privy. However, in this instance, the attempts at salience by either interlocutor do not prove central to meaning-making, and the examination proceeds.

Further on in this same encounter, Nurse Silke asks a question regarding the patient's diet, using a term more common in medical language – *diet pattern* – (e.g., Hu et al. 2016) than might be used in everyday speech.

31	Nurse Silke:	Okay. Then, what is your diet pattern? Diet pattern.
32	Patient:	Diet pattern? I think I eat pretty well. I drink lots of water, balanced diet, fruits and vegetables.
33	Silke:	Okay?
34	Patient:	Lots of protein.
35	Silke:	Okay. So, are you able to walk steady?

Perhaps anticipating the potential of unfamiliarity with this term, Nurse Silke utilizes repetition (*then what is your diet pattern? Diet pattern*). The Patient uses rising intonation to indicate temporary confusion about the term, but without waiting for clarification on its meaning, proceeds to draw upon prior knowledge of expectations surrounding what a health professional might want to know about one's eating, and lists several features of his diet (*eat pretty well*; *drink lots of water*; *balanced diet*; *fruits and vegetables*). Nurse Silke acknowledges this list without asking for additional information (*Okay*), but the Patient adds, unsolicited, an additional piece of information (*lots of protein*), again likely drawing upon the inner, private world of salience as described in SCA to infer the type of information likely to be requested in this context. Silke acknowledges the additional item, then changes the subject to proceed with the next phase of the health assessment.

5.4.1 Healthcare providers and linguistic home territory

A MELF encounter, viewed through the lens of an SCA approach (Kecskes 2014; 2010; Kecskes & Zhang 2009), focuses particularly on the search for core common ground. As discussed previously (see Chapter 2.4), core common ground comprises three sub-characteristics: common sense (general knowledge); cultural sense (general knowledge about a particular set of cultural norms, behaviours, expectations, etc.); and formal sense (general knowledge about the language system being used). Bigi and Rossi assert that it is the cultural and formal senses which "seem to be the critical dimensions that may contribute to generating the worst misunderstandings in multilingual communication, or to presenting interpreters and mediators with the biggest challenges" (2020: 28).

An SCA approach posits that given the inherently egocentric nature of communication, speakers begin an exchange by selecting the linguistic resources most readily available to them, and it is only afterward that they rely on the actual context for verification of meaning (Bigi & Rossi 2020). Speaking specifically of physicians in the context of a medical interview, the process is described as follows.

> it is likely that, acting within such a socially well-defined and structured context, doctors are inclined to take for granted the mind-set, knowledge, procedures and requirements of the context itself. These are primarily expressed through language use, be it the use of technical terms (e.g., glycemic values, instead of blood sugar) or of formulaic language (e.g., the habit of using acronyms). When in the exercise of their professional practice, doctors are in their 'territory' and it is likely that they lose awareness of how distant it is from their patients' 'land of origin'. (Bigi & Rossi 2020: 30)

Nurse Silke, at home in her "territory" as a healthcare professional, uses a more medically oriented term (*diet pattern*), and what appears to be formulaic language (*door is closed to maintain the privacy*). Disambiguation follows only when an interlocutor signals non-understanding, and in this instance, the Patient did not wait for his signal (*diet pattern*?) to be verified, nor did Nurse Silke presumably deem his answer off-point.

In this sense, effective medical communication relies heavily on the patient, despite being from a different "land of origin". Consider the following extract from another health assessment simulation.

Extract RE-SIM7

102	Nurse (L1 Malayalam):	Can you take deep breath? Okay. Okay. So, uh, you have, uh, tactile fremitus is, uh, bilateral and symmetric and you have, uh, sym= bilateral, symmetrical chest expansion, also. That is normal and great. Then, I will do the, uh, percussion on you.
103	Patient (L1 English):	Okay.
108	Nurse (L1 Malayalam):	Here also on the lungs side, lungs part I got the resonant sound? And, uh, the right side is your liver, so there is dullness. And on the left side is your stomach, that is tympany, all good.
109	Patient:	Okay.

5.4 Sociocognitive approach (SCA) — 149

As she proceeds through the assessment, Nurse on several occasions seems to "think aloud" her findings, using biomedical language, with minimal or no explanatory comment. Her patient's response (*okay*) does not explicitly reference understanding of the medical terminology (e.g., *tactile fremitus*; *percussion*; *tympany*); it is therefore unclear whether the patient's *okay* in turn 103 is an indication of consent to the percussion procedure, or a response to the *normal and great* finding (turn 102). Similarly, it is not clear whether the *okay* in turn 109 indicates the patient's comprehension of *resonant sound*, *dullness* and/or *tympany* and the Nurse's interpretation of those findings, or is simply a response to the *all good* conclusion.

As the interaction draws to a close, Nurse summarizes the findings of her assessment, again utilizing technical language familiar to her home "territory" as a healthcare professional.

117	Nurse:	When I auscultated, the right side, I got the, uh, normal vesicular on the lungs, right side. On the vesicular sound on the peripheral, uh, peripheral lungs. And on the trachea, I got the, um, bronchial sound. And on the lung side, I got the bronchovesicular, and the peripheral side, I got the vesicular sounds. Okay. Now, I have completed the respiratory assessment for you. Anything more you want to, so- anything more you want to, uh, you want me to tell?
118	Patient:	Yes, was, was it the results normal? Or was there [crosstalk 00:13:59]
119	Nurse:	Yeah, the results are within normal range, and that's why doctor has told you, told that there is that you can go home by tomorrow.
120	Patient:	Yes.

At Nurse's invitation for her patient to request further information (*anything more . . . you want me to tell*), the patient asks whether the results of the assessments were normal. Nurse responds to this query with further biomedical formulaic language (*the results are within normal range*). The patient's *yes* seems to signal understanding of the link between the results of the assessment and his impending discharge from hospital.

In medical encounters where the "distance travelled" between a patient's "land of origin" and the healthcare professional's "territory" may be considerable, the onus is often on the patient to signal non-understanding. As the Nurse draws upon her inner, private world for the most readily accessible linguistic resources (the biomedical descriptions of respiratory assessment findings), it falls upon the patient to initiate clarification processes. In the constraints of the medical interview as an activity type, the asymmetry of relations in medical consultations (Irwin & Richardson 2006), and the practical realities of time pressures upon successful clinical communication (Hemsley, Balandin & Worrall 2012), the patient may opt to seek only – as it appears the patient in this instance does – the "bottom line" of the assessment (*was it the results normal?*). Such constraints are not unique to MELF, but it is not difficult to see how attempts at salience may be additionally challenged when ELF interlocutors differ in formal and cultural senses of common communicative ground.

5.4.2 Biomedical think aloud and common communicative ground

We note throughout our data a propensity for healthcare professionals to select clinical language as the go-to, default starting point in salience. The following extracts illustrate how medical language appears to be the most readily available linguistic resource upon which nurses draw as they communicate with their patients.

Extract NE-SIM1B

51	Patient (L1 Malayalam):	And I think I'm taking also, anti-platelet, Coumadin.
52	Nurse (L1 Malayalam):	Coumadin also.
53	Patient:	Yes.
54	Nurse:	This all once daily you are taking or uh, variated?
55	Patient:	What?
56	Nurse:	Uh how frequent you are taking this medicine.

Extract NE-SIM3B

| 117 | Nurse (L1 Malayalam): | Okay. So her GCS is here, she's eyes opening spontaneously. It is full, and she is oriented and obeying my commands. Her GCS is 15 out of 15, and her . . . she's oriented to time, place, and person. Now I will go to your pupillary reaction. So for you, I will just check your pupillary reaction. So just, uh, can you look at my? (.) Okay. So I will ch= I will check your pupillary reaction to the light. ↓Okay. So just, uh . . . Uh, her pupils are constricting to light. Can you |

just, uh . . . I will just move to . . . near to you. Just look at this, uh, pentose. Okay? Okay. Her accommodation is normal. For the pupils are bilaterally equal to in size and the consa= and reacting to light and accommodation is normal. Now we will check your motor state. Okay? I will check the strength of your body. So I will check your upper . . . upper extremity strength. For (.) that, I will give you my two fingers. You are to grasp strongly. Okay? Grasp. Okay. Okay. Now both hand . . . this one. Okay. Can you grasp tighter? Okay.

Extract RE-SIM1C

31	Nurse (L1 Malayalam):	Okay what about the food patterns?
32	Patient (L1 English):	Umm food patterns. You mean uh my diet?
33	Nurse:	Yeah. You are you vegetarian or non-vegetarian?
34	Patient:	Um, yeah, I, uh, non-veg, yes.
35	Nurse:	Oh non-veg?
36	Patient:	Both yeah
37	Nurse:	You are a absolutely are a nutrition good. Okay okay what's your name?

Extract NE-SIM4B

19	Patient L1 Malayalam):	I have a stroke three days ago, my thumb with my
20	Nurse Mally (L1 Malayalam):	When it start?
21	Patient:	Three days ago, I've been here for three days now.
22	Mally:	Okay. Is it worse with any activity or is it worse with uh, any other um, associated problems?
23	Patient:	Yeah, when I uh um, doing some stuff it's worse on this side.
24	Mally:	Is it radiating to any other uh, places?
25	Patient:	No just this side.

In the first extract and third extract, the nurses' use of a more clinical term prompts signals of non-understanding from the patients: (*variated* prompts the response *what,* followed by a reformulation; *food patterns* prompts a clarification question: *you mean my diet?*) In contrast, in NE-SIM4B, the patient appears to understand the use of *associated problems* (response: *Yeah when I . . . doing some stuff it's worse on this side*) and whether these problems were *radiating to any other . . . places* (response: *No just this side*).

In NE-SIM3B, we see the "biomedical think aloud" phenomenon, where the nurse verbalizes her findings using biomedical language as the assessment proceeds. In this instance, the nurse alternates between descriptions of the patient in the third person (e.g., *her GCS[10] is fifteen out of fifteen; she's oriented to time place and person; her accommodation is normal*) and addressing the patient directly in instructions and explanations (*I will check your pupillary reaction to the light; now we will check your motor state; you are to grasp strongly*). This biomedical think aloud may well be of value to the medical professional: for example, perhaps as a means of self-assurance that all items in an assessment list have been checked off, or perhaps to demonstrate to the patient the nurse's expertise and authority. But it is not *communication* as such; in that the nurse speaks in the third person, only uses personal pronouns when asking the patient directly for a response, and the patient's understanding or non-understanding of the utterance content seems entirely inconsequential. To illustrate, we imagine an airline pilot verbalizing the technical pre-takeoff checklist to cabin passengers over the airplane's public address system; while it might reassure passengers that procedures are being followed, as a vehicle for communication it would be of little value. Most passengers will likely not comprehend the technical language, and in fact passengers' comprehension or non-comprehension is irrelevant to carrying out the procedures.

While acknowledging the utility of the biomedical think aloud phenomenon from the standpoint of the healthcare professional, it may also serve to inaccurately frame the information. In the following extract, Nurse Ruth reformulates the Patient's response, presumably to fit a biomedical assessment checklist, in a way that may inaccurately reflect the original utterance.

Extract NE-SIM6
44 Nurse Ruth (L1 Kannada):   May I know your daily routine food habits?
45 Patient (L1 English):   My daily routine. Uh, up in the morning, have cereal. My wife goes to work, we have a coffee.
46 Ruth: Okay.

---

[10] GCS – Glasgow Coma Scale: a protocol standard for assessing a patient's level of consciousness. A score of 15 is considered normal. See Durant and Sporer (2011).

47	Patient:	Um, she's at work all day, I'm retired. So, I, I have a lunch. Um, and I watch some TV. I'll, I'll, uh, call my children on Skype, or on computer at home.
48	Ruth:	Okay.
49	Patient:	Then I make dinner. Wait for my wife to come home.
50	Ruth:	So, your food habit is regular. And may I know your weight, please?

Nurse Ruth's query in turn 44 seems to be asking either for daily nutrition patterns (as in Extract RE-SIM1, above), considered an essential component of nursing health assessment (Jensen, 2018), or to discern the regularity of meals. The Patient's responses, however, would seem to indicate an interpretation which combined the two ideas: *daily routine* and *food habits*. Turn 45 begins with a partial repetition (*my daily routine*), and then goes on to recount daily activities (*watch TV*; *call my children on Skype*; *make dinner*; *wait for my wife to come home*), and to a lesser extent what he actually eats (*have cereal*; *have a coffee*). To this Ruth summarizes, *so your food habit is regular*, and moves on to the next portion of the assessment.

If Nurse Ruth is attempting to gage whether the Patient was eating regular meals, her question can be considered successful. If she is seeking to understand whether her Patient is eating nutritionally, this portion of the health assessment remains incomplete. Given the importance of nutrition evaluation in the overall health assessment process (Jensen 2018), the imprecise expression *daily routine food habits* leads to the interlocutors "talking past each other" (Roberts et al. 2005: 470), with the Patient recounting both daily routines and food habits. In any case, the point we raise here is Nurse Ruth's use of what appears to be another example of a biomedical think aloud summary to close this phase of the Patient interview, without expectation of a patient response (*so your food habit is regular*), yet with a non-understanding reframe.

While we considered the "pedagogical effect" as a potential cause for this (over)use of biomedical language, we noted in a previous chapter how a number of factors present in the simulation environment serve to significantly reduce the impact of this effect. In fact, the explicitly stated learning goals of patient-centred communication ought to have the opposite outcome: we would anticipate much *less* use of biomedical language with nurses aware they were being evaluated on therapeutic communication. In Chapter 3, we noted as well that the pedagogical effect would be further diminished by well-coached standardized patients; experienced nurses; and high-fidelity simulations which effectively mimicked real-world clinical settings.

5.5 Summary

We have considered here how the health assessment as activity type impacts upon ELF interaction, and how even within the limits this activity type places upon participants' turns, MELF interlocutors employ strategies for effective nursing communication. At the same time, the search for common communicative ground among interlocutors is often carried out in the context of nurses' "biomedical think alouds", which appear to serve as the primary starting point in efforts at salience. While perhaps of use to the healthcare provider, such strategies were not seen to enhance nurse-patient communication. The constraints of a health assessment activity type as brought to bear upon ELF interactions, again draw our attention to the distinctions between MELF communication and ELF in general. The dynamic transitory nature of interactions said to characterize ELF is brought into sharp relief when contrasted with the more prescribed and static character of MELF, impacted as it is by the constraints of activity type.

Chapter 6
Implications and conclusion: Healthcare education in MELF contexts

Chapter key points:
- Effective use of communication strategies identified in other domains of ELF are critically important in MELF.
- Language support to prepare MELF users for healthcare communication in contact zones of global mobility includes the ability to navigate exonormative medical language norms.
- Multimodal communication is an important dimension in the meaning-making resources of MELF users and is largely overlooked in ESP instruction.
- Integrated language instruction for MELF users draws upon, but also extends and transcends, traditional aural skills pedagogy as utilized in ESP.

6.1 Introduction

We have thus far conceptualized MELF from various micro- and macro-levels, attempting to understand the phenomenon from analysis of discussional turns between healthcare providers and patients, from its place within the broader context of healthcare communication in general, and from consideration of the larger social and linguistic context in which our observations are set. From a macro-perspective, the notion of community of practice was demonstrated to be particularly appropriate for examining the language practices of healthcare professionals, and the environment of the Gulf Cooperation Council nations (GCC) especially so. The language diversity of Qatar, accompanied by the escalated disruption of linguistic norms characteristic in a migrant destination, were seen to set the context for new degrees of linguacultural accommodation. At a micro-level, interactions between healthcare providers and their patients were viewed through the search for the common ground of co-constructed meaning, where socially framed expectations for conversational turns were seen to exert powerful influence on language use. Throughout the book, we have asserted that the conditions under which MELF interactions typically take place serve to distinguish it in several important ways from other domains where ELF has been studied to date.

In this chapter, we will attempt to weave all of these perspectives together, in order to arrive at some implications of our exploratory micro-/macro-level conceptualization of medical English as a lingua franca. We do so tentatively, for several reasons; not the least of which is that we acknowledge the preliminary nature of our inquiry, conducted as it is in a specific setting, with a particular set of data – a limitation common to all social research. There is also the challenge of drawing upon conceptual and methodological pluralism for our inquiry and the attendant difficulty of integrating those diverse perspectives, a limitation we have attempted to acknowledge throughout this volume. We speak tentatively as well in our unenviable position of outsiders (De Four-Babb, Pegg & Beck 2015) to the academic space of both ELF and healthcare communication. As outsiders to healthcare specifically, we are keenly aware of medicine's infamous "antipathy toward attempts by others outside the profession to improve practice" (Leape & Berwick 2005: 2387). Yet, outcomes of healthcare research, at least in principle, should be applied to improving health and to improving healthcare policy (Saks & Allsop 2019). As mentioned at the beginning of this book, our interest in healthcare communication lies not only in our professional interests, but as healthcare "users" and "consumers" (Saks & Allsop 2019: 7–9): as patients seeking quality care. It is from this perspective ultimately that we proffer the exploratory implications arising from our research. However, these personal interests intersect with our professional lives as language teachers, so we would be remiss if we did not include the implications for language instruction practices that prepare healthcare professionals to work in MELF environments.

We have organized our discussion in this chapter as follows. First, we briefly review the social context of our study, and its role in shaping language use of MELF users in our data – an important backdrop to the discussion of pedagogical implications which are to follow. The chapter then makes a case for the important role language use plays in quality healthcare and patient safety, and asserts the contrarian perspective that mobile translingual practices may, in the case of MELF, require more, not less, recognition of external norms. We then consider the intersection between simulation training, subject content from healthcare disciplines, and English language support courses, particularly with respect to multimodal communicative resources. Drawing upon a typology of approaches to classroom listening (Rost 2016), we propose a number of implications for language classrooms which support effective healthcare communication. Finally, we offer some hopeful possibilities for the contribution of medical ELF to the broader work of healthcare communication research.

6.2 Social context and language use

As we began to conceptualize MELF as it is utilized in our research setting, it became increasingly clear to us that we could not understand individual nurse-nurse or nurse-patient conversations in isolation from the broader social, linguistic and occupational context of the GCC. In the confluence of ethnic, linguistic and cultural influences which is Qatar and its Gulf Cooperation Council neighbours, and along with it an expatriate labour force whom in many cases share living quarters with workplace colleagues, conditions are set for both the sustained mutual engagement of a CoP, and thus the degree of ELF contact, to be both heightened and intensified. A Sri Lankan nurse attends a training event at her GCC clinic with a colleague from the Philippines, with whom she also shares accommodation, provided by their host country's Ministry of Health as part of the compensation package. Their Tanzanian colleague, who works as a surgical assistant at a different clinic, shares the same living quarters, and the three of them later that day discuss potential implications of the new Ministry policies presented during the training. We discussed previously (see Chapter 2.5) social network theory as a lens through which to view the impact of such conditions on language use in MELF.

The nurses in the simulation trainings, whose utterances form part of the data for our exploration of medical ELF, enrol in the institution either from, or while still a part of, an environment where lines of separation between work and home are blurred, or even non-existent. Mann (2011: 64) describes medical training where "learners are being socialised as they learn", and for many of the nurse learners in our research context, exceptionally so.

The nurses' "sustained mutual relationships", heightened by the blurred work-home environment – doubtless including elements which are "harmonious or conflictual" – provide fertile ground for other CoP characteristics described by Wenger (Wenger 1998: 125–126), and in particular those features related to language (see Chapter 2.3). An "absence of introductory preambles, as if conversations and interactions were merely the continuation of an ongoing process" are inevitable in this context, as are the development of "local lore, shared stories, inside jokes, knowing laughter". Their profession is infamous for its use of "jargon and shortcuts to communication", and these are reinforced and further refined through the course of their nursing studies. All of these elements are brought to bear on the nurses' ELF interactions and cannot but impact the very nature of the linguistic forms which emerge and are reinforced through sustained, intensified usage.

Healthcare education researchers Cruess et al assert that medicine has always functioned as a community of practice (2018: 185). Cruess and colleagues find in the training and post-training work of physicians clear examples of the specified domain; strong sense of community; and practice of specialized skills, all said to be characteristic of a CoP (cf. Snyder & Wenger 2004). The work of nurses has also been variously described through the lens of a CoP framework (Seibert 2015). Andrew and Ferguson, for example, describe a CoP context for nursing development mirroring what we observe in many GCC healthcare environments: "a combination of social engagement and collaborative working in an authentic environment" with "skills and talents of like and unlike diverse populations . . . harnessed to challenge and develop professional practice" (2008: 1; 12). In attempting to define a healthcare CoP with reference specifically to nursing, Seibert highlights the central role of community, "distinguished by relationships and interactions" as well as "meaningful, sustained relationships and shared ways of engaging" (2015: 71). The centrality of social dimensions for community are underscored by other nursing researchers who draw upon a CoP framework, and who emphasize the role of social activities, effective communication, interdependence, trust and the like in establishing and maintaining these meaningful relationships and interactions (e.g., Thrysoe et al. 2012; Thrysoe et al. 2010; Andrew et al. 2009; Andrew & Ferguson 2008; White et al. 2008).

It is within this framework, of linguistic norms shaped by the sustained engagement with a larger professional community, that we turn to the implications of our exploratory findings of MELF.

Communication textbooks exhort doctors to encourage more talk and to listen better, but such prescriptions are modelled on monolingual, mono-cultural consultations, where ordinary talk itself is not the problem (Roberts et al. 2005: 74).

6.3 Language matters: Implications for patient safety

A first and primary implication is the obvious reality that language *matters*. Claims that language barriers of "foreign" healthcare professionals may cause harm to patients makes for attention-grabbing headlines in popular media, and so seem to regularly recycle through news reports, and make their way into speeches of populist politicians. A headline like "EU doctor suspended from UK work for 'poor English test'" (BBC News 2015), or "Drug doses lost in translation" (Bladd 2008) not only make good press copy, but can be used by political leaders to defend one's point of view on lowered immigration quotas, or on Brexit, or to press for more funded places for local graduates in medical schools, or any number of other political intentions.

We have consistently maintained a non-alarmist perspective in this volume. Our findings indicate that by and large, ELF healthcare professionals effectively manage medical communication across lingua-cultures, through multiple accommodation strategies, and within a larger social context through which such accommodation strategies are fostered and supported.

And yet, language does matter. As we have shown, in the relatively few instances where ELF healthcare miscommunication did occur, it did so in areas of critical importance to patient health: in potential adverse drug events, in lexical ambiguity leading to missed diagnoses, and in extended hospital stays.

We return here to an instance in our initial exploration (Tweedie & Johnson 2018a; 2018b) where practicing nurses were recorded discussing the condition of an elderly patient (pulmonary edema) during a shift handover. Nurse A, attempting to articulate the patient's increasing disorientation, says, *he's feeling funny* and *I wonder maybe he's crazy, something, he's telling that way*. In sharp contrast, Nurse A had begun the shift handover report with the formulaic phrase *responding well*.

When asked to consider the role specifically of language use in this recorded patient handover, senior nursing instructors expressed alarm about the lexical imprecision of these terms, particularly given the disorientation associated with rising potassium levels, as indicated by the patient's lab reports. As one instructor put it:

> *you know,* funny, *what does that really mean, you know, is he unconscious you know is he responding to verbal commands, to painful stimuli, like all those impact patient care. And she did mention that the potassium was high, so that would lead me to believe that these were more serious concerns than acting* funny. *And that nursing other nursing intervention should be taken immediately, instead of just you know making a referral at some point in time.*
>
> (filler words removed)

Some critics of ELF research have noted a tendency to over-interpret communication as successful, with misunderstandings infrequent or inconsequential, and thus downplaying the potential for miscommunication. Mackenzie (2014: 140–141) describes this propensity:

> There is never the slightest suggestion that ELF speakers, like users of any other language, might range from the enviably articulate, co-operative and successful to the alarmingly inarticulate, unpleasant and inept. Despite the occasional reference to code-switching, there is hardly any acknowledgement that ELF users' English might be in any way wanting, not allowing them to express everything they wish to say, even though most bilingualism researchers stress that few bi- or multilinguals speak all their languages equally well, or use them for all domains of life, and so might easily have lexical gaps in many fields.

In this case, Nurse A (a postdiploma student who was already a practicing nurse in GCC hospitals) encountered a patient with rising potassium levels, accompanied by a growing *disorientation* or perhaps *delirium*, precise terms which she seemed unable to access in communicating to the nurse coming on-shift. Undetected disorientation, particularly in elderly patients like this one, can have life-threatening consequences (Brich et al. 2019).

We make no claim that such medical errors are unique to MELF users. Indeed, missed diagnoses of delirium appear unsettlingly prevalent (Barron & Holmes 2013), even without adding language barriers. We do however assert that ELF adds another layer of complexity to the process of medical communication, and one to which patient safety demands attention be paid. For the most part, our observation of MELF communication aligns with that of Firth's (2009: 149) summary of ELF research: "typically characterized by a high degree of interactional robustness, co-operation, consensus-seeking behavior and affiliation, and that explicit and overt miscommunications are rare, despite variance in language form and proficiency". Yet, the high-stakes nature of MELF communication can make even "rare" "explicit and overt miscommunications" of dire consequence. This particular simulation enacted a shift handover, an event of particular risk: the transfer or hand-off of patients may account for 80 percent of all preventable adverse medical events (Frankel et al. 2012).

6.3.1 Language errors in ELF and MELF

As instructors of English for Specific Purposes, preparing ELF users to deliver healthcare services in a multilingual environment, we are caught in a bind. On the one hand, we affirm an ELF view, drawn from both Complexity Theory and translanguaging perspectives, on the correction of (so-called) language errors. On the other hand, as shown in the example above, an ELF users' linguistic resource (in this case, inadequate range of expression) may impact the delivery of safe and effective healthcare. As Mackenzie asks, "what is the poor English teacher to do?" (2014: 165).

A translanguaging perspective as enacted in ELF rejects the traditional notion of "error" as deviation from a central set of standard and codified native speaker norms. As Horner and colleagues articulated in advocating a translingual approach, differences in language ought to be seen "not as a barrier to overcome or as a problem to manage, but as a resource for producing meaning" (2011: 303). Such approaches do not preclude attention to language conventions as such, but rather challenge the notion that they should be taken only at face value. A translanguaging perspective advocates a pedagogy which no longer focuses on identifying errors which deviate from a prescribed native speaker variety, but embracing a linguistic diversity which will help to "prepare students for new challenges of the increased global mobility and contact zone interactions" (Kimura & Canagarajah 2018: 304).

However, as in the case of MELF, what if part of preparing our students for "increased global mobility and contact zone interactions" involves *more*, not less, attention to language conventions? The nursing instructors commenting on the shift report described above suggested several biomedical formulaic terms which might have been helpful in preventing the potentially lethal outcome of Nurse A's missed diagnosis: *disorientation*; *delirium*; *responding to verbal commands*; *responding to stimuli*. Each of these terms may serve to activate a schema of professional knowledge in Nurse B (the incoming shift nurse, recipient of the patient handover), and thus provide an opportunity for appropriate and timely nursing intervention.

We embrace the linguistic innovation and creativity of ELF users, fostered by the intensified global mobility and zones of language contact which translanguaging perspectives so aptly describe. We have absolutely no interest in promoting English as *the* global language of healthcare delivery. In fact, we find an incongruence in the fact that healthcare across the GCC is often delivered in English when many of its patients have Arabic as a first language. We similarly reject the notion that errors are simply divergences from idealised native speaker norms. But in the language classroom, where we are at work preparing healthcare professionals to be effective ELF users in a linguistically diverse setting, we find our ideals challenged daily by several realities. First, linguistic innovation, if not aligned with precision communication, can have fatal outcomes in healthcare contexts. Second, the leadership of some Gulf Cooperation Council countries *choose*, for a variety of reasons, to utilize English as the language of healthcare education and delivery. Third, the Nepali radiographer and her Qatari patient find themselves in a situation where English is the only available communicative option. Fourth, our learners express a desire to add medical English to their multilingual repertoire. In light of realities such as these, we reformulate Mackenzie's (2014: 165) question slightly: What is a poor content-based English language teacher to do?

Similarly, an ELF perspective drawing upon Complexity Theory, with its understanding of language as a complex adaptive system, asserts that "there should be no one usage that is universally privileged, independent of purpose and audience" (Larsen-Freeman 2018: 55). Errors by ELF users, then, given that they occur by definition in multilingual contexts, may not be errors at all: "what appears to be an error from a monolingual English point of view may, in fact, be an innovation from a multilingual point of view" (Larsen-Freeman 2018: 56). We agree. Yet, in Chapter 4 we recounted an unsuccessful instance of communication regarding a patient's medication, a high-risk activity given the adverse effects of drug-to-drug interactions and other consequences (Bohand et al. 2009). The nurse's question *Can you tell me which of medicine you are taking* does not align with the question form usage of many monolingual English speakers. In the multilingual discussion between the ELF users in this instance, researchers may classify this as an innovative question form. But whether an error or an innovation, the nurse's utterance and subsequent ones did not have the necessary communicative effect: maintaining patient safety. Patient safety considerations required her to find out *how much* of *which* medication each day at *which* times. Whether from a multilingual point of view or a monolingual one, most observers would agree that the failure to establish this constitutes a communicative error. As language teachers of ESP, our priority is not "correcting" this nurse's question form to more closely align with Inner Circle usages, but to helping her avoid one or more "wrong patient, wrong diagnosis, wrong drug, wrong dose, wrong delivery, wrong timing" medication errors (Hudson & Guchelaar 2003: 1010).

The postmodern epistemology which underlies translingual orientations de-emphasize traditional fixed communities in light of the mobility characterizing today's world, transcending fixed geographical boundaries (Blommaert 2010; Pennycook 2012; Canagarajah 2013). In zones of contact (Pratt 1991) where globally mobile populations assemble, diverse groups of languages and cultures intersect, developing new communication norms and means. Indeed, a hallmark of a translingual orientation is the recognition that competence, rather than ability to adhere to a standard set of linguistic norms, is inherently performative in nature (Kimura & Canagarajah 2018), dependent in its entirety on the requirements of the communicative circumstance.

From a pedagogical perspective, fostering learners' competency for communication in zones of contact involves helping students understand "linguistic norms are ideological constructs that are fluid and negotiable" (Kimura & Canagarajah 2018: 304). Translingual pedagogical practices therefore aim to prepare learners for effectively navigating these diverse environments, as opposed to modelling and teaching adherence to norms of an established community.

But what if preparing learners for global mobility and effective interaction in contact zones actually *does* involve readying them for precise adherence to prescribed norms? To formulaic biomedical language? To internationally promoted health mnemonics and accompanying terms, and prescribed language for healthcare record-keeping? Here we admit a struggle to integrate translingual ideologies with the daily reality of preparing learners for the precise communicative requirements of medical ELF. We have no objection in principle to naming (and shaming) ideological constructs that pervade our content-based language for nursing curriculum. For example, perhaps we could devote classroom time to a discussion of why the World Health Organization issues its publications in only six "official" languages. Or, we might ask our learners to identify political considerations underlying healthcare delivery through English in countries where other languages are much more widely understood. Some of our learners openly express a desire to work as nurses in Europe or North America, so we might as a class discuss some of the ethical issues of healthcare migration, and how language ideologies undergird international recruitment and licensure. As a matter of *practice* though, our language support curriculum is crowded with eye-watering amounts of medical language to align with nursing content instructors' lectures, readings, learning tasks, and assessments. It is difficult in practical terms to find the time to incorporate "critical linguistics for nurses" lessons into the already limited classroom time. Plus, our learners seem far less interested in challenging language norms at the ideological level than in learning how to provide practical care to the suffering. To our learners, being prepared for a mobile world and its zones of contact means mastering external language norms, where the ability to adequately perform in these may be a matter of life and death. And they demand us as language teachers to provide direct instruction in these *so that* they are well prepared to function in the zones of contact in a globalized, mobile world.

At times, this means pointing out language "errors" to our learners, which may in some respects put MELF at cross-purposes with ELF theory. Identifying errors is not because we ideologically privilege a certain usage over another, but because the communicative situation (safe and effective healthcare delivery) requires it.

ELF research has tended to view what may be lexical gaps in terms of innovation and creativity. Identifying an "error" is described as "not a particularly ELF-compatible way of thinking about language" (Cogo & Dewey 2012: 78). Semantic approximations (e.g., Hülmbauer 2009) or creative innovations (e.g., Pitzl 2018) are more positive ways to express ELF usage that differs from others'. Hülmbauer rightly points out that semantic approximation may be of communicative benefit in contexts where ELF users share a similar language origin, an assertion born out in an autoethnographic account of MELF intraprofessional communication (Botis & Tweedie: in press).

However, as mobile multilinguals ourselves, we are keenly aware from our own experience that there is such a thing as a lexical gap. In describing lexical resources across different varieties of English, Meierkord states what to us is an obvious reality of our own multilingual repertoires: "Characteristically, a learner's lexicon contains gaps, the sizes of which vary according to the stage of second language acquisition which the learner has reached" (Meierkord 2005: 93). A nurse's inability to access the medical term *delirium* in a shift handover report may produce an attempt at semantic approximation (Hülmbauer 2009); a word transferred in some fashion from her L1 (Pitzl 2012); code-meshing (Canagarajah 2006); an example of a "less deeply entrenched memory representation" (Mauranen 2012: 37); or a demonstration of one of her multimodal "resources for producing meaning" (Kimura & Canagarajah 2018: 297). We have no misgivings about any of these descriptions as potential causes, but as language instructors preparing her for precision medical communication, we must also consider the possibility that her unsuccessful attempt to substitute *funny* or *crazy* for *delirium* represents a lexical gap, which, left unaddressed, may leave her unable to meet the communicative requirements of future MELF interactions, which, unfortunately, can entail life-threatening consequences.

It must be acknowledged that the analyst's interpretation of an utterance or conversation forms an important piece in the resultant description. According to Mackenzie:

> It is all too rarely acknowledged in ELF research that what can be described, when seen from one angle, as the active, skillful, innovative, creative and resourceful adapting, blending, manipulating, reshaping and co-constructing of lexico-grammatical and pragmatic forms and speakers' linguistic resources to produce localized repertoires can also be reasonably analysed in terms of a lack of proficiency, incomplete learning, fossilization or learner language. (2014: 143)

6.4 Multimodal resources to support effective MELF communication

At the same time, we are indebted to translingual perspectives in understanding human communication as not limited to language and its words alone, but "one of the many sign systems that involve different symbolic means of representation working in alignment with diverse modalities, media, and ecologies" (Canagarajah 2014: 78–79). Our data indicates that MELF communication derives common understanding by multimodal means, and we consider in this section how that might be applied to language education which prepares learners for effective interactions in multilingual healthcare environments.

The term multimodality is said to describe "approaches that understand communication and representation to be more than about language, and which attend to the full range of communicational forms people use – image, gesture, gaze, posture, and so on – and the relationship between these" (Jewitt 2014: 15). As a unit for analysis, the *mode* in multimodality is defined as a "socially shaped and culturally given resource for making meaning" (Kress 2014: 60), with examples expressed in spoken language including lexis, intonation, pitch variation, lexis, tone, vowel quality, pauses and so on. Norris (2004) identified how meaning-making is achieved through other modes, such as posture and distance between interlocutors, which we suggest may have special application to healthcare communication. Multiple modes of different types may function together in a communicative event in order to create meaning (Jewitt 2014). Though speaking of written texts specifically, Bezemer and Kress use the term "multimodal ensemble" to describe how modes interact for communicative effect (2008: 168); as readers, the use of *ensemble* conjures up for us images of an orchestra, with multiple musical instruments sounding together for an audience.

Non-verbal communication, despite its importance to quality healthcare, has been underrepresented in research literature on medical communication (Roter et al. 2006). However, researchers have demonstrated the important role non-verbal modes like eye contact, posture, nods, and tone of voice play in successful medical consultations (e.g., Ambady et al. 2002; Roter et al. 2006). Reductions in doctors' workload, patient satisfaction, and patient compliance with treatment have all been shown to be associated positively with non-verbal communication (Vogel, Meyer & Harendza 2018).

The most important thing in communication is to hear what isn't being said. – Peter Drucker (in Ratcliffe 2016).

This underrepresentation of non-verbal modes of communication is not limited to healthcare research, but our own field as well. Block (2014) finds a "lingual bias" in applied linguistics research which largely overlooks non-linguistic forms of communication language takes, a reality he finds "surprising: in that Hymes and Goffman, both extensively quoted in applied linguistics, "showed a deep understanding of multimodality in their work" (Block 2014: 62). Block notes how Hymes, for example, urged researchers to consider not only linguistic codes "but whole systems of communication, involving particular . . . alternative modalities" (2014: 62; cf., Hymes 1974).

In ELF specifically, the pioneering work of Matsumoto (2015; 2018; 2019) moved beyond lingual bias to consider multimodal means of expression in ELF contexts. Matsumoto finds non-verbal, embodied actions as central – not merely supplemental – elements in ELF communication, and observes how these resources are together marshalled for communicative success.

Though the application of multimodal analysis to the study of medical interactions is in its early stages, researchers have recognized its potential to inform healthcare research and education (Rachul & Varpio 2020). Bezemer (2017; 2014) focuses on the role of gestures and non-verbal communication in surgical procedures.

Frankel and colleagues (2012) considered non-verbals such as gesture, posture, and physical distance, finding that non-verbal aspects of communication in the patient handover process could play an important role in maintaining quality and safety in healthcare. In particular (and not surprisingly) joint focus of attention – where healthcare providers pay visual attention to the same thing at the same time – was found to be of particular importance.

To the best of our knowledge, the first consideration of non-verbals intersecting both healthcare and ELF is from Ting and Cogo (in press). Their analysis of doctor-patient MELF consultations in Hong Kong show a two-way use of non-verbals (gestures in particular), accompanied with verbal confirmations, which serve to pre-empt non-understandings. Sequences of asking-answering-repeating, and repeating-and-adding, supported by other-repetition, are used to good effect by physicians, but strategies of repetition are used as well by patients as meaning is co-constructed (see also Cox & Maryns 2021).

In our data, we observed a prompt-model-invitation-confirmation sequence, with playback used to positive communicative effect (our commentary is indicated by [square brackets]).

NE-SIML4

213	Roxane:	You have to do first l:ike this (.) on your knees [Nurse models and describes desired action] both the hands.
214	Patient:	Y:eah I can't. [Patient attempts action unsuccessfully; verbally indicates thus]
215	Roxane:	This one you cannot do. [Nurse verbally confirms]
216	Patient:	Right. [Patient re-confirms]
217	Roxane:	So this one you cannot >can< d:o [Nurse initiates next physical assessment: (Patient's other hand)]

Here we see Nurse Roxane efficiently proceeding through the health assessment, multimodally utilizing linguistic and non-linguistic resources in effective collaboration. Her verbal instructions are followed by embodied actions, then she provides verbal confirmation of the patient's utterance, closing the communication loop. But how might such important multimodal communication practices inform the language classroom?

Though it is well established that non-verbals play a significant role in communication, this reality has rarely translated into English for Specific Purposes curriculum, teaching materials or teacher training. To the credit of Anthony's (2018) *Introducing English for Specific Purposes*, a list of sub-skills includes, under the heading of Listening, "participating through active listening (e.g., giving non-verbal and verbal encouragements, making gestures, providing back channels and feedback" (2018: 85). Under Speaking is listed the sub-skill of "adjusting the message through volume, speed, stress, intonation and silence" (85–86). While we have seen attention drawn to this productive Speaking sub-skill in (a few) ESP classes – usually in passing, perhaps as a rubric item for grading a group presentation – we have observed instruction on the "active listening" sub-skill only very rarely, if at all.

The introduction of something like an *Effective Multimodal Communication for Nursing English* course offering would present a radical departure from what instructors – and students – have come to expect in English for Specific Purposes classes. Yet our findings indicate that multimodal resources are an important part of effective MELF communication, and largely untouched in traditional "four skills" curricula. Developing such a course would require close cooperation with nursing content instructors, who can make direct connections between multimodal communication and the content of courses in health assessment, community nursing, nursing of families, integrated nursing practice, etc. (see Cox & Li 2020).

This type of collaboration between language instructors and content specialists is likely to face a number of challenges, of course, all of which are well documented in ESP research. A first hurdle for ESP instructors to overcome is the well known "tendency to work *for* rather than *with* subject specialists" (Hyland & Hamp-Lyons 2002: 3; emphasis in original). At times this tendency can be attributed to practical matters, such as the challenge of scheduling planning meetings between language and content area departments, the realities of time constraints, or institutional bureaucracy for modifications to course content. With some organizational creativity, workarounds can usually be found for such obstacles.

However, there are other challenges to the language-subject area integration which are not so easily overcome. For example, institutional leadership must understand the critical role that language instruction plays in subject area success, and enact administrative policy which reflects that understanding. If integration is to proceed effectively, content specialists must value the expertise of language instructors enough to put in the extra effort collaboration requires. This collaborative effort goes both ways of course, so ESP instructors must be willing to explore new and potentially unfamiliar areas of subject content. Multimodal resources for communication are likely to be a new area for many ESP instructors, and so will require a revisit of existing teaching practices and course materials. Despite these obstacles, we remain optimistic about the possibilities for improved content and language integration which explores multimodal communication resources, and anticipate the emergence of many innovative and novel applications to ESP pedagogy and curriculum in future.

6.4.1 Multimodality in simulation training and ESP

Rachul and Varpio (2020) suggest three areas of healthcare education and research where multimodal analysis might be of particular utility. The first is in the area of technological innovations, such as electronic patient records, specifically the manner in which such technologies help or hinder effective healthcare provider-patient communication. To what extent, for example, is a nurse's health assessment – and the patient's perception of it – impacted by looking at patient data on a laptop, as opposed to eye contact, posture and other non-verbal modes of communication? Similarly, multimodal analysis could be applied to the evaluation of new technologies for healthcare education. Rachul and Varpio report on technological innovations in medical education which streamlined efficiency, but at the same time reduced learning opportunities afforded by social interaction. Third, multimodal analysis offers an extralinguistic window into ways intra- and interprofessional healthcare teams function. In a 2017 study by Gordon and colleagues, non-verbals played a significant role in the leadership communication of interprofessional teams, and reflective use of video was instrumental in challenging team members' practices (Gordon et al. 2017).

In this regard, video-recorded medical simulation training (VMST) offers significant potential for exploring both linguistic and non-linguistic resources in MELF communication, along with the opportunity to inform subject area content and ESP in a multidirectional manner. At present, the benefits afforded by video recorded simulation training for MELF research on nonverbal modes of communication, and the subsequent applications to healthcare education, remain largely underutilized. We suggest several reasons why this might be so.

First, using VMST to feed back and feed forward into both language support and subject courses requires exceptional levels of collaboration between subject specialists, ESP instructors, and simulation training specialists. Collaborative hurdles between language support instructors and subject specialists were described above, but an additional challenge to reaping the full benefits of simulation learning is effective coordination between nursing instructors and simulation specialists (Jeffries et al. 2015; Beroz 2017).

Second, language support is often delivered pre-enrolment, which has the unintended effect of siloing ESP curriculum from the very content it is intended to serve. In the GCC, ESP is often delivered in departmentalized "Foundations" programs. Departmentalized all too often becomes synonymous with compartmentalized, and siloed language courses may struggle to make direct and meaningful connections to subject area content. Further, in many GCC contexts pre-enrolment language courses perform an additional function as admission gatekeepers, which has an inevitable washback effect on pedagogy, further restraining the available curriculum resources for multidirectional input.

Finally, this potential for siloed compartmentalization is not unique to language support and specialist courses. A similar sense of disconnect may exist between nursing courses and the simulation training events they are meant to support: curriculum integration of simulation for medical trainees has proven to be a persistent challenge (e.g., Adamson 2010; Sole, Guimond & Amidei 2013; Cox & Li 2020).

These difficulties notwithstanding, we find that the potential benefits of using VMST for multidirectional input into nursing courses, nursing simulation experiences, and English for nursing exert a powerful influence on our motivation to persist in moving forward. Though largely aspirational at present, we see encouraging signs of a multiplex process of interdisciplinary collaboration, where nursing course subject content feeds directly into ESP curriculum and pedagogy, and to simulation training. Recorded VMST sessions then feed back into nursing content courses, and into ESP course design. Aspirationally, the integration of VMST findings would not be delayed until future iterations of nursing and ESP courses, but would provide real-time synchronous input into weekly instructional planning.

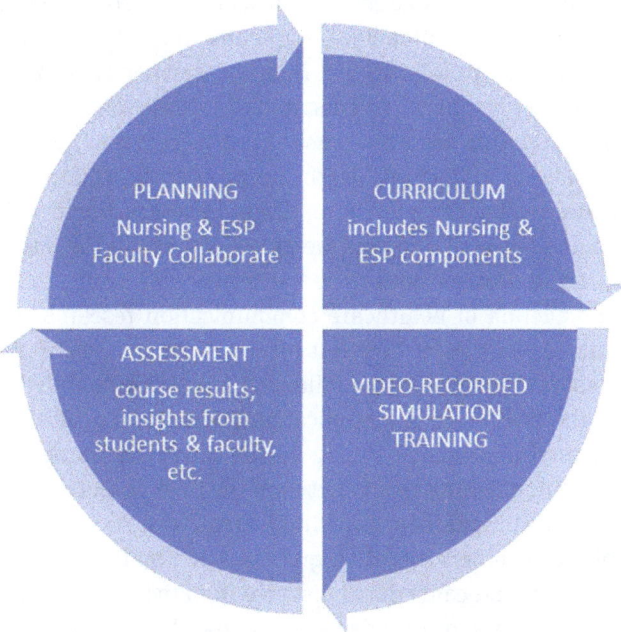

Figure 6.1: Video-recorded medical simulation training for nursing and ESP curriculum.

Given our emphasis on the use of VMST in the language classroom, it could be surmised that we are strong advocates of the use of authentic materials to support language instruction for medical purposes. We have no desire to become adherents of the "cult of authenticity" (Day 2004: 101–102), and so readily acknowledge that there are many instances when instructor-created materials can be more effective than authentic ones (Widdowson 1996; 1998), and that removing a text from its context by definition removes its authenticity (Belcher 2009). Yet, we find compelling the argument for, whenever possible, using instructional content that aligns as closely as possible with the language requirements learners will face in real world MELF encounters. Simulation has at its heart the intention to mimic high fidelity to actual clinical conditions, and its benefits for healthcare providers' learning are well known (Gliva-McConvey, Nicholas & Clark 2020); it seems logical that when possible, a similar "high fidelity" approach be taken to support their language development.

6.5 Implications for healthcare communication training in MELF contexts

Healthcare communication literature, like medical research in general, is directly oriented to improving health outcomes – typically quantifiable ones. Communication in healthcare research is studied from the perspective of measurable improvements in overall health of patients, and of healthcare providers. Though exact definitions of health are notoriously hard to come by, and of course vary considerably among individual healthcare providers (Julliard, Klimenko & Jacob 2006), concerns like the absence of disease and functional well-being in physical, mental and spiritual domains are prominent across the board. Pragmatic concerns around improving both patients' health and medical care overwhelmingly drive the agenda of healthcare communication research. We take the risk of stating this obvious point here lest readers more at home in the discourse of critical linguistics find some of the following discussion slightly jarring. Research studies in the healthcare communication literature, for example, given their outcomes-oriented perspective, rarely devote time to defining *language*, or *languages*, or to distinguishing clearly between the finer points of bilingualism, multilingualism, plurilingualism, translingualism, and so on. Many healthcare communication researchers might be quite puzzled by Pitzl's (2018) use of an asterisk (*language) to indicate critical distance from the notion of language as a bounded linguistic entity, or Holliday's (2005) use of single quotation marks around 'native speaker' for similar reasons. Terms like *English, language, native speaker* and *first language* are typically considered self-explanatory in healthcare communication literature, and are most often left undefined. Similarly, the pragmatic focus of healthcare communication research and its orientation toward quantifiable health outcomes makes it appear oblivious to sociolinguistic realities of which we in applied linguistics are especially aware: ideologies of "standard" language, "Centre" and "Periphery" users of English, English versus Englishes, translingual practice, and so on. Readers should not make the mistake of assuming, when we draw upon and engage with healthcare communication literature, that we are unaware of, or unconcerned with, the contested and political dimensions of such terms. Rather, we see this as one of the risks of interdisciplinary research (another contested term), as we attempt to straddle the boundaries of the radically different cultures (Snow 1998) separating the hard sciences from humanities and social sciences. In our opening chapter, we alluded to a discussion of interdisciplinarity, where Fuchs (2018) suggests that "the basic requirement for scholarly engagement across research domains is the capacity to adapt a fundamentally open and experimental approach to disciplines, research questions as well as their potential for addressing societal issues" (s3). We hope the reader will adopt this open stance in considering what follows, and bear with us as we attempt to navigate the intersections of two very different perspectives in language for healthcare.

Rost (2016: 186), on autonomous listening strategies:
For teaching purposes, two distinctions seem most important to make. First, if strategies are decisions that the user (the learner) makes, the mental decision or mental action that the learner undertakes must be psychologically valid, that is, it must be clear to the learner when he or she is and is not engaging the strategy. Only psychologically valid strategies need to be considered for instruction. Second, strategies that are associated with improved, or expert, performance are those that need to be identified, modeled, and practiced. Only success strategies need to be taught.

6.5.1 Teaching listening for MELF contexts

In the previous section we have envisioned the multidirectional flow of input between simulation training, nursing content and ESP instruction, as findings from each feed forward in an iterative cycle of content and language. What might instruction in the ESP component of this cycle look like?

To begin with, since the goal under consideration here is preparing learners for effective communication in high stakes MELF settings, we see limited value for this purpose in many of the activities traditionally associated with the teaching of listening in English language classrooms. Readers will be familiar with activities where listeners provide a non-oral response to an audio recording: like scoring a written representation of an utterance either right or wrong, or selecting the best representation of the utterance from a list of multiple written items. In our view, these kinds of discrete item approaches to listening, where a non-oral action is taken in response to an audio prompt, fall short in at least two respects.

First, the nature of healthcare communication in general requires a less passive approach. Even in medical history-taking, where a healthcare provider may be noting down on a prescribed form the patient's responses to questions about current medications, previous surgeries, and so on, it would not be considered good practice to passively write while the patient speaks. The healthcare provider would be expected to actively confirm medication names and dosages, ask additional follow-up questions for clarification, and even share decision-making (Fortin et al. 2019). This more active, two-way approach to listening is not only considered best practice for patient-centred approaches to communication (Keifenheim et al. 2015), but as we have seen throughout this volume, essential to patient safety. We find it therefore mystifying that well-known international assessments which utilize these kinds of approaches to the evaluation of listening remain acceptable to licensure regulators as a means of evaluating English language proficiency for healthcare professionals (e.g., see BCCNM 2020).

Second, we have shown previously how effective MELF communication in our data aligns with strategies utilized by ELF users in other domains, such as repetition, playback, reformulation, spelling out words, and other active approaches to meaning-making. Given the precision communication demanded by healthcare contexts, it would seem that these types of strategies are even more important in MELF interactions than in ELF generally. A receptive-only approach to listening, limited to non-oral actions in response to input, seems wholly incongruent with what we observe to be characteristic of effective MELF communication. Our approach resists the historical tendency of ELT to separate the four skills into discrete, standalone compartments for instruction (Hinkel 2010), but views communication as multimodal in nature, and therefore asserts that instruction be designed accordingly.

Rost (2016: Ch. 9) provides a helpful typology of listening practices in the language classroom, and this next section draws upon the five types to suggest what an integrated approach might look like in a language classroom designed to support MELF users' multimodal communicative resources.

Intensive listening. Intensive listening focuses on micro-elements of the speaker's utterance, at phonological, lexical and syntactic levels. Rost notes that this type of listening is not required in most everyday situations, so while emphasizing its importance for nuanced understanding, suggests it be included only as a "small part of each learning session" (2016: 170–171). However, for healthcare professionals preparing for work in ELF environments, where they will encounter variable levels of English proficiency and a range of accents, nuanced understanding of phonological distinctions may well be an everyday requirement. The phonological difference between opioids Percocet and Procet, for example, is slight, but the difference in uses between the two is of critical importance. Or consider a phone call between two ELF users, physician and pharmacist, regarding a prescription: it is possible to envision interlocutors' confusion between the sounding of Prenexa or Ranexa. Any temporary confusion would likely be clarified quickly; if not, a patient expecting treatment for vitamin deficiency in pregnancy would unknowingly receive angina medication.

In language support classes which prepare learners for ELF healthcare contexts, we therefore advocate the regular and sustained inclusion of classroom activities requiring authentic intensive listening. Dictation activities in their various forms are associated with intensive listening, but as traditionally practiced, we find many of them inauthentic for the demands of real time MELF communication. However, the combination of more authentic dictation tasks with reflexive collaboration presents a promising means of intensive listening pedagogy to support healthcare providers in ELF environments. For example, Cooke (2013) describes a classroom process where group transcription activities are used in conjunction with reflective discussion questions to help learners notice potential areas for skill improvement. We see several advantages of such an approach to learner awareness-raising in the classrooms providing language support for MELF. First, the collaborative approach to intensive listening in Cooke's activities represents a welcome departure from the insulated nature of traditional dictation practice, where a listener constructs meaning in response to a teacher's dictation in isolation from other learners – to consult others' versions of the prompt would be considered "cheating". Traditional dictation practices such as these are more akin to testing listening than teaching and learning (Brown 2011). Second, a collaborative approach, where meaning-making of utterances are co-constructed with other listeners, mirrors what actually takes place in daily intra- and interprofessional interactions among healthcare providers and with their patients. Collaborative clarification, checking and rechecking information with patients and medical colleagues, is an important element in patient safety (Michaels et al. 2007). Another advantage of this approach for MELF language support is that the post-listening reflective processing in Cooke's activities allows for increased metacognition in listening (Vandergrift & Goh 2012). Learning to identify *why* a particular item was misheard (phonological likeness to another similar word, syllable stress, etc.) is an important asset for MELF users' multimodal communicative resource, and so the inclusion of a reflective component provides an important extension to intensive listening activities. When compared with teacher-led correction characteristic of traditional dictation tasks, student-initiated repair has been shown to produce higher levels of transcription accuracy (Lynch 2007).

Given the importance of phonemic recognition, particularly for pharmacological interventions in healthcare, we also highlight here the potential of shadowing activities (Hamada 2016) in developing MELF users' intensive listening skills. Shadowing, a technique whereby learners actively track auditory input and vocalize it, has been shown to improve phonological recognition. Drawing its theoretical base from Baddeley's (2007) working memory model, shadowing is thought to strengthen the phonological loop (a sub-component of Baddeley's model) through more efficient processing. Shadowing also adopts tenets of the cohort model from cognitive psychology (Taft & Hambly 1986; Marslen-Wilson & Welsh 1978) whereby listeners process phonemes first, drawing upon a cohort of known, similar phonemes. The following excerpt from a shadowing text has been adapted for explanatory purposes from Hamada (2016: 44), who used it in a research study in a Japanese context.

[Recorded] Audio [stimuli]: In the service of Kublai Khan, "the most powerful man in people and in lands" . . .

S[tudent]: In the service of Kublai Khan, "the most powerful man in people and in lands" . . .

Hamada's study utilized the entirety of the text from this excerpt is taken in an eight-stage process where learners shadowed the same text (with and without written support for their listening) as many as six times, with the final result being improved phoneme recognition for all participants, across proficiency levels.

In classrooms designed to support content-based instruction for healthcare professionals, simulation data provides rich texts upon which to design shadowing activities. An audio or video recording of the discussion from which the following extract is drawn presents many possibilities for effective shadowing activities.

NE-SIM1B

40	Nurse:	Hypertension, okay. And for this hypertension, are you taking any medicine?
45	Patient:	Take uh, Metaprolo.
46	Nurse:	Okay.
47	Patient:	And I'm taking Novax.
48	Nurse:	Okay.
49	Patient:	And uh, Aspirin.
50	Nurse:	Okay.
51	Patient:	And I think I'm taking also, anti-platelet, Coumadin.
52	Nurse:	Coumadin also.

Adapting Hamada's (2016) sequence, the activity might begin with learners silent shadowing while hearing the recorded stimuli, without a written text, followed by shadowing with a text. After two to three more attempts at shadowing, learners might work in pairs of groups to discuss features of the pronunciation of the medications, and suggest potential areas of confusion these names might present. The activity might conclude with a final listening of the passage, or pair role plays with similar medication names.

In the absence of stimuli from the simulation lab, the instructor and her students might consult the "List of confused drug names" (ISMP 2019) to co-create shadowing activities.

Lest the reader think we are advocating a return to the linguistic behaviourism of the audiolingual model, or arguing for the imposition of exonormative pronunciation models, we want to stress that the goal of shadowing is not duplicating particular pronunciation features of other speakers, but ultimately to foster learner autonomy (Benson 2013), through raising awareness of phoneme recognition – given its importance in medication interventions – and learner self-reflection on strategies for more accurate listening in improved patient care.

Selective listening. Rost's typology of listening instruction uses the term selective listening to describe what Morley (1972; 1980) called "purposeful listening", which to us is a much preferable label to describe the aural skills required of healthcare professionals. Purposeful listening in Morley's instructional program encompassed attention to details like numbers, measurements and amounts, and abbreviations and spellings, all of which were deemed important in preparing learners for more complex aural tasks. For healthcare professionals, accurate apprehension of numbers, measurements and amounts are of course critical in avoiding "wrong patient, wrong diagnosis, wrong drug, wrong dose, wrong delivery, wrong timing" errors in pharmacological interventions (Hudson & Guchelaar 2003: 1010).

A typical activity in language classrooms for purposeful listening is note-taking (Rost 2016), as listeners select important information from an extended oral text, retrieving and storing it for access by self or others. The ready application of note-taking activities in language support classes for healthcare professionals is medical record-keeping. Accurate, precise, current and jargon-free records are considered central to patient safety and quality healthcare (Prideaux 2011), and have legal ramifications (Dimond 2005). Conversely, poor record-keeping has been shown to lower standards of care and negatively impact patient safety (Wang, Hailey & Yu 2011).

Teaching note-taking strategies in language classrooms designed to support healthcare professionals requires exceptional collaboration between the content instructor, local health authorities, and the language specialist. Specific requirements for healthcare record-keeping, though framed within national and international standards, are often determined by local jurisdictions. Close collaboration between the language instructor and instructors overseeing learners' clinical education would yield abundant authentic materials for instruction in note-taking that leads to effective patient record-keeping in future. Beyond documentation involving attention to dosage measurements and timings, language instruction for note-taking might also consider how to document non-biomedical aspects of patient care. Documentation of psychosocial elements of therapeutic care is considered important in effective record-keeping, but often neglected (Aitken, Manias & Dunning 2006).

Increasingly, medical record-keeping by healthcare professionals is performed electronically (e.g., Archibald et al. 2014), so listening/note-taking strategies in the language classroom will want to align with local clinical practices. It appears the jury is still out on whether electronic note-taking is as effective as handwritten notes in actual information processing (Wood et al. 2012; Mueller & Oppenheimer 2014), and the presence of mobile recording-capable devices at the bedside raises ethical issues surrounding patient privacy and consent (Nerminathan et al. 2017). Both of these issues carry over into the language classroom, so students and instructors will likely benefit from open discussions on the relative merits of electronic note-taking on actual engagement with patient information, and on how to make effective use of mobile devices in class while preserving fellow classmates' privacy and that of their patients in future. Interestingly, a study by Pyörälä and colleagues (2019) found that while medical students utilized digital devices for note-taking during their studies, usage declined in the clinical components of their programs due to matters of practicality. For language teachers, this finding points, again, toward the importance of orienting language instruction to the context for which learners are being prepared.

Interactive listening. The defining feature of interactive listening is collaborative conversation. We have already seen how MELF users effectively employed collaborative and cooperative strategies to pre-empt non- or misunderstandings, an especially important skill for medical communication, since healthcare services are often delivered in teams. Interactive listening for MELF involves explicit instruction on means of seeking clarification; confirming information; turn-taking regulation; backchannelling; joint construction of meaning; and referencing available resources (Rost 2016). The language instructor preparing learners for MELF environments will find immediate and direct links to these communicative skills in healthcare's emphasis on patient-centred communication. Naughton (2018), quoting a report of the National Cancer Institute) lists the following as core to patient-centred care:

(1) eliciting and understanding patient perspectives (e.g., concerns, ideas, expectations, needs, feelings, and functioning), (2) understanding the patient within his or her unique psychosocial and cultural contexts, and (3) reaching a shared understanding of patient problems and the treatments that are concordant with patient values.   (2018: 20)

It is not difficult to see how strategies for interactive listening such as clarification-seeking, confirmation of information, and backchannelling are important in facilitating the above core values of patient-centred care.

In this regard, ESP instructors may consider facilitating discussions among MELF users on how pragmalinguistic resources function in medical contexts across cultures. Dahm et al (2015: 829), give the following illustration drawn from an ENL context: "A doctor may, for example, use a direct approach to instruct a patient to undress, as in 'Take your shirt off', or a more mitigated way in order to avoid the impression of brusqueness, as in 'Would you mind just taking your shirt off for a moment?'" (p. 829). Nurses in our simulation data consistently showed a peremptory approach to providing direction to patients, akin to the first example provided by Dahm and colleagues. In some contexts, such direct approaches would be viewed as unnecessarily direct and non-conducive to patient-centred care, while in others, such as among ELF users, direct instructions might be viewed neutrally, or even positively, as efficient communication.

The study by Dahm and colleagues analyzed feedback by clinical educators on communication styles of International Medical Graduates in an Australian context. Evaluators' feedback included lack of attentive listening; overuse of biomedical language; "tokenistic" expressions of empathy; foregone opportunities to explore the deeper concerns of patients and express empathy; and "inappropriate" expressions such as "keep your chin up, you will be fine" (2015: 833).

We emphasize the word *discussion* here as we consider how to incorporate instruction on elements of socio- and pragmalinguistic medical communication into the language classroom. Means of showing empathy, for example, or what constitutes an "inappropriate" expression, are culturally situated. The call by North American and European healthcare systems for patient-centred communication may conflict with cultural expectations elsewhere for more hierarchical framings of doctor-patient relationships elsewhere (e.g., Claramita et al. 2013; Moore 2009). Discussions in the language classroom might lead MELF users to reflect on how core principles of patient-centred communication might translate (or not) across cultural boundaries, with instructors providing a wide range of language choices for directness or indirectness; for softening strategies (Dahm & Yates 2014); for expressing empathy; for clarification; for backchannelling and the like. The ability to draw upon an extensive breadth of in-time socio-pragmalinguistic strategies seems a critical skill for mobile MELF users in globalized contact zones (Canagarajah 2014).

Extensive listening. As the name suggests, the focus of this type of listening practice is on larger amounts of comprehensible input (Renandya & Farrell 2011). As such, extensive listening emphasizes global meaning and metacognitive skills like inference (Rost 2016). Instructional practices in extensive listening aim at developing self-regulated learners, who are metacognitively aware of their own processes of learning. Vandergrift and Goh (2012: 87–88) propose three broad areas of metacognitive knowledge which can be brought to bear on listening for language learning: person knowledge (awareness of the self, and one's own attitudes); task knowledge (of the demands of particular listening tasks); and strategy knowledge (for means of approaching listening endeavours).

Fostering metacognitive awareness is recognized as an important element in the education of healthcare providers (e.g., Quirk 2006), and its importance has been considered specifically with regard to medical communication (e.g., Falcone, Claxton & Marshall 2014). An area of metacognition highlighted in healthcare communication literature is awareness of, and management of the healthcare provider's emotions, which is said to have a critical impact on the caregiver's own well-being (Elwy et al. 2016), as well as patient care (Martin et al. 2015). Healthcare professionals at times have to deliver bad news, particularly those who work in cancer care, and so communication skills training is a well-established practice in oncology. A systematic review by Moore and colleagues (2013) found that communication skills training for cancer caregivers largely focused on awareness-raising, and that the self-awareness and specific skills gained through this kind of training were effective in improving healthcare professionals' empathy, and "reducing the likelihood of their giving facts only without individualising their responses to the patient's emotions or offering support" (2013: 2). These "difficult healthcare conversations" with patients (Martin et al. 2015: 1248) require, in the words of Mishra and colleagues (2018: 418), "empathy, clarity, and realism coupled with optimism; a balance of qualities that is difficult to strike but nonetheless teachable and achievable".

The ability to communicate with empathy, clarity, realism and optimism – and the ability to strike an effective balance between them – requires a considerable degree of metacognitive awareness, so we find in healthcare communication skills training a wealth of content which can be exploited in the English for Medical Purposes classroom. The review by Moore et al of self-awareness practices for healthcare communication skills training included direct instruction on verbal and non-verbal communication; role plays and extended simulations with explicit feedback; self-reflection, often through watching video; repeated practice; active learning in small groups; and the assistance of experienced facilitators (2013: 5). Given close coordination with the healthcare content specialist, all of the activities listed provide abundant opportunities for the development of extensive listening for the language support classroom, encompassing person, task and strategy knowledge (Vandergrift & Goh 2012).

Many ESP instructors will find daunting the task of helping healthcare professionals better break tragic news to patients, and feel very much out of their depth as language specialists. We do. However, a similar challenge is faced by all ESP instructors: providing language for a subject area in which we are not specialists. In this regard, the traditional argument that language specialists need to know about a subject area and its values rather than its specific content holds merit (Ferguson 1997), but we have found that there is no substitute for purposeful and systematic investigation of the specialist curriculum our language courses support (Basturkmen 2010). Though challenging, this process has also been energizing. We also rely heavily on collaborative relationships with subject instructors, the development of which take time and persistence. Perhaps most importantly though, and unfortunately often overlooked, is the role of students as a rich resource for ESP content. Learners can scaffold the specialist content for ESP instructors, and doing so may provide students with a motivational boost to their language learning (Belcher 2009).

Autonomous listening. The role of metacognition in this particular skill makes it closely related to the previous discussion of extensive listening. All natural language learning (i.e., without classrooms and teachers), by nature, includes autonomous listening (Rost 2016), so pedagogy to foster autonomy for healthcare communication largely involves helping learners become aware of their own already successful (or unsuccessful) strategies. Listening as a skill taught in the language classroom is notoriously teacher-led, so as a means of awareness-raising of effective strategies, instructors can give more autonomy to learners to select listening texts, design listening tasks for themselves and others, and develop their own means of post-listening reflection. Vandergrift and Goh propose a metacognitive pedagogy which integrates listening input with metacognitive awareness-raising, and in a sequence of instructional tasks, supports learner autonomy with activities which draw students' attention to their own strategies (2012: 127).

In language classes to support healthcare professionals, learners might create their own role plays for classmates: designing a healthcare scenario; using their disciplinary knowledge to specify what types of information are especially important to hear within that scenario; and identifying obstacles to accurate listening – both linguistic (e.g., phonological; lexical [complex medical terminology]) and non-linguistic (e.g., time pressures; hierarchical authority structures). Post-role play reflection activities, oral or written, individually or within pairs/groups, can be used to consolidate the learning. Here again, we see healthcare simulation training recordings, where available, as a rich instructional resource in awareness-raising to develop autonomous listening. The instructor might augment the creation of learner-designed communication role plays through exemplar listening texts drawn from simulation recordings. The following extract was discussed in a previous chapter.

43	Roz (L1 Arabic):	Father, mother, they have diabetes and arthritis.
44	Nurse B:	Father, mother have diabetes↑
45	Ragia:	Mm-hmm (affirmative).
46	Roz:	And arthritis.
47	Nurse B:	Arthritis.↓ Okay. Uh, your father and mother, they are alive
48	Roz:	No.
49	Nurse B:	Okay. Okay. Which age they are died
50	Roz:	Father was 70.
51	Nurse B:	70
52	Roz:	Mother was 65.
53	Nurse B:	60↑
54	Ragia:	65
55	Nurse B:	65, mother. Okay.

An instructor might use a recording of a simulation text such as this one to draw out from listeners successful meaning-making strategies, such as playback, repetition, and use of falling or rising intonation. *How did Nurse B make sure she knew the mother's age? How did Nurse B confirm she understood what the patient said about the family disease history?* The goal of discussing intonation is not, of course, to teach Inner Circle usage, but to lead learners' to reflect on how intonation is used (or not used) in the English communication of patients with different first languages. This text could also lead to discussions on therapeutic communication: *Did Nurse B show empathy? How?* Therapeutic communication has a considerable element of cultural-dependency (Fujimori & Uchitomi 2009), so learners might share experiences on how care is expressed in and through different cultural backgrounds. Such reflections are an important part of preparing for effective healthcare in zones of contact (Kimura & Canagarajah 2018). Reflective tasks such as these, supported by authentic texts and used in conjunction with learner-designed activities, can aid in developing the self-evaluation and self-monitoring elements of autonomous listening (Rost 2016).

6.6 Closing remarks

As we write the concluding comments of this book, healthcare organizations and medical professionals across the globe are attempting to cooperate on a scale without historical precedent, as they share information and strategies to contain the SARS-CoV-2 pandemic. This global attention to the work of healthcare professionals, and the reality of our interconnectedness and interdependence across international borders, for better or for worse, make our initial exploration of medical English as a lingua franca especially timely.

We have attempted, throughout this volume, to make the case that MELF is *different*: that the very nature of its global links press upon MELF interactions an insistence for language regulation and codification not evident in ELF contexts studied to date. The social settings and speech acts which frame MELF communication, such as the medical interview, exert significant influence on its linguistic forms. Yet we also find in MELF much that is common to ELF use in other domains: innovation, creativity, and an attention to communicative function over form. We observe MELF users effectively employing a full range of multimodal resources for healthcare communication, often skilfully and innovatively accommodating across linguacultures. We also observe features of MELF communication which are common challenges in healthcare communication generally: excessive biomedical language unhelpful to patients, orienting to authoritative stances at the expense of communication, and the very real potential for errors with life-threatening consequences.

It is this direct connection of ELF research to the broader field of medical communication that leaves us the most hopeful. We mentioned previously that medicine, by its own admission, tends to be adverse to input from outsiders for suggestions in improving practice (Leape & Berwick 2005). Yet, given the scope of healthcare worker migration and the role of English for international medical communication, we suggest that the field of ELF has much to contribute to understanding how medical communication takes place. We are by nature optimists, so hold to the possibility that ELF will be considered a potential frame for analysis not just by applied linguists but by healthcare communication researchers, and that insights from ELF will therefore be taken on board for achieving the primary goal of healthcare research: improvement in the quality of patient care and medical practice.

Appendix: Transcription Glossary

The transcription symbols used in the research follow Jefferson (2005); the explanations here have been adapted from the same source.

(0.5)	Time gap in tenths of a second.
(.)	A pause in talk less than two-tenths of a second.
=	Latching between utterances, or overlap between speakers' turns.

    S1:   yeah September seventy six it would be=
    S2:   =yeah that's right

    S1:   yeah September [seventy six=
    S2:   [September
    S1:   =it would be (examples from Jefferson 2005)

(guess)	Transcriber's best guess when an utterance is unclear.
word.	Period: falling tone; not always an indicator of an end of an utterance
word,	Comma: intonation indicating continuation.
word?	Question mark: rising reflection; not always indicating questions.
↑↓	Falling or rising intonation.
Under	Speaker emphasis.
CAPITALS	Louder speech.
° °	Quieter speech.
> <	Quicker speech than the surrounding utterances
< >	Slower speech than the surrounding utterances.
→	Specific parts of an utterance discussed in the text.
[NE-SIML4]	Researchers' organization labels for transcription extracts.

References

Adams, Patrick & Fiona Fleck (2015): Bridging the language divide in health. *Bulletin of the World Health Organization* 93(6). 365–366. doi:10.2471/BLT.15.020615.
Adamson, Katie (2010): Integrating human patient simulation into associate degree nursing curricula. *Clinical Simulation in Nursing* 6(3). e75–e81. doi:10.1016/j.ecns.2009.06.002.
Ahn, Meejung, Mona Choi & YoungAh Kim (2016): Factors associated with the timeliness of electronic nursing documentation. *Healthcare Informatics Research 22* (4).270. doi:10.4258/hir.2016.22.4.270.
Ahpra (2020): Registration standards: English language skills. *Nursing and midwifery Board* https://www.nursingmidwiferyboard.gov.au/registration-standards/english-language-skills.aspx (date accessed 24/ 11/2020).
Ainsworth-Vaughn, Nancy (2005): The discourse of medical encounters. In Deborah Schiffrin, Deborah Tannen & Heidi E. Hamilton (eds.), *The Handbook of Discourse Analysis*, 453–469. Malden: Wiley. doi:10.1002/9780470753460.ch24.
Aitken, Robyn, Elizabeth Manias & Trcisha Dunning (2006): Documentation of medication management by graduate nurses in patient progress notes: a way forward for patient safety. *Collegian* 13(4). 5–11. doi:10.1016/S1322-7696(08)60533-8.
Alderson, P. (1998): Theories in health care and research: the importance of theories in health care. *BMJ 317*(7164). 1007–1010. doi:10.1136/bmj.317.7164.1007.
Alexander, Maryann, Carol F. Durham, Janice I. Hooper, Pamela R. Jeffries, Nathan Goldman, Suzie Kardong-Edgren, Karen S. Kesten, et al. (2015): NCSBN Simulation Guidelines for prelicensure nursing programs. *Journal of Nursing Regulation* 6(3). 39–42. doi:10.1016/S2155-8256(15)30783-3.
Ali, Moi (2018): Communication skills 5: Effective listening and observation. *Nursing Times* 114(4). 56–57.
Ali, Nasreen (2003): Fluency in the consulting room. *The British Journal of General Practice: The Journal of the Royal College of General Practitioners* 53(492). 514–5.
Alkhatib, Hadeel (2017): Status and function of the English language in Qatar: a social semiotic perspective. *Journal of World Languages* 4(1). 44–68. doi:10.1080/21698252.2017.1406878.
Allen, David (2016): Investigating washback to the learner from the IELTS test in the Japanese tertiary context. *Language Testing in Asia* 6(1). 7. doi:10.1186/s40468-016-0030-z.
Allen, Marshall (2009): Foreign nurses can slip into communication gap. *Las Vegas Sun*.
Almost, Joan, Diane M. Doran, Linda McGillis Hall & Heather K. Spence Laschinger (2010): Antecedents and consequences of intra-group conflict among nurses. *Journal of Nursing Management* 18(8). 981–992. doi:10.1111/j.1365-2834.2010.01154.x.
Alshammari, Mukhlid, Jed Duff & Michelle Guilhermino (2019): Barriers to nurse–patient communication in Saudi Arabia: an integrative review. *BMC Nursing* 18(1). 61. doi:10.1186/s12912-019-0385-4.
Aluttis, Christoph, Tewabech Bishaw & Martina W. Frank (2014): The workforce for health in a globalized context – global shortages and international migration. *Global Health Action* 7 (1). 23611. doi:10.3402/gha.v7.23611.
Ambady, Nalini, Debi LaPlante, Thai Nguyen, Robert Rosenthal, Nigel Chaumeton & Wendy Levinson (2002): Surgeons' tone of voice: a clue to malpractice history. *Surgery 132*(1). 5–9. doi:10.1067/msy.2002.124733.

American Medical Association (2020): Reducing disparities in health care. https://www.ama-assn.org/delivering-care/patient-support-advocacy/reducing-disparities-health-care (date accessed 17/ 03/2020).

Anderson, Judith, Linda Malone, Kerry Shanahan & Jennifer Manning (2015): Nursing bedside clinical handover – an integrated review of issues and tools. *Journal of Clinical Nursing* 24(5–6). 662–671. doi:10.1111/jocn.12706.

Andrew, Nicola, Dorothy Ferguson, George Wilkie, Terry Corcoran & Liz Simpson (2009): Developing professional identity in nursing academics: the role of communities of practice. *Nurse Education Today* 29(6). 607–611. doi:10.1016/j.nedt.2009.01.012.

Andrew, Nicola O & Dorothy Ferguson (2008): Constructing communities for learning in nursing. *International Journal of Nursing Education Scholarship* 5(1). 1–15. doi:10.2202/1548-923X.1579.

Andrew, Nicola, Debbie Tolson & Dorothy Ferguson (2008): Building on Wenger: communities of practice in nursing. *Nurse Education Today* 28(2). 246–252. doi:10.1016/j.nedt.2007.05.002.

Anthony, Laurence (2018): *Introducing English for Specific Purposes*. Abingdon: Routledge.

Archibald, Douglas, Colla J Macdonald, Judith Plante, Rebecca J Hogue & Javier Fiallos (2014): Residents' and preceptors' perceptions of the use of the iPad for clinical teaching in a family medicine residency program. *BMC Medical Education* 14(1). 174. doi:10.1186/1472-6920-14-174.

Ariss, Steven M. (2009): Asymmetrical knowledge claims in general practice consultations with frequently attending patients: limitations and opportunities for patient participation. *Social Science & Medicine* 69(6). 908–919. doi:10.1016/j.socscimed.2009.06.045.

Arora, Neeraj K., Kathryn E. Weaver, Marla L. Clayman, Ingrid Oakley-Girvan & Arnold L. Potosky (2009): Physicians' decision-making style and psychosocial outcomes among cancer survivors. *Patient Education and Counseling* 77(3). 404–412. doi:10.1016/j.pec.2009.10.004.

Atkinson, J. Maxwell & Paul Drew (1979): *Order in court: the organization of verbal interactions in judicial settings*. London: Palgrave Macmillan.

Avram, Andrei A. (2018): On the relationship between Arabic Foreigner Talk and Pidgin Arabic. In Stefano Manfredi & Mauro Tosco (eds.), *Arabic in Contact*, 251–273. Amsterdam: John Benjamins. doi:10.1075/sal.6.13avr.

Azaizeh, Hassan, Bashar Saad, Edwin Cooper & Omar Said (2010): Traditional Arabic and Islamic Medicine, a re-Emerging health aid. *Evidence-Based Complementary and Alternative Medicine* 7(4). 419–424. doi:10.1093/ecam/nen039.

B-Line Medical (2019): SimCapture. *SimCapture* https://www.blinemedical.com/simcapture.html (date accessed 21/ 12/2020).

Bachman, Lyle F (2005): Building and supporting a case for test use. *Language Assessment Quarterly*. Taylor & Francis. 2(1). 1–34. doi:10.1207/s15434311laq0201_1.

Baddeley, Alan D. (2007): *Working memory, thought and action*. Oxford: Oxford University Press.

Baid, Heather (2006): The process of conducting a physical assessment: a nursing perspective. *British Journal of Nursing* 15(13). 710–714. doi:10.12968/bjon.2006.15.13.21482.

Baid, Heather, Christine Bartlett, Susan Gilhooly, Andrea Illingworth & Suzanne Winder (2009): Advanced physical assessment: the role of the district nurse. *Nursing Standard* 23(35). 41–46. doi:10.7748/ns2009.05.23.35.41.c6958.

Baker, Will (2011): Intercultural awareness: modelling an understanding of cultures in intercultural communication through English as a lingua franca. *Language and Intercultural Communication* 11(3). 197–214. doi:10.1080/14708477.2011.577779.

Baker, Will (2015): *Culture and identity through English as a lingua franca: rethinking concepts and goals in intercultural communication*. Berlin: De Gruyter Mouton.

Baker, Will (2016): English as an academic lingua franca and intercultural awareness: student mobility in the transcultural university. *Language and Intercultural Communication* 16(3). 437–451. doi:10.1080/14708477.2016.1168053.

Baker, Will (2018): English as a lingua franca and intercultural communication. In Jennifer Jenkins, Will Baker & Martin Dewey (eds.), *The Routledge handbook of English as a Lingua Franca*, 25–36. Abingdon: Routledge.

Barančicová, Jana & Jana Zerzová (2015): English as a lingua franca used at international meetings. *Journal of Language and Cultural Education* 3(3). 30–51. doi:10.1515/jolace-2015-0018.

Barnawi, Osman Z. (2018): *Neoliberalism and English language education policies in the Arabian Gulf*. Abingdon: Routledge.

Barron, Colin (2003): Problem-solving and EAP: themes and issues in a collaborative teaching venture. *English for Specific Purposes* 22(3). 297–314. doi:10.1016/S0889-4906(02)00016-9.

Barron, Ewan Alexander & John Holmes (2013): Delirium within the emergency care setting, occurrence and detection: a systematic review. *Emergency Medicine Journal* 30(4). 263–268. doi:10.1136/emermed-2011-200586.

Basturkmen, Helen (2010): *Developing courses in English for Specific Purposes*. Houndmills: Palgrave Macmillan.

BBC News (2010): GP Daniel Ubani struck off over fatal overdose. *BBC News*.

BBC News (2015): EU doctor suspended from UK work for 'poor English test'. *BBC News*.

BBC News (2016): EU nurses face language checks. *BBC News*.

BCCNM (2020): English language proficiency. *Internationally Educated Nurses, British Columbia College of Nurses & Midwives* https://www.bccnm.ca/LPN/applications_regis tration/how_to_apply/IENapplicant/Pages/English_proficiency.aspx (date accessed 13/12/2020).

Beijer, H.J.M. & C.J. de Blaey (2002): Hospitalisations caused by adverse drug reactions (ADR): a meta-analysis of observational studies. *Pharmacy World and Science* 24(2). 46–54. doi:10.1023/A:1015570104121.

Belcher, Diane (2009): What ESP is and can be: an introduction. In Diane Belcher (ed.), *English for specific purposes in theory and practice*, 1–20. Ann Arbor: University of Michigan Press ELT.

Benner, J. S., L. Erhardt, M. Flammer, R. A. Moller, N. Rajicic, K. Changela, C. Yunis, et al. (2008): A novel programme to evaluate and communicate 10-year risk of CHD reduces predicted risk and improves patients' modifiable risk factor profile. *International Journal of Clinical Practice* 62(10). 1484–1498. doi:10.1111/j.1742-1241.2008.01872.x.

Benson, Phil (2013): Learner autonomy. *TESOL Quarterly* 47(4). 839–843. doi:10.1002/tesq.134.

Berger, Zackary D., Emily F. Boss & Mary Catherine Beach (2017): Communication behaviors and patient autonomy in hospital care: a qualitative study. *Patient Education and Counseling* 100(8). 1473–1481. doi:10.1016/j.pec.2017.03.006.

Beroz, Sabrina (2017): A statewide survey of simulation practices using NCSBN Simulation Guidelines. *Clinical Simulation in Nursing* 13(6). 270–277. doi:10.1016/j.ecns.2017.03.005.

Bezemer, Jeff, Alexandra Cope, Terhi Korkiakangas, Gunther Kress, Ged Murtagh, Sharon-Marie Weldon & Roger Kneebone (2017): Microanalysis of video from the operating room: an underused approach to patient safety research. *BMJ Quality & Safety 26*(7). 583–587. doi:10.1136/bmjqs-2016-005816.

Bezemer, Jeff, Alexandra Cope, Gunther Kress & Roger Kneebone (2014): Holding the scalpel: achieving surgical care in a learning environment. *Journal of Contemporary Ethnography 43*(1). 38–63. doi:10.1177/0891241613485905.

Bezemer, Jeff & Gunther Kress (2008): Writing in multimodal texts. *Written Communication 25*(2). 166–195. doi:10.1177/0741088307313177.

Bigi, Sarah & Maria Grazia Rossi (2020): Considering mono- and multilingual interactions on a continuum: an analysis of interactions in medical settings. In Christiane Hohenstein & Magdalène Lévy-Tödter (eds.), *Multilingual healthcare: a global perspective on communicative challenges*, 11–37. Hamburg: Gabler Verlag. doi:10.1007/978-3-658-27120-6_2.

Bizri, Fida (2014): Unity and diversity across Asian migrant Arabic pidgins in the Middle East. *Journal of Pidgin and Creole Languages 29*(2). 385–409. doi:10.1075/jpcl.29.2.07biz.

Björkman, Beyza (2018): Morphosyntactic variation in spoken English as a lingua franca interactions. In Jennifer Jenkins, Will Baker & Martin Dewey (eds.), *The Routledge handbook of English as a Lingua Franca*, 255–266. Abingdon: Routledge.

Bladd, Joanne (2008): Drug doses lost in translation. *Arabianbusiness.com* http://www.arabianbusiness.com/drug-doses-lost-in-translation-51171.html.

Block, David (2014): Moving beyond 'lingualism': multilingual embodiment and multimodality in SLA. In Stephen May (ed.), *The multilingual turn: implications for SLA, TESOL and bilingual education2*, 54–77. New York: Routledge.

Blommaert, Jan (2010): *The sociolinguistics of globalization*. Cambridge: Cambridge University Press.

Blommaert, Jan (2013): *Ethnography, superdiversity and linguistic landscapes: chronicles of complexity*. Bristol: Multilingual Matters.

Bohand, Xavier, Laurent Simon, Eric Perrier, Hélène Mullot, Leslie Lefeuvre & Christian Plotton (2009): Frequency, types, and potential clinical significance of medication-dispensing errors. *Clinics 64*(1). 11–16. doi:10.1590/S1807-59322009000100003.

Botis, Valeria-Alina & M. Gregory Tweedie Challenges of intraprofessional healthcare communication when English is a lingua franca: an autoethnographic study. In M. Gregory Tweedie & Robert C. Johnson (eds.), *Perspectives on medical English as a lingua franca*. Newcastle upon Tyne: Cambridge Scholars.

Bowles, Hugo (2006): Conversation analysis and health communication: updating a developing relationship. In Maurizio Gotti & Françoise Saleger-Meyer (eds.), *Advances in medical discourse analysis: oral and written contexts*, 43–64. Bern: Peter Lang.

Boyd, Elizabeth & John Heritage (2006): Taking the history: questioning during comprehensive history-taking. In John Heritage & Douglas W. Maynard (eds.), *Communication in medical care. Interaction between primary care physicians and patients*, 151–184. Cambridge: Cambridge University Press.

Boyle, Ronald (2012): Language contact in the United Arab Emirates. *World Englishes 31*(3). 312–330. doi:10.1111/j.1467-971X.2012.01749.x.

Boyle, Ronald (2014): Economic migrants, social networks, and the prospect of koinéization in the United Arab Emirates. *English World-Wide 35*(1). 32–51. doi:10.1075/eww.35.1.03boy.

Bremer, Katharina (1996): Causes of understanding problems. In Katharina Bremer, Celia Roberts, Marie-Therese Vasseur, Margaret Simnot & Peter Broeder (eds.), *Achieving understanding: discourse in intercultural encounters*, 37–64. London: Routledge. doi:10.4324/9781315844954-9.

Brich, Jochen, Verena Baten, Judith Wußmann, Miriam Heupel-Reuter, Evgeniy Perlov, Stefan Klöppel & Hans-Jörg Busch (2019): Detecting delirium in elderly medical emergency patients: validation and subsequent modification of the German Nursing Delirium Screening Scale. *Internal and Emergency Medicine* 14(5). 767–776. doi:10.1007/s11739-018-1989-5.

Brodin Danell, Jenny-Ann & Rikard Danell (2007): Spiritualised medicine? A bibliometric study of complementary and alternative medicine. *Proceedings of ISSI 2007*, 154–161.

Brown, Megan E.L. & Angelique N. Dueñas (2020): A medical science educator's guide to selecting a research paradigm: building a basis for better research. *Medical Science Educator 30*. 545–553. doi:10.1007/s40670-019-00898-9.

Brown, Steven (2011): *Listening myths: applying second language research to classroom teaching*. Ann Arbor: University of Michigan Press.

Brugha, Ruairí & Sophie Crowe (2015): Relevance and effectiveness of the WHO Global Code Practice on the international recruitment of health personnel–ethical and systems perspectives. *International Journal of Health Policy and Management* 4(6). 333–6. doi:10.15171/ijhpm.2015.103.

Brutt-Griffler, Janina & Keiko K. Samimy (2001): Transcending the nativeness paradigm. *World Englishes*. Wiley Online Library. 20(1). 99–106. doi:10.1111/1467-971X.00199.

Buck, Gary (2001): *Assessing listening*. Cambridge: Cambridge University Press.

Butcher, Carmen Acevedo (2005): The case against the 'native speaker'. *English Today*. Cambridge Univ Press. 21(02). 13–24. doi:10.1017/S0266078405002038.

Calkins, David R., Roger B. Davis, Peggy Reiley, Russell S. Phillips, Katherine L. Pineo, Thomas L. Delbanco & Lisa I. Iezzoni (1997): Patient-physician communication at hospital discharge and patients' understanding of the postdischarge treatment plan. *Archives of Internal Medicine* 157(9). 1026–1030. doi:10.1001/archinte.1997.00440300148014.

Callahan, Daniel (1998): Managed care and the goals of medicine. *Journal of the American Geriatrics Society* 46(3). 385–388. doi:10.1111/j.1532-5415.1998.tb01060.x.

Campbell, Suzanne Hetzel & Karen M. Daley (2018): *Simulation scenarios for nursing educators: making it real*. New York: Springer.

Canagarajah, A. Suresh (2005): *Reclaiming the local in language policy and practice*: Mahwah: Lawrence Erlbaum.

Canagarajah, A. Suresh (2006): The place of World Englishes in composition: pluralization continued. *College Composition and Communication* 57(4). 586–619.

Canagarajah, A. Suresh (2012): Teacher development in a global profession: an autoethnography. *TESOL Quarterly* 46(2). 258–279. doi:10.1002/tesq.18.

Canagarajah, A. Suresh (2013): *Translingual practice: global Englishes and cosmopolitan relations*. Abingdon: Routledge. doi:10.4324/9780203073889.

Canagarajah, A. Suresh (2014): Theorizing a competence for translingual practice at the contact zone. In Stephen May (ed.), *The multilingual turn: implications for SLA, TESOL and bilingual education*, 78–102. New York: Routledge.

Cappuzzo, Barbara (2015): Allo-repetition in academic settings. Cooperation, understanding co-construction and knowledge negotiation in the medical section of the ELFA corpus. *ESP Across Cultures 12*. 33–54.

Carnet, Didier & Jean-Pierre Charpy (2017): Discours de professionnels et discours pour professionnels : le travail collaboratif au service de l'enseignement de l'anglais médical. *ASp* (71). 47–68. doi:10.4000/asp.4952.

Carter, Lorraine & Patti Dickieson (2010): Scenario testing in undergraduate nursing education: assessment for learning. *Canadian Journal for the Study of Adult Education* 22(2). 65–76.

Carter, Robert (2005): The history and prehistory of pearling in the Persian Gulf. *Journal of the Economic and Social History of the Orient* 48(2). 139–209. doi:10.1163/1568520054127149.

Carvalho, Irene P, Vanessa G Pais, Filipa R Silva, Raquel Martins, Margarida Figueiredo-Braga, Raquel Pedrosa, Susana S Almeida, et al. (2014): Teaching communication skills in clinical settings: comparing two applications of a comprehensive program with standardized and real patients. *BMC Medical Education* 14(1). 92. doi:10.1186/1472-6920-14-92.

Cassell, Eric J. (1985): *Talking with patients, Volume II: clinical technique*. Cambridge: MIT Press.

CELBAN (2020): About the Canadian English Language Benchmark Assessment for Nurses. *The CELBAN Centre* https://www.celbancentre.ca/about.aspx (date accessed 24/ 11/2020).

Centre for the Advancement of Interprofessional Education (2020): What is CAIPE? https://www.caipe.org/about-us (date accessed 19/ 03/2020).

Chen, Jennifer & Taylor McCormick (2015): "Am I having a heart attack, doc?" Patient-physician communication for possible acute coronary syndromes. *Annals of Emergency Medicine* 66(6). 677–683. doi:10.1016/j.annemergmed.2015.10.009.

Cheng, Liying (2013): Consequences, impact, and washback. In Anthony John Kunnan (ed.), *The Companion to Language Assessment*, 1130–1145. Hoboken: John Wiley & Sons, Inc. doi:10.1002/9781118411360.wbcla071.

CHIA (2002): *California standards for healthcare interpreters: ethical principles, protocols, and guidance on roles and intervention*. Sacramento.

Child, J. C., S. B. Sepples & K. Chambers (2007): Designing simulations for nursing education. In Pamela R. Jeffries (ed.), *Simulation in nursing education: from conceptualization to evaluation*, 42–58. New York: National League for Nursing.

Chou, Calvin & Laura Cooley (2018): *Communication Rx: transforming healthcare through relationship-centred communication*. New York: McGraw-Hill Education.

Chow, E. P. Y. (1984): Traditional Chinese medicine: a holistic system. In W. J. Salmon (ed.), *Alternative medicines: popular and policy perspectives*, 114–137. New York: Tavistock.

Churchouse, Christopher & Chris McCafferty (2012): Standardized patients versus simulated patients: is there a difference? *Clinical Simulation in Nursing* 8(8). e363–e365. doi:10.1016/j.ecns.2011.04.008.

Claramita, Mora, Mubarika D. F. Nugraheni, Jan van Dalen & Cees van der Vleuten (2013): Doctor–patient communication in Southeast Asia: a different culture? *Advances in Health Sciences Education* 18(1). 15–31. doi:10.1007/s10459-012-9352-5.

Clark, Herbert H. (1996): *Using language*. Cambridge: Cambridge University Press.

Cockbain, Beatrice Clare, Sanja Thompson, Helen Salisbury, Pamina Mitter & Lola Martos (2015): A collaborative strategy to improve geriatric medical education. *Age and Ageing* 44(6). 1036–1039. doi:10.1093/ageing/afv100.

Cogo, Alessia & Martin Dewey (2012): *Analysing English as a lingua franca: a corpus-driven investigation*. Continuum: London.

Cogo, Alessia & Marie-Luise Pitzl (2016): Pre-empting and signalling non-understanding in ELF. *ELT Journal 70*(3). 339–345. doi:10.1093/elt/ccw015.

Cohen, A. L., F. Rivara, E.K. Marcuse, H. McPhillips & R. Davis (2005): Are language barriers associated with serious medical events in hospitalized pediatric patients? *PEDIATRICS 116*(3). 575–579. doi:10.1542/peds.2005-0521.

Cooke, Simon D. (2013): Examining transcription, autonomy and reflective practice in language development. *RELC Journal 44*(1). 75–85. doi:10.1177/0033688212473271.

Coomber, Peter, Alexandra Clavarino, Emma Ballard & Karen Luetsch (2018): Doctor–pharmacist communication in hospitals: strategies, perceptions, limitations and opportunities. *International Journal of Clinical Pharmacy 40*(2). 464–473. doi:10.1007/s11096-018-0592-1.

Cox, Antoon (2020): Venturing into interdisciplinary research as an applied linguist: challenges and opportunities. *Bulletin de Linguistique et Des Sciences Du Langage 31*. 13–37.

Cox, Antoon & Shuangyu Li (2020): The medical consultation through the lenses of language and social interaction theory. *Advances in Health Sciences Education 25*(1). 241–257. doi:10.1007/s10459-018-09873-2.

Cox, Antoon & Katrijn Maryns (2021): Multilingual consultations in urgent medical care. *The Translator* 1–19. doi:10.1080/13556509.2020.1857501.

CRICO Strategies (2015): *Malpractice risks in communication failures: 2015 annual benchmarking report*. Boston.

Cruess, Richard L., Sylvia R. Cruess & Yvonne Steinert (2018): Medicine as a community of practice. *Academic Medicine 93*(2). 185–191. doi:10.1097/ACM.0000000000001826.

Crystal, David (2003): *English as a global language*. 2nd edn. Cambridge: Cambridge University Press.

Crystal, David (2008): Two thousand million? *English Today 24*(1). 3–6. doi:https://doi.org/10.1017/S0266078408000023.

Crystal, David (2009): *A dictionary of linguistics and phonetics*. 6th edn. Hoboken: Wiley.

Cullati, Stéphane, Naike Bochatay, Fabienne Maître, Thierry Laroche, Virginie Muller-Juge, Katherine S. Blondon, Noëlle Junod Perron, et al. (2019): When team conflicts threaten quality of care: a study of health care professionals' experiences and perceptions. *Mayo Clinic Proceedings: Innovations, Quality & Outcomes 3*(1). 43–51. doi:10.1016/j.mayocpiqo.2018.11.003.

Dahm, Maria R. & Lynda Yates (2014): English for the workplace: doing patient-centred care in medical communication. *TESL Canada Journal 30*(7). 21–44. doi:10.18806/tesl.v30i7.1150.

Dahm, Maria R, Lynda Yates, Kathryn Ogden, Kim Rooney & Brooke Sheldon (2015): Enhancing international medical graduates' communication: the contribution of applied linguistics. *Medical Education 49*(8). 828–837. doi:10.1111/medu.12776.

Dashti, Abdulmohsen (2015): The role and status of the English language in Kuwait. *English Today 31*(3). 28–33. doi:10.1017/S026607841500022X.

Davies, Alan (2003): *The native speaker: myth and reality*. Clevedon: Multilingual Matters.

Davies, Bethan (2005): Communities of practice: legitimacy not choice. *Journal of Sociolinguistics 9*(4). 557–581. doi:10.1111/j.1360-6441.2005.00306.x.

Davis, Kathryn A. (1995): Qualitative theory and methods in applied linguistics research. *TESOL Quarterly 29*(3). 427–453. doi:10.2307/3588070.

Day, Richard R. (2004): A critical look at authentic materials. *The Journal of Asia TEFL 1*(1). 101–114.

Denzin, Norman K & Yvonna S Lincoln (2018): *The SAGE handbook of qualitative research*. 5th edn. Los Angeles: Sage.

Deterding, David (2013): *Misunderstandings in English as a lingua franca: an analysis of ELF interactions in South-East Asia*. Boston/Berlin: De Gruyter Mouton.

Deuster, Lindsay, Stephanie Christopher, Jodi Donovan & Michael Farrell (2008): A method to quantify residents' jargon use during counseling of standardized patients about cancer screening. *Journal of General Internal Medicine 23*(12). 1947–1952. doi:10.1007/s11606-008-0729-3.

Dewey, M (2009): English as a lingua franca: heightened variability and theoretical implications. In Anna Mauranen & Elina Ranta (eds.), *English as a Lingua Franca: studies and findings*, 60–83. Newcastle upon Tyne: Cambridge Scholars.

Diamond, Lisa C. & Elizabeth A. Jacobs (2010): Let's not contribute to disparities: the best methods for teaching clinicians how to overcome language barriers to health care. *Journal of General Internal Medicine 25* (S2).189–193. doi:10.1007/s11606-009-1201-8.

Dimond, Bridgit (2005): Exploring the principles of good record keeping in nursing. *British Journal of Nursing 14*(8). 460–462. doi:10.12968/bjon.2005.14.8.17931.

Divi, Chandrika, Richard G. Koss, Stephen P. Schmaltz & Jerod M. Loeb (2007): Language proficiency and adverse events in US hospitals: a pilot study. *International Journal for Quality in Health Care 19*(2). 60–67. doi:10.1093/intqhc/mzl069.

Dolan, Gabrielle (2019): The single biggest problem with communication. *CEO Magazine*. Sydney.

Drew, Paul & John Heritage (1992a): *Talk at work: interaction in institutional settings*. Cambridge: Cambridge University Press.

Drew, Paul & John Heritage (1992b): Analyzing talk at work: an introduction. *Talk at work: interaction in institutional settings*, 3–65. Cambridge: Cambridge University Press.

Drljača Margić, Branka (2017): Communication courtesy or condescension? Linguistic accommodation of native to non-native speakers of English. *Journal of English as a Lingua Franca 6*(1) doi:10.1515/jelf-2017-0006.

Duncan-Hewitt, Wendy & Zubin Austin (2005): Pharmacy schools as expert communities of practice? A proposal to radically restructure pharmacy education to optimize learning. *American Journal of Pharmaceutical Education 69*(3). 54. doi:10.5688/aj690354.

Dupont, C (2002): Quality of referral letters. *The Lancet 359*(9318). 1701. doi:10.1016/S0140-6736(02)08583-5.

Durant, Edward & Karl A Sporer (2011): Characteristics of patients with an abnormal Glasgow Coma Scale score in the prehospital setting. *The Western Journal of Emergency Medicine 12*(1). 30–36.

Eberhard, David M., Gary F. Simons & Charles D. Fennig (2020): *Ethnologue: languages of the world*. 23rd edn. Dallas: SIL International.

Eckert, Penelope & Sally McConnell-Ginet (1992): Think practically and look locally: language and gender as community-based practice. *Annual Review of Anthropology 21*(1). 461–488. doi:10.1146/annurev.an.21.100192.002333.

Ehrenreich, Susanne (2009): English as a lingua franca in multinational corporations: exploring business communities of practice. *English as a lingua franca: studies and findings*, 126–151. Newcastle upon Tyne: Cambridge Scholars.

Ehrenreich, Susanne (2010): English as a business lingua franca in a German multinational corporation: meeting the challenge. *Journal of Business Communication 47*(4). 408–431. doi:10.1177/0021943610377303.

Ehrenreich, Susanne (2011): *The dynamics of English as a business lingua franca: a language contact perspective.* In Alasdair Archibald, Alessia Cogo & Jennifer Jenkins (eds.), *Latest trends in ELF research*, 11–34. Newcastle upon Tyne.

Ehrenreich, Susanne (2018): Communities of practice and English as a lingua franca. In Jennifer Jenkins, Will Baker & Martin Dewey (eds.), *The Routledge handbook of English as a Lingua Franca*, 37–50. Abingdon: Routledge.

Ellili-Cherif, Maha & Haitham Alkhateeb (2015): College students' attitude toward the medium of instruction: Arabic versus English dilemma. *Universal Journal of Educational Research 3*(3). 207–213. doi:10.13189/ujer.2015.030306.

ElShaer, Amr, Gianpiero Calabrese, Diogo Casanova & Isabel Huet (2016): Building a community of practice for engaging pharmacy students to learn in a collaborative research environment. *Currents in Pharmacy Teaching and Learning 8*(5). 698–707. doi:10.1016/j.cptl.2016.05.001.

Elwy, A. Rani, Kamal M. F. Itani, Barbara G. Bokhour, Nora M. Mueller, Mark E. Glickman, Shibei Zhao, Amy K. Rosen, et al. (2016): Surgeons' disclosures of clinical adverse events. *JAMA Surgery 151*(11). 1015–1021. doi:10.1001/jamasurg.2016.1787.

Enfield, Niicholas J. (2008): Common ground as a resource for social affiliation. In Istvan Kecskes & Jacob Mey (eds.), *Intention, common ground and the egocentric speaker-hearer*, 223–254. Berlin: Mouton de Gruyter.

Engel-Hills, Penelope & Rethy K. Chhem (2012): The nature of professional expertise. In Kathryn M. Hibbert, Rethy K. Chhem, Teresa van Deven & Shih-chang Wang (eds.), *Radiology education: the evaluation and assessment of clinical competence*, 3–9. Berlin, Heidelberg: Springer Berlin Heidelberg. doi:10.1007/978-3-642-27600-2_1.

Epomedicine (2020): Medical mnemonics. https://epomedicine.com/medical-mnemonics/ (date accessed 13/ 10/2020).

Epstein, R. M., Peter Franks, Cleveland Shileds, Sean Meldrum, Katherine Miller, Thomas Campbell & Kevin Fiscella (2005): Patient-centered communication and diagnostic testing. *The Annals of Family Medicine 3*(5). 415–421. doi:10.1370/afm.348.

Falcone, John L., René N. Claxton & Gary T. Marshall (2014): Communication skills training in surgical residency: a needs assessment and metacognition analysis of a difficult conversation objective structured clinical examination. *Journal of Surgical Education 71*(3). 309–315. doi:10.1016/j.jsurg.2013.09.020.

Fassaert, Thijs, Jaap Peen, Annemieke van Straten, Matty de Wit, Agnes Schrier, Henk Heijnen, Pim Cuijpers, Arnoud Verhoeff, Aartjan Beekman & Jack Dekker (2010): Ethnic differences and similarities in outpatient treatment for depression in the Netherlands. *Psychiatric Services 61*(7). 690–697. doi:10.1176/ps.2010.61.7.690.

Fassier, Thomas & Elie Azoulay (2010): Conflicts and communication gaps in the intensive care unit. *Current Opinion in Critical Care 16*(6). 654–665. doi:10.1097/MCC.0b013e32834044f0.

Ferguson, Gibson (1997): Teacher education and LSP: the role of specialised knowledge. In Ron Howard & Gillian Brown (eds.), *Teacher education for language for specific purposes*, 80–89. Clevedon: Multilingual Matters.

Ferguson, Gibson (2013): English for Medical Purposes. In Brian Paltridge & Sue Starfield (eds.), *The Handbook of English for Specific Purposes*, 243–261. Chichester: John Wiley & Sons. doi:10.1002/9781118339855.ch13.

Fernando, Asanga, Chris Attoe, Peter Jaye, Sean Cross, James Pathan & Simon Wessely (2017): Improving interprofessional approaches to physical and psychiatric comorbidities through simulation. *Clinical Simulation in Nursing 13*(4). 186–193. doi:10.1016/j.ecns.2016.12.004.

Ferrell, Betty Rolling & Judith A. Paice (2019): *Oxford textbook of palliative nursing*. 5th edn. Oxford: Oxford University Press.

Firth, Alan (1996): The discursive accomplishment of normality: on 'lingua franca' English and conversation analysis. *Journal of Pragmatics 26*(2). 237–259. doi:10.1016/0378-2166(96)00014-8.

Firth, Alan (2009): The lingua franca factor. *Intercultural Pragmatics 6*(2). 147–170. doi:10.1515/IPRG.2009.009.

Flickinger, Tabor E., Somnath Saha, Debra Roter, P. Todd Korthuis, Victoria Sharp, Jonathan Cohn, Susan Eggly, Richard D. Moore & Mary Catherine Beach (2016): Clinician empathy is associated with differences in patient–clinician communication behaviors and higher medication self-efficacy in HIV care. *Patient Education and Counseling 99*(2). 220–226. doi:10.1016/j.pec.2015.09.001.

Flin, Rhona, Lucy Mitchell & Bonnie McLeod (2014): Non-technical skills of the scrub practitioner the SPLINTS system. *ORNAC Journal 32*(3). 33–38.

Flores, G., M. B. Laws, S. J. Mayo, B. Zuckerman, M. Abreu, L. Medina & E. J. Hardt (2003): Errors in medical interpretation and their potential clinical consequences in pediatric encounters. *PEDIATRICS 111*(1). 6–14. doi:10.1542/peds.111.1.6.

Forman, Dawn, Marion Jones & Jill Thistlethwaite (2016): *Leading research and evaluation in interprofessional education and collaborative practice*. London: Palgrave Macmillan UK. doi:10.1057/978-1-137-53744-7.

Foronda, Cynthia, Brent MacWilliams & Erin McArthur (2016): Interprofessional communication in healthcare: an integrative review. *Nurse Education in Practice 19*. 36–40. doi:10.1016/j.nepr.2016.04.005.

Fortin, Auguste H, Richard M Frankel, Brenda Lovegrove Lepisto & Robert C Smith (2019): *Smith's patient-centred interviewing: an evidence-based method*. 4th edn. New York: McGraw-Hill Education.

Four-Babb, Joyanne De, Jerine Pegg & Makini Beck (2015): Reducing intellectual poverty of outsiders within academic spaces through informal peer mentorship. *Mentoring & Tutoring: Partnership in Learning 23*(1). 76–93. doi:10.1080/13611267.2015.1011038.

Frankel, Richard M. (1984): From sentence to sequence: understanding the medical encounter through microinteractional analysis. *Discourse Processes 7*(2). 135–170. doi:10.1080/01638538409544587.

Frankel, Richard M. (1990): Talking in interviews: a dispreference for patient-initiated questions. In George Psathas (ed.), *Interaction competence*, 231–262. Washington, DC: University Press of America.

Frankel, Richard M, Mindy Flanagan, Patricia Ebright, Alicia Bergman, Colleen M. O' Brien, Zamal Franks, Andrew Allen, Angela Harris & Jason J Saleem (2012): Context, culture and (non-verbal) communication affect handover quality. *BMJ Quality & Safety 21* (Suppl 1). i121 LP-i128. doi:10.1136/bmjqs-2012-001482.

Freeman, Thomas R. (2016): *McWhinney's textbook of family medicine*. 4th edn. Oxford: Oxford University Press.
French, Roger (2003): *Medicine before science: the business of medicine from the Middle Ages to the Enlightenment*. Cambridge: Cambridge University Press. doi:10.1017/CBO9780511614989.005.
Fromherz, Allen J. (2017): *Qatar: a modern history*. Washington, DC: Georgetown University Press.
Fuchs, Milena Žic (2018): Crossing over to the future: interdisciplinarity in research and higher education. *European Review 26*(S2). S1–S5. doi:10.1017/S1062798718000327.
Fujimori, M. & Y. Uchitomi (2009): Preferences of cancer patients regarding communication of bad news: a systematic literature review. *Japanese Journal of Clinical Oncology 39*(4). 201–216. doi:10.1093/jjco/hyn159.
Fussell, Blair (2011): The local flavour of English in the Gulf. *English Today 27*(4). 26–32. doi:http://dx.doi.org/10.1017/S0266078411000502.
García, Ofelia (2009): *Translanguaging: bilingual education in the 21st century*. Oxford: Wiley Blackwell.
García, Ofelia & Li Wei (2014): *Translanguaging: language, bilingualism and education*. London: Palgrave Macmillan UK. doi:10.1057/9781137385765.
Gasiorek, Jessica & Kris van de Poel (2012): Divergent perspectives on language-discordant mobile medical professionals' communication with colleagues: an exploratory study. *Journal of Applied Communication Research 40*(4). 368–383. doi:10.1080/00909882.2012.712708.
Gerwing, Jennifer & Meredith Allison (2009): The relationship between verbal and gestural contributions in conversation. *Gesture 9*(3). 312–336. doi:10.1075/gest.9.3.03ger.
Gerwing, Jennifer & Anne Marie Landmark Dalby (2014): Gestures convey content: an exploration of the semantic functions of physicians' gestures. *Patient Education and Counseling 96*(3). 308–314. doi:10.1016/j.pec.2014.07.014.
Giannoni, Davide Simone (2008): Medical writing at the periphery: the case of Italian journal editorials. *Journal of English for Academic Purposes 7*(2). 97–107. doi:10.1016/j.jeap.2008.03.003.
Gibson, Barbara E. (2008): Videorecording. In Lisa M. Given (ed.), *The SAGE encyclopedia of qualitative research methods*, 917–918. Thousand Oaks: SAGE Publications. doi:10.4135/9781412963909.n481.
Gliva-McConvey, Gayle, Catherine Nicholas & Lou Clark (2020): *Comprehensive healthcare simulation: implementing best practices in standardized patient methodology*. New York: Springer. doi:10.1007/978-3-030-43826-5.
Goffman, Erving (1974): *Frame Analysis: an essay on the organization of experience*. New York: Harper and Row.
Goffman, Erving (1981): *Forms of talk*. Philadelphia: University of Pennsylvania Press.
Goldman, Brian (1991): Ayurvedism: eastern medicine moves west. *Canadian Medical Association Journal 144*(2). 218–221.
González-Aguña, Alexandra, Marta Fernández-Batalla, Sara Gasco-González, Adriana Cercas-Duque, María Lourdes Jiménez-Rodríguez & José María Santamaría-García (2021): Taxonomic triangulation of care in healthcare protocols. *CIN: Computers, Informatics, Nursing 39*(3). 145–153. doi:10.1097/CIN.0000000000000662.
Gordon, Lisi, Charlotte Rees, Jean Ker & Jennifer Cleland (2017): Using video-reflexive ethnography to capture the complexity of leadership enactment in the healthcare

workplace. *Advances in Health Sciences Education 22*(5). 1101–1121. doi:10.1007/s10459-016-9744-z.

Goroll, Allan H., Carl Sirio, F. Daniel Duffy, Richard F. LeBlond, Patrick Alguire, Thomas A. Blackwell, William E. Rodak & Thomas Nasca (2004): A new model for accreditation of residency programs in internal medicine. *Annals of Internal Medicine 140* (11).902. doi:10.7326/0003-4819-140-11-200406010-00012.

Gotti, Maurizio (2011): *Investigating specialized discourse*. 3rd edn. Bern: Peter Lang.

Gotti, Maurizio (2016): Variations in medical discourse for academic purposes. In Pilar Ordóñez-López & Nuria Edo-Marzá (eds.), *Medical discourse in professional, academic and popular settings*, 9–30. Bristol: Multilingual Matters.

Government of Qatar (2020): Education and Training. *Topics* https://portal.www.gov.qa/wps/portal/topics/Education+and+Training (date accessed 21/ 12/2020).

Green, Molly (2017): Language barriers and health of Syrian refugees in Germany. *American Journal of Public Health 107*(4). 486–486. doi:10.2105/AJPH.2016.303676.

Greenfield, Sheldon, Sherrie H. Kaplan, John E. Ware, Elizabeth Martin Yano & Harrison J. L. Frank (1988): Patients' participation in medical care. *Journal of General Internal Medicine 3*(5). 448–457. doi:10.1007/BF02595921.

Grudzen, Corita R, Lillian L Emlet, Joanne Kuntz, Ashley Shreves, Erin Zimny, Maureen Gang, Monique Schaulis, Scott Schmidt, Eric Isaacs & Robert Arnold (2016): EM Talk: communication skills training for emergency medicine patients with serious illness. *BMJ Supportive & Palliative Care 6*(2). 219–224. doi:10.1136/bmjspcare-2015-000993.

Guchelaar, Henk-Jan, Hadewig B B Colen, Mathijs D Kalmeijer, Patrick T W Hudson & Irene M. Teepe-Twiss (2005): Medication errors. *Drugs 65*(13). 1735–1746. doi:10.2165/00003495-200565130-00001.

Gude, T., H. Grimstad, A. Holen, T. Anvik, A. Baerheim, O. B. Fasmer, P Hjortdahl & P. Vaglum (2015): Can we rely on simulated patients' satisfaction with their consultation for assessing medical students' communication skills? A cross-sectional study. *BMC Medical Education 15*(1). 225. doi:10.1186/s12909-015-0508-x.

Gullick, Janice G. & Sandra H. West (2016): Building research capacity and productivity among advanced practice nurses: an evaluation of the Community of Practice model. *Journal of Advanced Nursing 72*(3). 605–619. doi:10.1111/jan.12850.

Gumperz, Joseph John (1968): The speech community. In D. L. Sills (ed.), *International Encyclopedia of the Social Sciences*, 381–386. New York: MacMillan.

Gunnarsson, Britt-Louise (2009): *Professional discourse*. London: Continuum.

Gupta, Anthea Fraser (2010): Singapore Standard English revisted. In Lisa Lim, Anne Pakir & Lionel Wee (eds.), *English in Singapore: modernity and management (Asian Englishes Today)*, 57–89. Hong Kong: Hong Kong University Press.

Ha, Jennifer Fong & Nancy Longnecker (2010): Doctor-patient communication: a review. *The Ochsner Journal 10*(1). 38–43.

Hall, Judith A., Debra L. Roter & Cynthia S. Rand (1981): Communication of affect between patient and physician. *Journal of Health and Social Behavior 22*(1). 18. doi:10.2307/2136365.

Hall, Pippa (2005): Interprofessional teamwork: professional cultures as barriers. *Journal of Interprofessional Care 19*(sup1). 188–196. doi:10.1080/13561820500081745.

Hamada, Yo (2016): Shadowing: who benefits and how? Uncovering a booming EFL teaching technique for listening comprehension. *Language Teaching Research 20*(1). 35–52. doi:10.1177/1362168815597504.

Hampers, Louis C., Susie Cha, David J. Gutglass, Helen J. Binns & Steven E. Krug (1999): Language barriers and resource utilization in a pediatric emergency department. *Pediatrics 103*(6). 1253–1256. doi:10.1542/peds.103.6.1253.

Hampers, Louis C. & Jennifer E. McNulty (2002): Professional interpreters and bilingual physicians in a pediatric emergency department. *Archives of Pediatrics & Adolescent Medicine 156* (11).1108. doi:10.1001/archpedi.156.11.1108.

Hanamoto, Hiroki (2016): How participants in English as a Lingua Franca (ELF) employ communication strategies: multiple realities in minimal responses in ELF. *Asian Englishes 18*(3). 181–196. doi:10.1080/13488678.2016.1229832.

Harbison, Joseph, Omar Hossain, Damian Jenkinson, John Davis, Stephen J. Louw & Gary A. Ford (2003): Diagnostic accuracy of stroke referrals from primary care, emergency room physicians, and ambulance staff using the Face Arm Speech Test. *Stroke 34*(1). 71–76. doi:10.1161/01.STR.0000044170.46643.5E.

Harding, Mariann M. & Maureen Barry (2018): Introduction to medical-surgical nursing in Canada. In Sharon L. Lewis, Shannon Ruff Dirksen, Margaret M. Heitkemper, Linda Bucher, Maureen A. Barry, Sandra Goldsworthy, Jana Lok, Jane Tyerman & Mariann M. Harding (eds.), *Medical-surgical nursing in Canada*, 2–20. 4th edn. Milton: Elsevier Canada.

Hayden, Jennifer K., Richard A. Smiley, Maryann Alexander, Suzan Kardong-Edgren & Pamela R. Jeffries (2014): The NCSBN National Simulation Study: a longitudinal, randomized, controlled study replacing clinical hours with simulation in prelicensure nursing education. *Journal of Nursing Regulation 5*(2). S3–S40. doi:10.1016/S2155-8256(15)30062-4.

Health Workforce Department (2018): International platform on health worker mobility: an introduction. *Meeting of the International Platform on Health Worker Mobility*. Geneva: World Health Organization.

Heath, Christian (1992): The delivery and reception of diagnosis in the general practice consultation. In Paul Drew & John Heritage (eds.), *Talk at work: interaction in institutional settings*, 235–267. Cambridge: Cambridge University Press.

Hegland, Pål A., Hege Aarlie, Hilde Strømme & Gro Jamtvedt (2017): Simulation-based training for nurses: systematic review and meta-analysis. *Nurse Education Today 54*. 6–20. doi:10.1016/j.nedt.2017.04.004.

Helman, Cecil G. (1984): The role of context in primary care. *The Journal of the Royal College of General Practitioners 34*. 547–550.

Hemsley, Bronwyn, Susan Balandin & Linda Worrall (2012): Nursing the patient with complex communication needs: time as a barrier and a facilitator to successful communication in hospital. *Journal of Advanced Nursing 68*(1). 116–126. doi:10.1111/j.1365-2648.2011.05722.x.

Herdman, Heather T. & Shigemi Kamitsuru (2017): *NANDA international nursing diagnoses: definitions and classification, 2018-2019*. 11th edn. New York: Thieme.

Herfs, Paul G P (2014): Aspects of medical migration with particular reference to the United Kingdom and the Netherlands. *Human Resources for Health 12*(1). 59. doi:10.1186/1478-4491-12-59.

Heritage, John (2010): Questioning in medicine. In Alice F. Freed & Susan Lynn Ehrlich (eds.), *Why do you ask? The functions of questions in institutional discourse*, 42–68. Oxford: Oxford University Press.

Heritage, John & Douglas W. Maynard (2006): *Communication in medical care. Interaction between primary care physicians and patients*. Cambridge: Cambridge University Press.

Hillman, Sara & Emilio Ocampo Eibenschutz (2018): English, super-diversity, and identity in the State of Qatar. *World Englishes 37*(2). 228–247. doi:10.1111/weng.12312.

Hinkel, Eli (2010): 11. Integrating the four skills: current and historical perspectives. http://www.w.elihinkel.org/downloads/Integrating_the_four_skills.pdf (date accessed 13/ 12/2020).

HMC Patients and family rights. *Heart Hospital* https://www.hamad.qa/EN/Hospitals-and-services/HeartHospital/PatientsandVisitors/General_information/Pages/Patient-and-Family-Rights.aspx (date accessed 12/12/ 2020a).

HMC Interpreter services. *Patient Information* https://www.hamad.qa/EN/Patient-Information/Interpreter-Services/Pages/default.aspx (date accessed 12/12/ 2020b).

Hogan-Quigley, Beth, Mary Louise Palm & Lynn Bickley (2017): *Bates' nursing guide to physical examination and assessment*. 2nd edn. Philadelphia: Wolters Kluwer.

Holes, Clive D. (2011): Language and identity in the Arabian Gulf. *Journal of Arabian Studies 1* (2). 129–145. doi:10.1080/21534764.2011.628492.

Holliday, Adrian (2005): *The struggle to teach English as an international language*. Oxford: Oxford University Press.

Holmes, Janet & Miriam Meyerhoff (1999): The community of practice: theories and methodologies in language and gender research. *Language in Society 28*(2). S004740459900202X. doi:10.1017/S004740459900202X.

Holmes, Janet & Nick Wilson (2017): *Introduction to sociolinguistics*. 5th edn. Abingdon: Routledge.

Horner, Bruce (2018): Written academic English as a lingua franca. In Jennifer Jenkins, Will Baker & Martin Dewey (eds.), *The Routledge handbook of English as a Lingua Franca*, 413–426. Abingdon: Routledge.

Horner, Bruce, Min-Zhan Lu, Jacqueline Jones Royster & John Trimbur (2011): Language difference in writing: toward a translingual approach. *College English 73*(3). 303–321.

House, Juliane (2003): English as a lingua franca: a threat to multilingualism? *Journal of Sociolinguistics 7*(4). 556–578. doi:10.1111/j.1467-9841.2003.00242.x.

Hu, Frank B., Ambika Satija, Eric B. Rimm, Donna Spiegelman, Laura Sampson, Bernard Rosner, Carlos A. Camargo, Meir Stampfer & Walter C. Willett (2016): Diet assessment methods in the Nurses' Health Studies and contribution to evidence-based nutritional policies and guidelines. *American Journal of Public Health 106*(9). 1567–1572. doi:10.2105/AJPH.2016.303348.

Hudson, P.T.W. & Henk-Jan Guchelaar (2003): Risk assessment in clinical pharmacy. *Pharmacy World and Science 25*(3). 98–103. doi:10.1023/A:1024068817085.

Hughes, Jason, Nick Jewson & Lorna Unwin (2007): *Communities of practice: critical perspectives*. Abingdon: Routledge.

Hull, Melodie (2013): *Medical language: terminology in context*. Philadelphia: F.A. Davis.

Hull, Melodie (2016): Medical language proficiency: a discussion of interprofessional language competencies and potential for patient risk. *International Journal of Nursing Studies 54*. 158–172. doi:10.1016/j.ijnurstu.2015.02.015.

Hülmbauer, Cornelia (2009): 'We don't take the right way. We just take the way that we think you will understand' – the shifting relationship between correctness and effectiveness in ELF. In Anna Mauranen & Elina Ranta (eds.), *English as a lingua franca: studies and findings*, 323–347. Newcastle upon Tyne: Cambridge Scholars.

Hutchby, Ian & Robin Wooffitt (2008): *Conversation analysis*. 2nd edn. Cambridge: Polity Press.
Hyland, Ken (2014): Re-imagining literacy: english in Hong Kong's new university curriculum. In David Coniam (ed.), *English Language Education and Assessment*, 139–151. Singapore: Springer Singapore. doi:10.1007/978-981-287-071-1_9.
Hyland, Ken (2019): English for Specific Purposes: some influences and impacts. In Xuesong Gau (ed.), *Second handbook of English language teaching*, 337–353. Cham: Springer. doi:10.1007/978-3-030-02899-2_19.
Hyland, Ken & Liz Hamp-Lyons (2002): EAP: issues and directions. *Journal of English for Academic Purposes* 1(1). 1–12. doi:10.1016/S1475-1585(02)00002-4.
Hymes, Dell (1974): *Foundations in sociolinguistics: an ethnographic approach*. Philadelphia: University of Pennsylvania Press.
Hynninen, Niina & Anna Solin (2018): Language norms in ELF. In Jennifer Jenkins, Will Baker & Martin Dewey (eds.), *The Routledge handbook of English as a Lingua Franca*, 267–278. Abingdon: Routledge.
Ibnouf, Arwa, Lois Dou & Jane Knight (2014): The evolution of Qatar as an education hub: moving to a knowledge-based economy. *International Education Hubs*, 43–61. Dordrecht: Springer Netherlands. doi:10.1007/978-94-007-7025-6_4.
IELTS (2020): IELTS scoring in detail. https://www.ielts.org/ielts-for-organisations/ielts-scoring-in-detail (date accessed 25/ 11/2020).
IMedPub (2020): Health assessment. *Health Science Journal* https://www.imedpub.com/scholarly/health-assessment-journals-articles-ppts-list.php (date accessed 21/ 12/2020).
International Relations and Security Network (2009): Charter of the GCC. *Charter of the Gulf Cooperation Council* https://www.files.ethz.ch/isn/125347/1426_GCC.pdf (date accessed 04/ 07/2018).
Irwin, Richard S. & Naomi D. Richardson (2006): Patient-focused care. *Chest 130*(1). 73S-82S. doi:10.1378/chest.130.1_suppl.73S.
ISMP (Institute for Safe Medication Practices) (2019): List of confused drug names. https://www.ismp.org/recommendations/confused-drug-names-list (date accessed 14/ 12/2020).
Jackson, Carey (1998): Medical interpretation: an essential service for non-English-speaking immigrants. In Sana Loue (ed.), *Handbook of immigrant health*, 61–79. New York: Plenum.
Janardhan, N. (2009): Expatriates – a liability? *Khaleej Times*.
Jayasuriya-Illesinghe, Vathsala, Sepali Guruge, Bawantha Gamage & Sherry Espin (2016): Interprofessional work in operating rooms: a qualitative study from Sri Lanka. *BMC Surgery* 16(1). 61. doi:10.1186/s12893-016-0177-7.
Jefferson, Gail (2005): Glossary of transcript symbols with an introduction. In Gene H. Lerner (ed.), *Conversation analysis: studies from the first generation*, 13–31. Amsterdam: John Benjamins.
Jeffries, Pamela (2020): *Simulation in nursing education: from conceptualization to evaluation*. 3rd edn. Wolters Kluwer.
Jeffries, Pamela R, Kristina Thomas Dreifuerst, Suzie Kardong-Edgren & Jennifer Hayden (2015): Faculty development when initiating simulation programs: lessons learned from the National Simulation Study. *Journal of Nursing Regulation* 5(4). 17–23. doi:10.1016/S2155-8256(15)30037-5.
Jenkins, J. (2012): English as a Lingua Franca from the classroom to the classroom. *ELT Journal* 66(4). 486–494. doi:10.1093/elt/ccs040.

Jenkins, Jennifer (2000): *The phonology of English as an international language: new models, new norms, new goals*. Oxford: Oxford University Press.

Jenkins, Jennifer (2007): *English as a lingua franca: attitude and identity*. Oxford: Oxford University Press.

Jenkins, Jennifer (2011): Accommodating (to) ELF in the international university. *Journal of Pragmatics 43*(4). 926–936. doi:10.1016/j.pragma.2010.05.011.

Jenkins, Jennifer (2015): Repositioning English and multilingualism in English as a Lingua Franca. *Englishes in Practice 2*(3). 49–85. doi:10.1515/eip-2015-0003.

Jenkins, Jennifer, Alessia Cogo & Martin Dewey (2011): Review of developments in research into English as a lingua franca. *Language Teaching 44*(03). 281–315. doi:10.1017/S0261444811000115.

Jenks, Christopher (2018): Uncooperative lingua franca encounters. In Jennifer Jenkins, Will Baker & Martin Dewey (eds.), *The Routledge handbook of English as a Lingua Franca*, 279–291. Abingdon: Routledge.

Jensen, Sharon (2018): *Nursing health assessment: a best practice approach*. 3rd edn. Philadelphia: Wolters Kluwer.

Jewitt, Carey (2014): An introduction to multimodality. In Carey Jewitt (ed.), *The Routledge handbook of multimodal analysis*, 15–30. 2nd edn. Abingdon: Routledge.

Jin, Ying & Bernadette Maria Watson (2020): Playback: An investigation of the discursive implications and the pragmatic functions of repetition in traditional Chinese medical consultations. *Journal of Language and Social Psychology 39*(5–6). 716–737. doi:10.1177/0261927X20908614.

John-Baptiste, Ava, Gary Naglie, George Tomlinson, Shabbir M. H. Alibhai, Edward Etchells, Angela Cheung, Moira Kapral, et al. (2004): The effect of English language proficiency on length of stay and in-hospital mortality. *Journal of General Internal Medicine 19*(3). 221–228. doi:10.1111/j.1525-1497.2004.21205.x.

Julliard, Kell, Elena Klimenko & Mary S. Jacob (2006): Definitions of health among healthcare providers. *Nursing Science Quarterly 19*(3). 265–271. doi:10.1177/0894318406289575.

Kaba, R. & P. Sooriakumaran (2007): The evolution of the doctor-patient relationship. *International Journal of Surgery 5*(1). 57–65. doi:10.1016/j.ijsu.2006.01.005.

Kachru, Braj B. (1991): Liberation linguistics and the Quirk Concern. *English Today 7*(01). 3–13. doi:10.1017/S026607840000523X.

Kachru, Braj B. (1996): The paradigms of marginality. *World Englishes 15*(3). 241–255. doi:10.1111/j.1467-971X.1996.tb00112.x.

Kachru, Braj B (1985): Standards, codification and sociolinguistic realism: the English language in the outer circle. In Randolph Quirk & Henry G Widdowson (eds.), *English in the World: Teaching and learning the language and literatures*, 11–30. Cambridge: Cambridge University Press.

Kachru, Braj B (2008): The first step: the Smith paradigm for intelligibility in world Englishes. *World Englishes 27*(3–4). 293–296. doi:10.1111/j.1467-971X.2008.00567.x.

Kachru, Yamuna (1993): Social meaning and creativity in Indian English speech acts. In James E Alatis (ed.), *Georgetown University Round Table on Languages and Linguistics (GURT) 1992: language, Communication, and Social Meaning*, 378–387. Washington, DC: Georgetown University Press.

Kachru, Yamuna & Larry E Smith (2008): *Cultures, contexts and World Englishes*. New York: Routledge.

Kahane, Henry & Renee Kahane (1976): Lingua franca: the story of a term. *Romance Philology* 30(1). 25–41.

Kain, Zeev N., Jill E. Maclaren, Carrie Hammell, Cristina Novoa, Michelle A. Fortier, Heather Huszti & Linda Mayes (2009): Healthcare provider-child-parent communication in the preoperative surgical setting. *Pediatric Anesthesia* 19(4). 376–384. doi:10.1111/j.1460-9592.2008.02921.x.

Kalocsai, Karolina (2014): *Communities of practice and English as a lingua franca: a study of students in a central European context.* Berlin: De Gruyter Mouton.

Kane, Michael T. (1992): An argument-based approach to validity. *Psychological Bulletin* 112(3). 527–535. doi:10.1037/0033-2909.112.3.527.

Kane, Tanya (2014): Whose lingua franca? The politics of language in transnational medical education. *The Journal of General Education* 63(2–3). 94–112. doi:10.5325/jgeneeduc.63.2-3.0094.

Kankaanranta, Anne & Leena Louhiala-Salminen (2018): ELF in the domain of business – BELF. What does the B stand for? In Jennifer Jenkins, Will Baker & Martin Dewey (eds.), *The Routledge handbook of English as a Lingua Franca*, 309–320. Abingdon: Routledge.

Karliner, Leah S., Elizabeth A. Jacobs, Alice Hm Chen & Sunita Mutha (2007): Do professional interpreters improve clinical care for patients with Limited English Proficiency? A systematic review of the literature. *Health Services Research* 42(2). 727–754. doi:10.1111/j.1475-6773.2006.00629.x.

Karliner, Leah S., Sue E. Kim, David O. Meltzer & Andrew D. Auerbach (2010): Influence of language barriers on outcomes of hospital care for general medicine inpatients. *Journal of Hospital Medicine* 5(5). 276–282. doi:10.1002/jhm.658.

Karliner, Leah S., Eliseo J. Pérez-Stable & Ginny Gildengorin (2004): The language divide: the importance of training in the use of interpreters for outpatient practice. *Journal of General Internal Medicine* 19(2). 175–183. doi:10.1111/j.1525-1497.2004.30268.x.

Karmani, Sohail (2005): Petro-Linguistics: the emerging nexus between oil, English, and Islam. *Journal of Language, Identity & Education* 4(2). 87–102. doi:10.1207/s15327701jlie0402_2.

Kaur, Jagdish (2009a): Pre-empting problems of understanding in English as a Lingua Franca. In Anna Mauranen & Elina Ranta (eds.), *English as a lingua franca: studies and findings*, 107–123. Newcastle upon Tyne: Cambridge Scholars.

Kaur, Jagdish (2009b): *English as a lingua franca: co-constructing understanding.* Saarbrücken: VDM Verlag.

Kaur, Jagdish (2011): Intercultural communication in English as a lingua franca: some sources of misunderstanding. *Intercultural Pragmatics* 8(1). 93–116. doi:10.1515/IPRG.2011.004.

Kaur, Jagdish (2018): ELF in spoken genres in the international university: of contextual factors and non-linguistic resources. *Journal of English as a Lingua Franca* 7(2). 403–410. doi:10.1515/jelf-2018-0020.

Kecskes, Istvan (2003): *Situation-bound utterances in L1 and L2.* Berlin: Mouton de Gruyter.

Kecskes, Istvan (2008): Dueling contexts: a dynamic model of meaning. *Journal of Pragmatics* 40(3). 385–406. doi:10.1016/j.pragma.2007.12.004.

Kecskes, Istvan (2010): The paradox of communication: socio-cognitive approach to pragmatics. *Pragmatics and Society* 1(1). 50–73. doi:10.1075/ps.1.1.04kec.

Kecskes, Istvan (2014): *Intercultural pragmatics.* Oxford: Oxford University Press.

Kecskes, Istvan & Fenghui Zhang (2009): Activating, seeking, and creating common ground: a socio-cognitive approach. *Pragmatics & Cognition* 17(2). 331–355. doi:10.1075/pc.17.2.06kec.

Keifenheim, Katharina E., Martin Teufel, Julianne Ip, Natalie Speiser, Elisabeth J. Leehr, Stephan Zipfel & Anne Herrmann-Werner (2015): Teaching history taking to medical students: a systematic review. *BMC Medical Education* 15(1). 159. doi:10.1186/s12909-015-0443-x.

Kelly, Deborah V., Lisa Bishop, Stephanie Young, John Hawboldt, Leslie Phillips & T. Montgomery Keough (2013): Pharmacist and physician views on collaborative practice. *Canadian Pharmacists Journal / Revue des Pharmaciens du Canada* 146(4). 218–226. doi:10.1177/1715163513492642.

Khairat, Saif & Gong Yang (2010): Understanding effective clinical communication inmedical errors. In C. Safran, S. Reti & H.F. Marin (eds.), *Studies in Health Technology and Informatics*, 704–708. Cape Town: IOS Press. doi:10.3233/978-1-60750-588-4-704.

Kim, Jung Hee, Myung-Haeng Hur & Hyun-Young Kim (2018): The efficacy of simulation-based and peer-learning handover training for new graduate nurses. *Nurse Education Today* 69. 14–19. doi:10.1016/j.nedt.2018.06.023.

Kimura, Daisuke & Suresh Canagarajah (2018): Translingual practice and ELF. In Jennifer Jenkins, Will Baker & Martin Dewey (eds.), *The Routledge handbook of English as a Lingua Franca*, 295–308. Abingdon: Routledge.

Kincheloe, Joe L. (2001): Describing the bricolage: conceptualizing a new rigor in qualitative research. *Qualitative Inquiry* 7(6). 679–692. doi:10.1177/107780040100700601.

Kincheloe, Joe L. (2005): On to the next level: continuing the conceptualization of the bricolage. *Qualitative Inquiry* 11(3). 323–350. doi:10.1177/1077800405275056.

Kirkpatrick, Andy (2010a): *English as a lingua franca in ASEAN: a multilingual model.* Hong Kong: Hong Kong University Press.

Kirkpatrick, Andy (2010b): Researching English as a Lingua Franca in Asia: the Asian Corpus of English (ACE) project. *Asian Englishes* 13(1). 4–18. doi:10.1080/13488678.2010.10801269.

Kitzinger, Celia (2013): Repair. In Jack Sidnell & Tanya Stivers (eds.), *The handbook of conversation analysis*, 229–256. Malden: Blackwell. doi:10.1002/9781118325001.

Klagsbrun, J (2001): Listening and focusing: holistic health care tools for nurses. *The Nursing Clinics of North America* 36(1). 115–30.

Knight, Jane (2014): Understanding education hubs within the context of crossborder education. *International Education Hubs*, 13–27. Dordrecht: Springer Netherlands. doi:10.1007/978-94-007-7025-6_2.

Knighton, Andrew J., Kimberly D. Brunisholz & Samuel T. Savitz (2017): Detecting risk of low health literacy in disadvantaged populations using area-based measures. *eGEMs (Generating Evidence & Methods to Improve Patient Outcomes)* 5 (3).7, 1–10. doi:10.5334/egems.191.

Kohn, Linda T, Janet M Corrigan & Molla S Donaldson (2000): *To err is human: building a safer health system.* Washington, DC: National Academies Press. doi:10.17226/9728.

Kosmützky, Anna (2018): Tracing the development of international branch campuses: from local founding waves to global diffusion? *Globalisation, Societies and Education* 16(4). 453–477. doi:10.1080/14767724.2018.1512044.

Kress, Gunther (2014): What is mode? In Carey Jewitt (ed.), *The Routledge handbook of multimodal analysis*, 60–75. 2nd edn. Abingdon: Routledge.

Kurtz, Suzanne, Juliet Draper & Jonathan Silverman (2005): *Teaching and learning communication skills in medicine*. 2nd edn. Abingdon: Radcliffe.
Labov, William (1972): *Sociolinguistic patterns*. Philadelphia: University of Pennsylvania Press.
Larsen-Freeman, Diane (2018): Complexity and ELF. In Jennifer Jenkins, Will Baker & Martin Dewey (eds.), *The Routledge handbook of English as a Lingua Franca*, 51–60. Abingdon: Routledge.
Lauver, Diane R., Sandra E. Ward, Susan M. Heidrich, Mary L. Keller, Barbara J. Bowers, Patricia Flatley Brennan, Karin T. Kirchhoff & Thelma J. Wells (2002): Patient-centered interventions. *Research in Nursing & Health* 25(4). 246–255. doi:10.1002/nur.10044.
Lave, Jean & Etienne Wenger (1991): *Situated learning: legitimate peripheral participation*. Cambridge: Cambridge University Press.
Law, Jonathan & Elizabeth Martin (2020): *Concise medical dictionary*. (Ed.) Jonathan Law & Elizabeth Martin 10th edn. Oxford: Oxford University Press. doi:10.1093/acref/9780198836612.001.0001.
Leape, Lucian L. (1995): Systems analysis of adverse drug events. *JAMA: The Journal of the American Medical Association* 274(1). 35. doi:10.1001/jama.1995.03530010049034.
Leape, Lucian L. & Donald M. Berwick (2005): Five years after To Err Is Human. *JAMA* 293 (19). 2384. doi:10.1001/jama.293.19.2384.
Lee, Jeewon, Joonho Jung, Jai Sung Noh, Seungmin Yoo & You Sun Hong (2013): Perioperative psycho-educational intervention can reduce postoperative delirium in patients after cardiac surgery: a pilot study. *The International Journal of Psychiatry in Medicine* 45(2). 143–158. doi:10.2190/PM.45.2.d.
Lee, Karen C., Jonathan P. Winickoff, Minah K. Kim, Eric G. Campbell, Joseph R. Betancourt, Elyse R. Park, Angela W. Maina & Joel S. Weissman (2006): Resident physicians' use of professional and nonprofessional interpreters: a national survey. *JAMA* 296(9). 1049. doi:10.1001/jama.296.9.1050.
Lehtinen, Esa (2007): Merging doctor and client knowledge: On doctors' ways of dealing with clients' potentially discrepant information in genetic counseling. *Journal of Pragmatics* 39(2). 389–427. doi:10.1016/j.pragma.2006.05.006.
Leotsakos, A., H. Zheng, R. Croteau, J. M. Loeb, H. Sherman, C. Hoffman, L. Morganstein, et al. (2014): Standardization in patient safety: the WHO High 5s project. *International Journal for Quality in Health Care* 26(2). 109–116. doi:10.1093/intqhc/mzu010.
Levinson, Stephen C. (1992): Activity types and language. In Paul Drew & John Heritage (eds.), *Talk at work: interaction in institutional settings*, 66–100. Cambridge: Cambridge University Press.
Lewis, Christine; & David Deterding (2018): Word stress and pronunciation teaching in English as a Lingua Franca contexts. *CATESOL Journal* 30(1). 161–176.
Lipkin, Mack Jr., J.G. Carrol, R.M. Frankel, Samuel M. Putnam, Aaron Lazare, A. Keller, T. Klein & P.K. Williams (2011): *The medical interview: clinical care, education, and research*. Springer-Verlag.
Liu, Min, Therese Poirier, Lakesha Butler, Rhonda Comrie & Junvie Pailden (2015): Design and evaluation of interprofessional cross-cultural communication sessions. *Journal of Interprofessional Care* 29(6). 622–627. doi:10.3109/13561820.2015.1051215.
Lloyd, B W & P Barnett (1993): Use of problem lists in letters between hospital doctors and general practitioners. *BMJ* 306(6872). 247–247. doi:10.1136/bmj.306.6872.247.
Lu, Peih-ying & John Corbett (2012): *English in medical education: an intercultural approach to teaching language and values*. Bristol: Multilingual Matters.

Luo, Jing & Mark Garner (2017): The challenges and opportunities for English teachers in teaching ESP in China. *Journal of Language Teaching and Research* 8(1). 81. doi:10.17507/jltr.0801.10.

Lynch, T. (2007): Learning from the transcripts of an oral communication task. *ELT Journal* 61(4). 311–320. doi:10.1093/elt/ccm050.

Lyndon, Audrey, Marya G. Zlatnik & Robert M. Wachter (2011): Effective physician-nurse communication: a patient safety essential for labor and delivery. *American Journal of Obstetrics and Gynecology* 205(2). 91–96. doi:10.1016/j.ajog.2011.04.021.

MacKenzie, Ian (2014): *English as a lingua franca: theorizing and teaching English*. Abingdon: Routledge.

Maejima, Satoko & Ryuichi Ohta (2019): Physical assessment by Japanese community hospital nurses compared to that performed overseas: a cross-sectional study. *Journal of General and Family Medicine* 20(2). 55–61. doi:10.1002/jgf2.230.

Maguire, P. & Carolyn Pitceathly (2002): Key communication skills and how to acquire them. *BMJ* 325(7366). 697–700. doi:10.1136/bmj.325.7366.697.

Mahboob, Ahmar & Tariq Elyas (2014): English in the Kingdom of Saudi Arabia. *World Englishes* 33(1). 128–142. doi:10.1111/weng.12073.

Maher, J (1987): English as an international language of medicine. *Medical Education* 21(4). 283–284. doi:10.1111/j.1365-2923.1987.tb00363.x.

Maher, John (1986): The development of English as an international language of medicine. *Applied Linguistics* 7(2). 206–218. doi:10.1093/applin/7.2.206.

Mann, Karen V (2011): Theoretical perspectives in medical education: past experience and future possibilities. *Medical Education* 45(1). 60–68. doi:10.1111/j.1365-2923.2010.03757.x.

Mann, Michael (2014): *South Asia's modern history*. London: Routledge. doi:10.4324/9781315754550.

Manna, Aditya, SK Sarkar & LK Khanra (2015): PA1 An internal audit into the adequacy of pain assessment in a hospice setting. *BMJ Supportive & Palliative Care* 5 (Suppl1). A19.3-A20. doi:10.1136/bmjspcare-2015-000906.61.

Marslen-Wilson, William D & Alan Welsh (1978): Processing interactions and lexical access during word recognition in continuous speech. *Cognitive Psychology* 10(1). 29–63. doi:10.1016/0010-0285(78)90018-X.

Martin, Elliott B., Natalia M. Mazzola, Jessica Brandano, Donna Luff, David Zurakowski & Elaine C. Meyer (2015): Clinicians' recognition and management of emotions during difficult healthcare conversations. *Patient Education and Counseling* 98(10). 1248–1254. doi:10.1016/j.pec.2015.07.031.

Marvel, M. Kim, Ronald M. Epstein, Kristine Flowers & Howard B. Beckman (1999): Soliciting the patient's agenda. *JAMA* 281(3). 283. doi:10.1001/jama.281.3.283.

Matsumoto, Yumi (2015): *Multimodal communicative strategies for resolving miscommunication in multilingual writing classrooms*. Pennsylvania State University.

Matsumoto, Yumi (2018): Challenging moments as opportunities to learn: the role of nonverbal interactional resources in dealing with conflicts in English as a lingua franca classroom interactions. *Linguistics and Education* 48. 35–51. doi:10.1016/j.linged.2018.08.007.

Matsumoto, Yumi (2019): Exploring epistemological expansions of English as a Lingua Franca. *TESOL Quarterly* 53(2). 566–578. doi:10.1002/tesq.508.

Matthews, Peter Hugoe (2014): *The Concise Oxford Dictionary of Linguistics*. Oxford University Press. doi:10.1093/acref/9780199675128.001.0001.

Mauranen, Anna (2003): The corpus of English as Lingua Franca in academic settings. *TESOL Quarterly 37*(3). 513–527. doi:10.2307/3588402.
Mauranen, Anna (*2006*): Signaling and preventing misunderstanding in English as lingua franca communication. *International Journal of the Sociology of Language* 2006(177). 123–150. doi:https://doi.org/10.1515/IJSL.2006.008.
Mauranen, Anna (2010): Discourse reflexivity – a discourse universal? The case of ELF. *Nordic Journal of English Studies 9*(2). 13–40.
Mauranen, Anna (2012): *Exploring ELF: academic English shaped by non-native speakers*. Cambridge: Cambridge University Press.
Mauranen, Anna (2018): Conceptualising ELF. In Jennifer Jenkins, Will Baker & Martin Dewey (eds.), *The Routledge handbook of English as a Lingua Franca*, 7–24. Abingdon: Routledge.
Mauranen, Anna, Niina Hynninen & Elina Ranta (2010): English as an academic lingua franca: the ELFA project. *English for Specific Purposes* doi:10.1016/j.esp.2009.10.001.
Maxwell, Joseph Alex (2012): *A realist approach for qualitative research*. Thousand Oaks: Sage.
McArthur, Tom (1998): *The English languages*. Cambridge: Cambridge University Press.
McArthur, Tom (2002): *The Oxford Guide to World English*. Oxford: Oxford University Press.
Mead, Nicola & Peter Bower (2000): Patient-centredness: a conceptual framework and review of the empirical literature. *Social Science & Medicine 51*(7). 1087–1110. doi:10.1016/S0277-9536(00)00098-8.
Meierkord, Christiane (2005): Interactions across Englishes and their lexicon. In Claus Gnutzmann & Frauke Intemann (eds.), *The globalisation of English and the English language classroom*, 89–104. Tubingen: Gunter Narr.
Merritt, Marilyn (1977): The playback: an instance of variation in discourse. In Ralph W. Fasold & Roger W. Shuy (eds.), *Studies in language variation: semantics, syntax, phonology, pragmatics, social situations, ethnographic approaches*, 198–208. Washington, DC: Georgetown University Press.
Merton, Robert K. (1957): Some preliminaries to a sociology of medical education. In Robert K. Merton, George G. Reader & Patricia L. Kendall (eds.), *The student-physician: introductory studies in the sociology of medical education*, 3–79. Cambridge: Harvard University Press.
Meterko, Mark, Steven Wright, Hai Lin, Elliott Lowy & Paul D. Cleary (2010): Mortality among patients with acute myocardial infarction: the influences of patient-centered care and evidence-based medicine. *Health Services Research 45*(5p1). 1188–1204. doi:10.1111/j.1475-6773.2010.01138.x.
Meuter, Renata F. I., Cindy Gallois, Norman S. Segalowitz, Andrew G. Ryder & Julia Hocking (2015): Overcoming language barriers in healthcare: A protocol for investigating safe and effective communication when patients or clinicians use a second language. *BMC Health Services Research 15*(1). 371. doi:10.1186/s12913-015-1024-8.
Meyerhoff, Miriam (2004): Communities of practice. In J.K. Chambers, Peter Trudgill & Natalie Schilling-Estes (eds.), *The Handbook of language variation and change*, 526–548. Malden: Blackwell.
Michaels, Robert K., Martin A. Makary, Yasser Dahab, Frank J. Frassica, Eugenie Heitmiller, Lisa C. Rowen, Richard Crotreau, Henry Brem & Peter J. Pronovost (2007): Achieving the National Quality Forum's 'Never Events': prevention of wrong site, wrong procedure, and wrong patient operations. *Annals of Surgery 245*(4). 526–532. doi:10.1097/01.sla.0000251573.52463.d2.

Michalski, Kerstin, Nabeel Farhan, Edith Motschall, Werner Vach & Martin Boeker (2017): Dealing with foreign cultural paradigms: A systematic review on intercultural challenges of international medical graduates. (Ed.) Jacobus P. van Wouwe *PLOS ONE 12*(7). e0181330. doi:10.1371/journal.pone.0181330.

Miles, Leslie W, Linda Mabey, Sarah Leggett & Katie Stansfield (2014): Teaching communication and therapeutic relationship skills to baccalaureate nursing students: a peer mentorship simulation approach. *Journal of Psychosocial Nursing and Mental Health Services 52*(10). 34–41. doi:10.3928/02793695-20140829-01.

Miller, Karen-Lee & Pia C. Kontos (2013): The intraprofessional and interprofessional relations of neurorehabilitation nurses: a negotiated order perspective. *Journal of Advanced Nursing 69*(8). 1797–1807. doi:10.1111/jan.12041.

Milroy, Lesley (2004): Social networks. In J.K. Chambers, Peter Trudgill & Schilling-Estes (eds.), *The Handbook of language variation and change*, 549–572. Malden: Blackwell.

Mishra, Anuradha, David Browning, Miriam J. Haviland, Mary Lou Jackson, Donna Luff, Elaine C. Meyer, Katherine Talcott & Carolyn E. Kloek (2018): Communication skills training in ophthalmology: results of a needs assessment and pilot training program. *Journal of Surgical Education 75*(2). 417–426. doi:10.1016/j.jsurg.2017.08.011.

Mitchell, J. Clyde (1986): Network procedures. In Dieter Frick, Hans W. Hoefert, Heiner Legewie, Rainer Mackensen & Rainer K. Silbereisen (eds.), *Quality of urban life*, 73–92. Berlin: De Gruyter. doi:10.1515/9783110884968.

Moore, Malcolm (2009): What do Nepalese medical students and doctors think about patient-centred communication? *Patient Education and Counseling 76*(1). 38–43. doi:10.1016/j.pec.2008.11.018.

Moore, Philippa M, Solange Rivera Mercado, Mónica Grez Artigues & Theresa A Lawrie (2013): Communication skills training for healthcare professionals working with people who have cancer. *Cochrane Database of Systematic Reviews 2018*(7). 1–97. doi:10.1002/14651858.CD003751.pub3.

Morley, Joan (1972): *Improving aural comprehension*. Ann Arbor: University of Michigan Press.

Morley, Joan (1980): Active participation / purposeful listening in the language laboratory: aspects of theory and practice. *SPEAQ Journal 4*(3–4). 25–54.

Mortensen, Janus (2013): Notes on English used as a lingua franca as an object of study. *Journal of English as a Lingua Franca 2*(1). 25–46. doi:10.1515/jelf-2013-0002.

Mu, Congjun & Lawrence Jun Zhang (2018): Understanding Chinese multilingual scholars' experiences of publishing research in English. *Journal of Scholarly Publishing 49*(4). 397–418. doi:10.3138/jsp.49.4.02.

Mueller, Pam A. & Daniel M. Oppenheimer (2014): The pen is mightier than the keyboard. *Psychological Science 25*(6). 1159–1168. doi:10.1177/0956797614524581.

Müller-Staub, Maria, Ian Needham, Matthias Odenbreit, Mary Ann Lavin & Theo van Achterberg (2008): Implementing nursing diagnostics effectively: cluster randomized trial. *Journal of Advanced Nursing 63*(3). 291–301. doi:10.1111/j.1365-2648.2008.04700.x.

Murata, Kumiko (1995): Repetitions: a cross-cultural study. *World Englishes 14*(3). 343–356. doi:10.1111/j.1467-971X.1995.tb00078.x.

Murray, B.L. & E.J. Hauenstein (2008): Self harm and suicidal behaviour: children, adolescents, and adults. In Wendy Austin & Mary Ann Boyd (eds.), *Psychiatric Nursing for Canadian Practice*, 898–922. Philadelphia: Lippincott, Williams & Wilkins.

Mustafa, Mohammed, Andrew Carson-Stevens, David Gillespie & Adrian GK Edwards (2013): Psychological interventions for women with metastatic breast cancer. *Cochrane Database of Systematic Reviews* doi:10.1002/14651858.CD004253.pub4.
NAPRA (2014): Language proficiency requirements for licensure as a pharmacist in Canada. https://napra.ca/sites/default/files/2017-08/Language_Proficiency_Requirements_for_Licensure_Pharmacist_June2014_b2.pdf (date accessed 24/ 11/2020).
National League for Nursing (2015): Managing incivility. http://cms.montgomerycollege.edu/nursingsims/ (date accessed 21/ 09/2018).
Naughton, Cynthia (2018): Patient-centered communication. *Pharmacy* 6(1). 18. doi:10.3390/pharmacy6010018.
Nebel, Anne (2017): Linguistic superdiversity and English-medium higher education in Qatar. In L. Arnold, A. Nebel & L. Ronesi (eds.), *Emerging writing research from the Middle East – North Africa region*, 27–40. Fort Collins: The WAC Clearing House & University Press of Colorado.
Nehring, Wendy M. & Felissa R. Lashley (2010): *High-fidelity patient simulation in nursing training*. Sudbury: Jones & Bartlett Publishers.
Nelson, Cecil L (2011): *Intelligibility in World Englishes: theory and application*. New York: Routledge.
Nerminathan, Arany, Amanda Harrison, Megan Phelps, Karen M. Scott & Shirley Alexander (2017): Doctors' use of mobile devices in the clinical setting: a mixed methods study. *Internal Medicine Journal* 47(3). 291–298. doi:10.1111/imj.13349.
Nestel, Debra & Tanya Tierney (2007): Role-play for medical students learning about communication: guidelines for maximising benefits. *BMC Medical Education* 7(1). 3. doi:10.1186/1472-6920-7-3.
Newman-Toker, David E., Ernest Moy, Ernest Valente, Rosanna Coffey & Anika L. Hines (2014): Missed diagnosis of stroke in the emergency department: a cross-sectional analysis of a large population-based sample. *Diagnosis* 1(2). 155–166. doi:10.1515/dx-2013-0038.
Nguyen, Lisa, Steven Ropers, Esther Nderitu, Anneke Zuyderduin, Sam Luboga & Amy Hagopian (2008): Intent to migrate among nursing students in Uganda: measures of the brain drain in the next generation of health professionals. *Human Resources for Health* 6(1). 5. doi:10.1186/1478-4491-6-5.
Nicotera, Anne Maydan, Margaret M. Mahon & Kevin B. Wright (2014): Communication that builds teams. *Nursing Administration Quarterly* 38(3). 248–260. doi:10.1097/NAQ.0000000000000033.
Nielsen-Bohlman, Lynn, Allison M. Panzer & David A. Kindig (2004): *Health literacy: a prescription to end confusion*. Washington, DC: National Academy Press.
Norris, Sigrid (2004): *Analyzing multimodal interaction: a methodological framework*. New York: Routledge.
Nursing Council of New Zealand (2020): Internationally qualified nurses with other registrations (non-Australian). *Registration for International Nurses* https://www.nursingcouncil.org.nz/ (date accessed 25/ 11/2020).
O'Regan, John P. (2014): English as a lingua franca: an immanent critique. *Applied Linguistics* 35(5). 533–552. doi:10.1093/applin/amt045.
OECD (2019): *Recent trends in international migration of doctors, nurses and medical students*. Paris: OECD. doi:10.1787/5571ef48-en.

Oelke, Nelly D., Wilfreda E. Thurston & Nancy Arthur (2013): Intersections between interprofessional practice, cultural competency and primary healthcare. *Journal of Interprofessional Care 27*(5). 367–372. doi:10.3109/13561820.2013.785502.

OET (2020): Occupational English Test. *The OET: English language test for healthcare professionals* https://www.occupationalenglishtest.org/ (date accessed 24/ 11/2020).

Oliveira, Kathleen De, Sara North, Barbra Beck & Jane Hopp (2015): Promoting collaboration and cultural competence for physician assistant and physical therapist students: a cross-cultural decentralized interprofessional education model. *Journal of Educational Evaluation for Health Professions 12*. 20. doi:10.3352/jeehp.2015.12.20.

Oliveira, Vinicius C., Manuela L. Ferreira, Rafael Z. Pinto, Ruben F. Filho, Kathryn Refshauge & Paulo H. Ferreira (2015): Effectiveness of training clinicians' communication skills on patients' clinical outcomes: a systematic review. *Journal of Manipulative and Physiological Therapeutics 38*(8). 601–616. doi:10.1016/j.jmpt.2015.08.002.

Ong, L.M.L., J.C.J.M. de Haes, A.M. Hoos & F.B. Lammes (1995): Doctor-patient communication: A review of the literature. *Social Science & Medicine 40*(7). 903–918. doi:10.1016/0277-9536(94)00155-M.

Osimk-Teasdale, Ruth (2018): Analysing ELF variablity. In Jennifer Jenkins, Will Baker & Martin Dewey (eds.), *The Routledge handbook of English as a Lingua Franca*, 201–209. Abingdon: Routledge.

'Paper' (2020): Paper. *Cambridge Dictionary* https://dictionary.cambridge.org/dictionary/english/paper (date accessed 22/ 12/2020).

Patrick, Peter L. (2004): The speech community. In J.K. Chambers, Peter Trudgill & Natalie Schilling-Estes (eds.), *The Handbook of language variation and change*, 573–597. Malden: Blackwell.

Paulino, Nancy Armenta, María Sandín Vázquez & Francisco Bolúmar (2019): Indigenous language and inequitable maternal health care, Guatemala, Mexico, Peru and the Plurinational State of Bolivia. *Bulletin of the World Health Organization 97*(1). 59–67. doi:10.2471/BLT.18.216184.

Pelzang, Rinchen (2010): Time to learn: understanding patient-centred care. *British Journal of Nursing 19*(14). 912–917.

Pennycook, Alastair (2007): *Global Englishes and transcultural flows*. London: Routledge.

Pennycook, Alastair (2009): Plurilithic Englishes: towards a 3D model. In Kumiko Murata & Jennifer Jenkins (eds.), *Global Englishes in Asian contexts: current and future debates*, 194–207. Basingstoke: Palgrave Macmillan.

Pennycook, Alastair (2012): *Language and mobility: unexpected places*. Bristol: Multilingual Matters.

Peräkylä, Anssi (2006): Communicating and responding to diagnosis. In John Heritage & Douglas W. Maynard (eds.), *Communication in medical care. Interaction between primary care physicians and patients*, 214–247. Cambridge: Cambridge University Press.

Pfrimmer, Dale (2009): Teamwork and communication. (Ed.) Diane Twedell *The Journal of Continuing Education in Nursing 40*(7). 294–295. doi:10.3928/00220124-20090623-09.

Pilnick, Alison (2001): The interactional organization of pharmacist consultations in a hospital setting: a putative structure. *Journal of Pragmatics 33*(12). 1927–1945. doi:10.1016/S0378-2166(00)00079-5.

Pilnick, Alison, Diane Trusson, Suzanne Beeke, Rebecca O'Brien, Sarah Goldberg & Rowan H. Harwood (2018): Using conversation analysis to inform role play and simulated interaction in communications skills training for healthcare professionals: identifying avenues for further development through a scoping review. *BMC Medical Education 18*(1). 267. doi:10.1186/s12909-018-1381-1.

Pilotto, Louis S, Geraldine F Duncan & Jane Anderson-Wurf (2007): Issues for clinicians training international medical graduates: a systematic review. *Medical Journal of Australia 187*(4). 225–228. doi:10.5694/j.1326-5377.2007.tb01204.x.

Pitzl, Marie-Luise (2012): Creativity meets convention: idiom variation and remetaphorization in ELF. *Journal of English as a Lingua Franca 1*(1). 27–55. doi:10.1515/jelf-2012-0003.

Pitzl, Marie-Luise (2018): *Creativity in English as a lingua franca: idiom and metaphor.* Berlin: De Gruyter Mouton.

Pope, Barbara B., Lisa Rodzen & Gene Spross (2008): Raising the SBAR. *Nursing 38*(3). 41–43. doi:10.1097/01.NURSE.0000312625.74434.e8.

Pratt, Mary Louise (1991): Arts of the contact zone. *Profession* 33–40.

Prideaux, Antony (2011): Issues in nursing documentation and record-keeping practice. *British Journal of Nursing 20*(22). 1450–1454. doi:10.12968/bjon.2011.20.22.1450.

Purden, Margaret (2005): Cultural considerations in interprofessional education and practice. *Journal of Interprofessional Care 19*(sup1). 224–234. doi:10.1080/13561820500083238.

Pyörälä, Eeva, Saana Mäenpää, Leo Heinonen, Daniel Folger, Teemu Masalin & Heikki Hervonen (2019): The art of note taking with mobile devices in medical education. *BMC Medical Education 19*(1). 96. doi:10.1186/s12909-019-1529-7.

Quail, Michelle, Shelley B Brundage, Josh Spitalnick, Peter J Allen & Janet Beilby (2016): Student self-reported communication skills, knowledge and confidence across standardised patient, virtual and traditional clinical learning environments. *BMC Medical Education 16*(1). 73. doi:10.1186/s12909-016-0577-5.

Quirk, Mark E. (2006): *Intuition and metacognition in medical education: keys to developing expertise.* New York: Springer.

Rachul, Christen & Lara Varpio (2020): More than words: how multimodal analysis can inform health professions education. *Advances in Health Sciences Education 25*(5). 1087–1097. doi:10.1007/s10459-020-10008-9.

Raimes, Ann (1992): Instructional balance: from theories to practices in the teaching of writing. In James E. Alatis (ed.), *Georgetown University Round Table on Languages and Linguistics (GURT) 1991: linguistics and language pedagogy*, 238–249. Washington, DC: Georgetown University Press.

Ratcliffe, Susan (2016): *Oxford Essential Quotations.* (Ed.) Susan Ratcliffe 4th edn. Vol. 1. Oxford: Oxford University Press. doi:10.1093/acref/9780191826719.001.0001.

Ray, Joel D. & Angela S. Overman (2014): Hard facts about soft skills. *AJN, American Journal of Nursing 114*(2). 64–68. doi:10.1097/01.NAJ.0000443784.75162.b7.

Reilly, Amanda & Christine Spratt (2007): The perceptions of undergraduate student nurses of high-fidelity simulation-based learning: A case report from the University of Tasmania. *Nurse Education Today 27*(6). 542–550. doi:10.1016/j.nedt.2006.08.015.

Renandya, W. A. & T. S. C. Farrell (2011): 'Teacher, the tape is too fast!' Extensive listening in ELT. *ELT Journal 65*(1). 52–59. doi:10.1093/elt/ccq015.

Roberts, Celia, Becky Moss, Val Wass, Srikant Sarangi & Roger Jones (2005): Misunderstandings: a qualitative study of primary care consultations in multilingual settings, and educational implications. *Medical Education 39*(5). 465–475. doi:10.1111/j.1365-2929.2005.02121.x.

Robinson, Pauline C. (1991): *ESP today: a practitioner's guide.* Hertfordshire: Prentice-Hall.

Rosenberg, Ilene L., Todd Cassese & Dennis Barbon (2018): *Netter's clinical skills: pocket guide*. Elsevier.
Rost, Michael (2002): *Teaching and researching listening*. Harlow: Longman.
Rost, Michael (2016): *Teaching and researching listening*. 3rd edn. New York: Routledge.
Roter, Debra L., Richard M. Frankel, Judith A. Hall & David Sluyter (2006): The expression of emotion through nonverbal behavior in medical visits. Mechanisms and outcomes. *Journal of General Internal Medicine 21*(S1). S28–S34. doi:10.1111/j.1525-1497.2006.00306.x.
Roter, Debra L., Gail Geller, Susan M. Bernhardt, Barbara A. Larson & Teresa Doksum (1999): Effects of obstetrician gender on communication and patient satisfaction. *Obstetrics & Gynecology 93*(5). 635–641. doi:10.1016/S0029-7844(98)00542-0.
Roter, Debra L. & Judith A. Hall (2006): *Doctors talking with patients/patients talking with doctors: improving communication in medical visits*. 2nd edn. Westport: Praeger.
Sacks, Harvey, Emanuel A. Schegloff & Gail Jefferson (1974): A simplest systematics for the organization of turn-taking for conversation. *Language 50*(4). 696–735. doi:10.2307/412243.
Sagar, Priscilla (2012): *Transcultural nursing theory and models*. New York: Springer.
Sailaja, Pingali (2009): *Indian English*. Edinburgh: Edinburgh University Press.
Saks, Mike & Judith Allsop (2019): Introduction to researching health. *Researching health: qualitative, quantitative and mixed methods*, 3–15. 3rd edn. Thousand Oaks: SAGE.
Sawir, Erlenawati (2004): Keeping up with native speakers: the many and positive roles of repetition in the conversations of EFL learners. *Asian EFL Journal 6*(4). 1–32.
Schegloff, Emanuel A. (1987): Some sources of misunderstanding in talk-in-interaction. *Linguistics 25*(1). 201–218. doi:10.1515/ling.1987.25.1.201.
Schenker, Yael, Eliseo J. Pérez-Stable, Dana Nickleach & Leah S. Karliner (2011): Patterns of interpreter use for hospitalized patients with Limited English Proficiency. *Journal of General Internal Medicine 26*(7). 712–717. doi:10.1007/s11606-010-1619-z.
Schillinger, Dean, John Piette, Kevin Grumbach, Frances Wang, Clifford Wilson, Carolyn Daher, Krishelle Leong-Grotz, Cesar Castro & Andrew B Bindman (2003): Closing the loop: physician communication with diabetic patients who have low health literacy. *Archives of Internal Medicine 163*(1). 83–90. doi:10.1001/archinte.163.1.83.
Schneider, Edgar W. (2012): Exploring the interface between World Englishes and Second Language Acquisition – and implications for English as a Lingua Franca. *Journal of English as a Lingua Franca 1*(1). 57–91. doi:10.1515/jelf-2012-0004.
Schoenthaler, Antoinette, William F. Chaplin, John P. Allegrante, Senaida Fernandez, Marleny Diaz-Gloster, Jonathan N. Tobin & Gbenga Ogedegbe (2009): Provider communication effects medication adherence in hypertensive African Americans. *Patient Education and Counseling 75*(2). 185–191. doi:10.1016/j.pec.2008.09.018.
Schwei, Rebecca J., Sam Del Pozo, Niels Agger-Gupta, Wilma Alvarado-Little, Ann Bagchi, Alice Hm Chen, Lisa Diamond, Francesca Gany, Doreena Wong & Elizabeth A. Jacobs (2016): Changes in research on language barriers in health care since 2003: a cross-sectional review study. *International Journal of Nursing Studies 54*. 36–44. doi:10.1016/j.ijnurstu.2015.03.001.
Scollon, Ron, Suzanne Wong Scollon & Rodney H. Jones (2012): *Intercultural communication: a discourse approach*. 3rd edn. Chichester: John Wiley & Sons.
Seibert, Susan (2015): The meaning of a healthcare Community of Practice. *Nursing Forum 50*(2). 69–74. doi:10.1111/nuf.12065.

Seidlhofer, Barbara (2001): Closing a conceptual gap: the case for a description of English as a lingua franca. *International Journal of Applied Linguistics* 11(2). 133–158. doi:10.1111/1473-4192.00011.

Seidlhofer, Barbara (2009a): Orientations in ELF research: form and function. In Anna Mauranen & Elina Ranta (eds.), *English as a lingua franca: Studies and findings*, 37–59. Newcastle upon Tyne: Cambridge Scholars.

Seidlhofer, Barbara (2009b): Common ground and different realities: world Englishes and English as a lingua franca. *World Englishes* 28(2). 236–245. doi:10.1111/j.1467-971X.2009.01592.x.

Seidlhofer, Barbara (2011): *Understanding English as a lingua franca*. Oxford: Oxford University Press.

Shajani, Zahra & Diana Snell (2019): *Wright and Leahey's Nurses and Families: a guide to family assessment and intervention*. 7th edn. Philadelphia: F.A. Davis.

Shimoda, Jody, Marie-Claude Toriida & William D Kay (2016): Improving learning outcomes: creating and implementing a specialized corpus. *TESOL Arabia Perspectives* 24(1). 22–28.

Shuy, Roger W (1983): Three types of interference to an effective exchange of information in the medical interview. In Sue Fisher & Alexandra Dundas Todd (eds.), *Social organization of doctor-patient communication*, 189–202. Washington, DC: Centre for Applied Linguistics.

Siassakos, Dimitrios, Katherine Bristowe, Helen Hambly, Jo Angouri, Joanna F. Crofts, Catherine Winter, Linda P. Hunt & Timothy J. Draycott (2011): Team communication with patient actors. *Simulation in Healthcare: The Journal of the Society for Simulation in Healthcare* 6(3). 143–149. doi:10.1097/SIH.0b013e31821687cf.

Sidnell, Jack & Tanya Stivers (2013): *The handbook of conversation analysis*. Chichester: John Wiley & Sons. doi:10.1002/9781118325001.

Siegel, Jeff (2001): Koine formation and creole genesis. In Norval Smith & Tonjes Veenstra (eds.), *Creolization and contact*, 175–197. John Benjamins.

Skjeggestad, Erik, Jennifer Gerwing & Pål Gulbrandsen (2017): Language barriers and professional identity: a qualitative interview study of newly employed international medical doctors and Norwegian colleagues. *Patient Education and Counseling* 100(8). 1466–1472. doi:10.1016/j.pec.2017.03.007.

Slusser, Margaret, Luis L. Garcia, Carole-Rae Reed & Patricia Quinn McGinnis (2018): *Foundations of interprofessional collaborative practice in health care*. St Louis: Elsevier.

Smit, Ute (2010): *English as a lingua franca in higher education: a longitudinal study of classroom discourse*. Berlin: De Gruyter Mouton.

Smith, Emma (2008): Pitfalls and promises: the use of secondary data analysis in educational research. *British Journal of Educational Studies* 56(3). 323–339. doi:10.1111/j.1467-8527.2008.00405.x.

Smith, Larry E (1992): Spread of English and issues of intelligibility. In Braj B Kachru (ed.), *The Other Tongue: english across cultures*, vol. 2nd, 75–90. Urbana, IL: University of Illinois Press.

Smith, Larry E & Cecil L Nelson (1985): International intelligibility of English: directions and resources. *World Englishes* 4(3). 333–342. doi:10.1111/j.1467-971X.1985.tb00423.x.

Snow, C. P. (1998): *The two cultures and the scientific revolution (with Introduction by Stefan Collini)*. Cambridge: Cambridge University Press.

Snyder, William M. & Etienne Wenger (2004): Our world as a learning system: a communities-of-practice approach. In Marcia L. Connor & James G. Clawson (eds.), *Creating a learning culture: strategy, technology and practice*, 35–58. Cambridge: Cambridge University Press.

Sole, Mary Lou, Mary Elizabeth Guimond & Christina Amidei (2013): An analysis of simulation resources, needs, and plans in Florida. *Clinical Simulation in Nursing* 9(7). e265–e271. doi:10.1016/j.ecns.2012.03.003.

Sopel, Jon (2020): Coronavirus: The young doctors being asked to play god. *BBC News*.

Sorkhabi, Rasoul (2010): The Qatar oil discoveries. *GeoExPro* 7(1). 42–46.

Squires, Susan & Michael L. Van De Vanter (2012): Communities of practice. In D. Douglas Caulkins & Ann T. Jordan (eds.), *A companion to organizational anthropology*, 289–310. Chichester: John Wiley & Sons. doi:10.1002/9781118325513.ch14.

Stevens, Sue & Dianne Pickering (2010): Keeping good nursing records: a guide. *Community Eye Health* 23(74). 44–45.

Stewart, Moira, Judith Belle Brown, Wayne W. Weston, Thomas R. Freeman & Carol L. McWilliam (2014): Introduction. In Moira Stewart, Judith Belle Brown, Wayne W. Weston, Ian R. McWhinney, Carol L. McWilliam & Thomas R. Freeman (eds.), *Patient-centered medicine: transforming the clinical method*, 3–17. 3rd edn. London: Radcliffe.

Street, Richard L. Jr. (1991): Accommodation in medical consultations. In Howard Giles, Justine Coupland & Nikolas Coupland (eds.), *Contexts of accommodation: developments in applied sociolinguistics*, 131–156. Cambridge: Cambridge University Press.

Sun, Hao (2004): Opening moves in informal Chinese telephone conversations. *Journal of Pragmatics* 36(8). 1429–1465. doi:10.1016/j.pragma.2004.01.007.

Svennevig, Jan (2013): Reformulation of questions with candidate answers. *International Journal of Bilingualism* 17(2). 189–204. doi:10.1177/1367006912441419.

Svennevig, Jan, Jennifer Gerwing, Bård Uri Jensen & Meredith Allison (2019): Pre-empting understanding problems in L1/L2 conversations: evidence of effectiveness from simulated emergency calls. *Applied Linguistics* 40(2). 205–227. doi:10.1093/applin/amx021.

Sweeney, E. & Z. Hua (2010): Accommodating toward your audience: do native speakers of English know how to accommodate their communication strategies toward nonnative speakers of English? *Journal of Business Communication* 47(4). 477–504. doi:10.1177/0021943610377308.

Taavitsainen, Irma & Päivi Pahta (2004): *Medical and scientific writing in Late Medieval English*. Cambridge: Cambridge University Press.

Taft, Marcus & Gail Hambly (1986): Exploring the cohort model of spoken word recognition. *Cognition* 22(3). 259–282. doi:10.1016/0010-0277(86)90017-X.

Tamparo, Carol & Wilburta Lindh (2017): *Therapeutic communication for health care professionals*. 4th edn. Boston: Cengage Learning.

Tannen, Deborah (1987): Repetition in conversation: toward a poetics of talk. *Language* 63(3). 574–605. doi:10.2307/415006.

Tannen, Deborah (2005): *Conversational style: analyzing talk among friends*. Oxford: Oxford University Press.

Tannen, Deborah (2007): *Talking voices: repetition, dialogue and imagery in conversational discourse*. 2nd edn. Cambridge: Cambridge University Press.

Tattersall, Martin H N, Phyllis N Butow, Judith E Brown & John F Thompson (2002): Improving doctors' letters. *The Medical Journal of Australia* 177(9). 516–20.

Tay, Li Hui, Emily Ang & Desley Hegney (2012): Nurses' perceptions of the barriers in effective communication with inpatient cancer adults in Singapore. *Journal of Clinical Nursing* 21(17–18). 2647–2658. doi:10.1111/j.1365-2702.2011.03977.x.

Tayem, Yasin, Ahmad AlShammari, Nouf Albalawi & Marwa Shareef (2020): Language barriers to studying medicine in English: perceptions of final-year medical students at the Arabian Gulf University. *Eastern Mediterranean Health Journal 26*(2). 233–238. doi:10.26719/2020.26.2.233.

The Joint Commission (2016): Most commonly reviewed sentinel event types. https://www.join tcommission.org/-/media/deprecated-unorganized/imported-assets/tjc/system-folders /topics-library/event_type_2q_2016pdf.pdf?db=web&hash=9C250CCEFD47B11B33D CA8277F68134B (date accessed 10/ 03/2020).

Theodoropoulou, Irene (2015): Sociolinguistic anatomy of mobility: evidence from Qatar. *Language & Communication 40*. 52–66. doi:10.1016/j.langcom.2014.12.010.

Thistlethwaite, Jill & Monica Moran (2010): Learning outcomes for interprofessional education (IPE): literature review and synthesis. *Journal of Interprofessional Care 24*(5). 503–513. doi:10.3109/13561820.2010.483366.

Thomas, Santhosh A (2003): Spinal stenosis: history and physical examination. *Physical Medicine and Rehabilitation Clinics of North America 14*(1). 29–39. doi:10.1016/S1047-9651(02)00049-9.

Thong, J F, P Mok & D Loke (2010): A quality assurance survey to improve communication between ENT specialists and general practitioners. *Singapore Medical Journal 51*(10). 796–9.

Thrysoe, Lars, Lise Hounsgaard, Nina Bonderup Dohn & Lis Wagner (2010): Participating in a community of practice as a prerequisite for becoming a nurse – Trajectories as final year nursing students. *Nurse Education in Practice 10*(6). 361–366. doi:10.1016/j.nepr.2010.05.004.

Thrysoe, Lars, Lise Hounsgaard, Nina Bonderup Dohn & Lis Wagner (2012): Newly qualified nurses – experiences of interaction with members of a community of practice. *Nurse Education Today 32*(5). 551–555. doi:10.1016/j.nedt.2011.07.008.

Till, Alex, Hanish Sall & Jonathan Wilkinson (2014): Safe handover: safe patients – the electronic handover system. *BMJ Quality Improvement Reports 2*(2). u202926.w1359. doi:10.1136/bmjquality.u202926.w1359.

Ting, Shawnea Sum Pok & Alessia Cogo Repetition and rephrasing in English as a lingua franca medical consultations in Hong Kong. In M. Gregory Tweedie & Robert C. Johnson (eds.), *Perspectives on medical English as a lingua franca*. Newcastle upon Tyne: Cambridge Scholars.

Todd, Alexandra Dundas (1984): The prescription of contraception: negotiations between doctors and patients. *Discourse Processes 7*(2). 171–200. doi:10.1080/01638538409544588.

Tongue, John R., Howard R. Epps & Laura L. Forese (2005): Communication skills for patient-centered care. *The Journal of Bone and Joint Surgery-American Volume 87*(3). 652–658. doi:10.2106/00004623-200503000-00027.

Trummer, Ursula F., Ulrich O. Mueller, Peter Nowak, Thomas Stidl & Jürgen M. Pelikan (2006): Does physician–patient communication that aims at empowering patients improve clinical outcome? *Patient Education and Counseling 61*(2). 299–306. doi:10.1016/j.pec.2005.04.009.

Tweedie, M. Gregory & Robert C. Johnson (2018a): Listening instruction and patient safety: exploring Medical English as a Lingua Franca (MELF) for nursing education. *Journal of Belonging, Identity, Language, and Diversity 2*(1). 75–100.

Tweedie, M. Gregory & Robert C. Johnson (2018b): Listening instruction for ESP: exploring nursing education where English is a lingua franca. In Joseph Siegel & Anne Burns (eds.), *International Perspectives on Teaching the Four Skills in ELT*, 65–77. London: Palgrave. doi:10.1007/978-3-319-63444-9_5.

Tweedie, M. Gregory & Robert C. Johnson (2019): Research directions in medical English as a lingua franca (MELF). *Language and Linguistics Compass 13*(3). e12312. doi:10.1111/lnc3.12312.

Tweedie, M. Gregory & Johnson, Robert, C. (in press). Perspectives on medical English as a lingua franca. Newcastle upon Tyne: Cambridge Scholars.

U.S. Department of Health and Human Services Office of Minority Health (2013): *National standards on culturally and linguistically appropriate services (CLAS) in health and health care: a blueprint for advancing and sustaining CLAS policy and practice*.

Vandergrift, Larry & Christine C M Goh (2012): *Teaching and learning second language listening: metacognition in action*. New York: Routledge. doi:10.4324/9780203843376.

Vivar, Cristina Garcia (2006): Putting conflict management into practice: a nursing case study. *Journal of Nursing Management 14*(3). 201–206. doi:10.1111/j.1365-2934.2006.00554.x.

Vogel, Daniela, Marco Meyer & Sigrid Harendza (2018): Verbal and non-verbal communication skills including empathy during history taking of undergraduate medical students. *BMC Medical Education 18*(1). 157–163. doi:10.1186/s12909-018-1260-9.

Vora, Neha (2015): Is the university universal? Mobile (re)constitutions of American academia in the Gulf Arab states. *Anthropology & Education Quarterly 46*(1). 19–36. doi:10.1111/aeq.12085.

Wales, Marilyn A & D Lynn Skillen (1997): Using scenarios as a testing method in teaching health assessment. *Journal of Nursing Education 36*(6). 256–262. doi:10.3928/0148-4834-19970902-07.

Walker, James E. (2015): *Canadian English: a sociolinguistic perspective*. New York: Routledge.

Wallace, Peggy (2007): *Coaching standardized patients for use in the assessment of clinical competence*. New York: Springer.

Wang, Ning, David Hailey & Ping Yu (2011): Quality of nursing documentation and approaches to its evaluation: a mixed-method systematic review. *Journal of Advanced Nursing 67*(9). 1858–1875. doi:10.1111/j.1365-2648.2011.05634.x.

Wang, Ying (2018): Chinese English as a lingua franca: an ideological inquiry. In Jennifer Jenkins, Will Baker & Martin Dewey (eds.), *The Routledge handbook of English as a Lingua Franca*, 151–164. Abingdon: Routledge.

Warde, Fiona, Janet Papadakos, Tina Papadakos, Danielle Rodin, Mohammad Salhia & Meredith Giuliani (2018): Plain language communication as a priority competency for medical professionals in a globalized world. *Canadian Medical Education Journal 9*(2). e52–e59.

Warne, T. & S. McAndrew (2009): Constructing a bricolage of nursing research, education and practice. *Nurse Education Today 29*(8). 855–858. doi:10.1016/j.nedt.2009.04.002.

Waters, Alan (2007a): ELT and 'the spirit of the times'. *ELT journal. Oxford Univ Press. 61*(4). 353–359. doi:10.1093/elt/ccm053.

Waters, Alan (2007b): Native-speakerism in ELT: Plus ca change . . .? *System 35*. 281–292. doi:10.1016/j.system.2007.01.002.

Weissman, Joel S., Joseph Betancourt, Eric G. Campbell, Elyse R. Park, Minah Kim, Brian Clarridge, David Blumenthal, Karen C. Lee & Angela W. Maina (2005): Resident physicians' preparedness to provide cross-cultural care. *JAMA 294* (9).1058. doi:10.1001/jama.294.9.1058.

Wenger-Trayner, Etienne & Beverly Wenger-Trayner (2015): Learning in a landscape of practice: a framework. In Etienn Wenger-Trayner, Mark Fenton-O'Creevy, Steven Hutchinson, Chris Kubiak & Beverly Wenger-Trayner (eds.), *Learning in landscapes of practice: boundaries, identity, and knowledgeability in practice-based learning*, 13–31. Abingdon: Routledge.

Wenger, Etienne (1998): *Communities of practice: learning, meaning and identity*. Cambridge: Cambridge University Press.

White, Debbie, Esther Suter, I. Parboosingh & Elizabeth Taylor (2008): Communities of Practice: creating opportunities to enhance quality of care and safe practices. *Healthcare Quarterly 11*(sp). 80–84. doi:10.12927/hcq.2008.19654.

Widdowson, H.G. (1996): Comment: authenticity and autonomy in ELT. *ELT Journal 50*(1). 67–68. doi:10.1093/elt/50.1.67.

Widdowson, H G (1998): Review article. *Applied Linguistics. Oxford University Press / USA. 19* (1). 136–151. doi:10.1093/applin/19.1.136.

Widdowson, Henry (2015): ELF and the pragmatics of language variation. *Journal of English as a Lingua Franca 4*(2). 359–372. doi:10.1515/jelf-2015-0027.

Widdowson, Henry G (2004): A perspective on recent trends. In Anthony Philip Reid Howatt & Henry G Widdowson (eds.), *A history of English language teaching*, 353–372. 2nd edn. Oxford: Oxford University Press.

Willoughby, John (2006): Ambivalent anxieties of the South Asian – Gulf Arab labor exchange. In John W. Fox, Nada Mourtada-Sabbah & Mohammed Al-Mutawa (eds.), *Globalization and the Gulf*, 223–243. London: Routledge.

Wilson, Arnold T. (1928): *The Persian Gulf: An historical sketch from the earliest times to the beginning of the 20th century*. Abingdon: Routledge.

Wilson, Elisabeth, Alice H.M. Chen, Kevin Grumbach, Frances Wang & Alicia Fernandez (2005): Effects of limited English proficiency and physician language on health care comprehension. *Journal of General Internal Medicine 20*(9). 800–806. doi:10.1111/j.1525-1497.2005.0174.x.

Wilson, H. J (2000): The myth of objectivity: is medicine moving towards a social constructivist medical paradigm? *Family Practice 17*(2). 203–209. doi:10.1093/fampra/17.2.203.

Wolpe, Paul Root (1994): The dynamics of heresy in a profession. *Social Science & Medicine 39*(9). 1133–1148. doi:10.1016/0277-9536(94)90346-8.

Wood, Eileen, Lucia Zivcakova, Petrice Gentile, Karin Archer, Domenica De Pasquale & Amanda Nosko (2012): Examining the impact of off-task multi-tasking with technology on real-time classroom learning. *Computers & Education 58*(1). 365–374. doi:10.1016/j.compedu.2011.08.029.

World Health Organization (1988): *Learning together to work together for health: report of a WHO study group on multiprofessional education of health personnel: the team approach*. Geneva.

World Health Organization (2009): *WHO guidelines for safe surgery*. Geneva.

World Health Organization (2010): The WHO Global Code of Practice on the International Recruitment of Health Personnel. http://www.who.int/hrh/migration (date accessed 08/ 03/2020).

World Health Organization (2020a): Traditional, complementary and integrative medicine. https://www.who.int/traditional-complementary-integrative-medicine/activities/en/ (date accessed 25/ 05/2020).

World Health Organization (2020b): Health workforce – migration. *Health Workforce* https://www.who.int/hrh/migration/en/ (date accessed 08/ 03/2020).

Xu, Xiao-feng, Yan Wang, Yan-yan Wang, Ming Song, Wen-gang Xiao & Yun Bai (2016): Role-playing is an effective instructional strategy for genetic counseling training: an investigation and comparative study. *BMC Medical Education* 16(1). 235. doi:10.1186/s12909-016-0756-4.

Yaeger, Kimberly A., Louis P. Halamek, Mary Coyle, Allison Murply, Jodee Anderson, Kristi Boyle, Kirsten Braccia, Jennifer McAuley, Glenn De Sandre & Brad Smith (2004): High-fidelity simulation-based training in neonatal nursing. *Advances in Neonatal Care* 4(6). 326–331. doi:10.1016/j.adnc.2004.09.009.

Zhang, Baohui, Alexi A. Wright, Haiden A. Huskamp, Matthew E. Nilsson, Matthew L. Maciejewski, Craig C. Earle, Susan D. Block, Paul K. Maciejewski & Holly G. Prigerson (2009): Health care costs in the last week of life. *Archives of Internal Medicine* 169(5). 480. doi:10.1001/archinternmed.2008.587.

Zhang, Lawrence (2004): Awareness-raising in the TEFL phonology classroom. *ITL – International Journal of Applied Linguistics* 145–146. 219–268. doi:10.2143/ITL.145.0.562915.

Zhu, Hua (2015): Negotiation as the way of engagement in intercultural and lingua franca communication: frames of reference and Interculturality. *Journal of English as a Lingua Franca* 4(1). 63–90. doi:10.1515/jelf-2015-0008.

Zimmerman, D. (1992): The interactional organization of calls for emergency assistance. In Paul Drew & John Heritage (eds.), *Talk at work: interaction in institutional settings*, 418–469. Cambridge: Cambridge University Press.

(2017): Qatar to approve permanent residency for some expats. *Al Jazeera English*. Doha.

(2020): Rev. *Convert audio and video to text* https://www.rev.com/ (date accessed 21/12/2020).

(2021): lingua franca. *Cambridge Advanced Learner's Dictionary & Thesaurus* https://dictionary.cambridge.org/dictionary/english/lingua-franca (date accessed 05/08/2021).

Index

accommodation 7, 35, 42, 55, 56, 57, 59, 71, 122, 126, 131, 151, 152, 155, 157, 192, 212
activity type 15, 16, 32, 67, 68, 69, 70, 71, 72, 89, 90, 95, 106, 134, 135, 136, 137, 138, 140, 143, 144, 150, 154
agents
– antihypertensive 129
– antiplatelet 129
angina 173
Angle of Louis 135
Arabian Peninsula 74
Arabic
– broken 76
– Egyptian 2, 94
– Gulf Pidgin 76
– Modern Standard 8
assessment
– emergency 136
– neurological 129
– nursing 86, 136
– patient 67, 71, 116, 118, 138
– physical 131
– respiratory 137, 149
– stroke 131
assessments
– health 7
audiolingual model 175

Bachelor of Nursing (BN) 80
Bachelor of Nursing Regular Track (BNRT) 80
barriers
– communication 4
– language 4
biomedical
– language 110
– model 19, 10, 11, 17, 29
– summaries 136
– think aloud 34, 134, 152, 153
biomedical formulaic terms 161
blood clot 67

centrist perspective 36
Cerebrovascular Accident 140

Clinical Professional Development (CPD) 106
co-constructed 143, 155, 167, 173
Code of Practice 21, 215
codified 15, 54, 160
Collaborative repair 113
Colloquial Singapore English 73
common communicative ground 150
common ground
– core 61
– emergent 61
communication
– breakdown 25
– cooperative 59
– cross-cultural 29, 105, 203
– cross-linguistic 29
– doctor-patient 23
– effective 4
– ineffective 20
– intercultural 8
– interlingual 19, 17, 43
– international 14
– interprofessional 23, 31
– intralingual 42
– medical 19, 4, 7, 9, 12, 13, 16, 20, 22, 25, 31, 32, 33, 49, 56, 67, 72, 91, 101, 105, 131, 136, 144, 148, 159, 160, 164, 165, 176, 177, 178, 181, 191
– multilingual 148
– multimodal 7, 132, 156, 164, 165, 167, 168, 169, 172, 173, 181, 188, 200, 202, 207, 209
– non-linguistic 3, 7, 165, 167, 169, 180, 201
– nursing 118
– physician-patient 91
– therapeutic 114, 119, 121, 122, 127, 135, 139
communicative constellations
– fleeting and temporal 114
community of practice 15, 2, 3, 32, 33, 40, 41, 44, 46, 47, 48, 51, 56, 72, 89, 90, 155, 157, 193, 198, 213
complementary and alternative medicine 17, 189
Complexity Theory 160, 161

confluence 94
constellations 114
content-based language 163
context
– business 46
– cultural 83
– healthcare 40
– linguistic 73
– local 75
– multilingual 74
– occupational 157
– situational 59
– social 41
contrarian perspective 156
conversation analysis 12, 18, 89, 108, 115, 194, 202, 208, 211
conversational turns 155
cooperative pre-emption 113
COVID-19 10, 27
CRICO Strategies 25
cultural gap 67

departmentalized 169
diet pattern 147
discoloration 135
discourse planning 70
Dynamic Model of Meaning (DMM) 145

egocentrism 40, 59
encounter
– ad hoc 55
– medical 59
– transient 55
English as a lingua franca (ELF) 19, 32
English as a Native Language (ENL) 15
English for Specific Purposes (ESP) 88
epistemic authority 140
epistemology 13
error
– communication 57, 85
– medical 7
– medication 6
essentialist 8, 9
expatriate labour force 157
exploratory implications 156

foreign-born 20
foreign-trained 20
formulaic language 58
frame-activating power 60

Gulf Cooperation Council (GCC) 3

Harvard Medical Institutions 25
health system 20
Health Workforce Department 21
healthcare
– interprofessional 106
– professional 40
– provider 25
– providers 29, 30, 80, 155, 167, 171, 173, 178, 200
– simulation 115
– system 80
healthcare curriculum 114
Hematochezia 145
Hematuria 145
high-stakes 6, 160
Hypertension 174

illness 25
incongruence 161
individual identity 44
inferential schemata 68
Inner Circle 38
institutional talk 3, 32, 69, 70, 89
institutional bureaucracy 168
intelligibility 12, 51, 82, 83, 86, 101, 105, 200, 211
interaction
– medical 2
– nurse-patient 40
– pharmacist-client 69
– physician-patient 23
– professional-patient 40
Interactive listening 176
intercultural 74
interlocutor 2
international branch campuses (IBCs) 79
international medical graduates (IMG) 30
interpreter 26, 27, 52
interprofessional interaction 28

joint enterprise 44

language diversity 155
language variety 73
learner autonomy 175, 180
legitimate peripheral 44
lesion 138
lexical
– ambiguity 159
– gaps 159
– imprecision 159
Lexical simplification 136
lingua franca
– medical section 121
– uncooperative encounter 118
linguacultural ambiguity 53
linguacultures 8
linguistic behaviourism 175
linguistic norms 41, 94, 155, 158, 162
linguistic resource 46
linguistic superdiversity 94
longitudinal 51

meaning-making 12
medical
– consultation 7
– simulation 73
– treatment 29
– use 67
medical English as a lingua franca MELF 38
medical jargon 4, 91, 111, 223
medication
– dosages. *See* also, drugs
– names. *See* also, drugs
MELF
– definition 19
– distinctives 15, 19
MELF interactions 19
metacognition 173, 178, 180, 193, 209, 214
metacognitive
– awareness 178, 180
– skills 178
migration. *See* also, Migrate, migrant, migratory, global movement, international movement
– Healthcare professional 20

– labour 20
– medical 15, 4, 6, 13, 24, 29, 32, 50, 59, 72, 106, 197
misunderstanding 27, 28, 66, 86, 93, 101, 113, 115, 126, 127, 137, 201, 205, 210
mobile medical professionals (MMPs) 31
mutual engagement 44
myocardial infarction 67

NANDA International (NANDA-I) 54
nasal flaring 111
native speaker 8, 9, 15, 34, 51, 82, 125, 126, 160, 161, 171, 189, 191
nativization process 76
non-comprehension 122, 152
non-native speaker 8
non-understanding 7, 92, 101, 113, 119, 122, 124, 128, 148, 149, 151, 152, 153, 191
non-verbal
– communication 16, 7, 96, 99, 113, 129, 132, 165, 166, 167, 169, 178, 194, 214
norm development 35
Nursing Interventions Classification (NIC) 54
Nursing Outcomes Classification 54

oncology 178
Organisation for Economic Co-operation and Development (OECD) 20
other-initiated repair (OIR) 126
outcomes
– healthcare 26
– negative 25
– patient 20, 22, 54

palpate 138
patient handover process 167
patient safety 17, 6, 7, 13, 20, 26, 30, 84, 85, 86, 87, 88, 93, 101, 103, 115, 129, 133, 135, 156, 158, 160, 162, 172, 173, 175, 185, 188, 203, 204, 213
patient-centred approaches 172
patient-centred care (PCC) 13, 29
pedagogical effect 110
perception 6, 23, 57, 67, 122, 169
percussion 148
peripheral participant 47
pharmacist. *See* also, pharmacists

phonological loop 174
physical proximity 41
physiotherapist. *See* also, physiotherapists
playback
– affirmative forms of 131
– queryback 131
pluralism
– methodological 73
Post-diploma Bachelor of Nursing (PDBN) 80
postmodern. *See* also, postmodernist; post-modern
post-modern 13, 59
postmodernist 9, 10, 113
pragmalinguistic 177
Pre-emption strategies 116
probing 118
professional
– educated 20
– foreign-trained 21
professional competency 46
proficiency
– language 6, 13, 30, 31, 36, 37, 84, 172, 187, 198, 200
ptosis 135
pulmonic 136

racial blends 75
radiographer 17
radiologist. *See* also, radiologist
recipient design 144
recruitment 21
reformulation 115
regulation
– language. *See* also, regulatory
request for clarification 122
respiratory effort 138
rhythmic oscillation 135

SARS-CoV-2 181
scaffold 180
self-correction 122
sense
– common 61
– culture 61
– current 61
– formal 61
– shared 61
sentinel event 25
shared repertoire 44
simulation laboratory 87, 88
simulation training 13
situated learning 44
social grouping 41
social network theory 40, 70, 72, 94, 95, 157
socio-cognitive approach (SCA) 40, 59
sociocultural backdrop 40
sociolinguistic analysis 43
speech community 9, 33, 35, 41, 43, 44, 54, 61, 113, 114, 196, 208
standard normative English 74
standardization 19, 2, 38
Standardized patients 109
suicidal ideation 98
Surgical Safety Checklist 51
surgical technicians 42
suturing incision 42
symmetrical chest wall 139

tactile fremitus 148, 149
TESOL 8, 9, 187, 188, 189, 191, 204, 205, 211
thrombus 67
transcription accuracy 174
Transient International Groups (TIGs) 57
translanguaging 13, 16, 126, 160
translingual practices 156
treatment 6
turn-taking 3, 4, 68, 69, 70, 102, 105, 106, 140, 210
tympany 148, 149
typology 156, 172, 175

Variability 113
variable settings 114
variation in ELF 114
video-recorded medical simulation training (VMST) 169

World Englishes (WE) 15, 53
World Health Organization (WHO) 7

www.ingramcontent.com/pod-product-compliance
Lightning Source LLC
Chambersburg PA
CBHW050524170426
43201CB00013B/2071